S0-EGR-756

# *The* LITERARY SPOTLIGHT

# *The* LITERARY SPOTLIGHT

WITH A PREFACE BY

JOHN FARRAR

WITH PORTRAIT CARICATURES
BY WILLIAM GROPPER

*Essay Index Reprint Series*

BOOKS FOR LIBRARIES PRESS
FREEPORT, NEW YORK

Reprinted 1970 by arrangement

INTERNATIONAL STANDARD BOOK NUMBER:
0-8369-1874-6

LIBRARY OF CONGRESS CATALOG CARD NUMBER:
70-117789

PRINTED IN THE UNITED STATES OF AMERICA

# PREFACE

The character studies in the following pages were written by over a dozen different individuals, all of them fairly well known in the world of American letters. In most cases the critic chosen to limn a particular author was an acquaintance rather than an intimate of that author's. I wanted frankness; but certainly not the very bitterest truth. Our debt for the idea to the anonymous "Mirrors of Downing Street" and the other "Mirror" books is obvious. The scheme of its literary application I owe to my always helpful publisher, Mr. George H. Doran.

The spirit of the sketches varies. With so many anonymous contributors it was impossible to keep the book homogeneous. They range from the most radical youngsters to exceedingly conservative gentlemen of middle age who do not shiver at the sight of a frock coat in their cupboards; but quake a bit at certain aspects of sex. If I were to relate all of the experiences attendant on securing these essays, it would form a most complicated study of contemporary writing: the hates, the loves, the pettinesses, the qualms of conscience, the injured pride. Yet, in the main, it has been worth the trouble, though the book itself is far from satisfactory to me. Some of the chapters are too bitter, others too laudatory; some carelessly written, some lacking in taste. Yet the contributors have been uniformly enthusiastic on the final stretch. One or two, I confess, seem to me to be brilliant studies. Three chapters were suppressed, two of these appeared in THE BOOKMAN, one never went further than galley proofs. It was one that I wrote myself. I lost courage. It will never see the light of day. The other two were concerning ladies, and for reasons best known to myself I did not choose to offend these ladies further by including sketches which had annoyed their friends in this book. One or two gentlemen have also been offended; but their backs are broad. They should be able to stand criticism, even if they do squirm somewhat noisily under the really not so strenuous lashing.

The period of American writing during which these sketches have been published has been, in some ways, a peculiarly interesting one. I shouldn't be surprised if it came to be known as the most self-conscious time in our literary history. Following the war, we became conscious of our small towns, of our realtors, of our flappers, of our grandmothers, of a quotation-marked "Younger Generation," of sex as if it were a new discovery, of gland treatment, of Bolshevism, of Mr. Mencken, of Joe Cook, of what not! We have had several years of violent journalistic fiction writing, and the best journalism is nothing but realism, after all. Slowly, our young writers are drifting back to romanticism, our middle-aged writers are writing realism better than the youngsters, and our granddads are saying, "I told you so!" Presently the writing folk will settle down to writing again, and the public will struggle on toward a millennium when they will really know what fine writing is, and appreciate it. Meanwhile, a book like this, which attempts to criticize and flatly does not intend to be amiable, can do no harm. Perhaps it may even help, a trifle, to clear the atmosphere.

Just who comprises the company of anonymous authors? I trust that half the fun of reading the book will be in attempting to guess the answer to that question. To any guesses I should feel that I might offer lies and that they should be considered "white." Did Burton

Rascoe contribute to the series? "Yes!" He has already included one of the sketches in a forthcoming book of essays. He *must,* then, have written it. If he is not ashamed of the fact, I'm not. He wrote several. Did H. L. Mencken contribute? "No!" Did I? "Yes," and my friends have assured me that my efforts are the worst of the series. One gentleman turned the spotlight on himself, one completely rewrote another's article which I sent him in proof. Among the other contributors are two critics of first rank, a famous playwright, a major poet, a popular novelist, an editor of one of our largest magazines, a publisher, etc., etc. I wish that I could say that a circus clown had contributed to the series; but, there again, it is not so. I should be pleased to hear what your surmises are as to authorship. If any one is clever enough to guess the entire list correctly, I'll be glad to acknowledge his success on one condition—that he will not make public his list. I should promptly deny his statement, of course; for while in some cases the authors are not sensitive concerning revealment, in others there have been "over my dead body" clauses in the contract. So, guess away! I can tell you that it took me only five minutes to guess who wrote the sketch of myself.

The choice of authors to be discussed has been more or less hit-or-miss; but as the book stands I think we can boast that it covers a wide field with some completeness. I have tried to pick examples of various "schools" and of various "lives." Meanwhile, I trust that you will not find this a mean-spirited book. On the whole, I believe it to be a fair one. After all, what is criticism, if it does not criticize; and I believe that there is in these pages as much constructive as destructive thinking.

J. F.

*New York City.*

# CONTENTS

## *Part One*

## *Part Two*

BOOKS FOR GENERAL REFERENCE

REFERENCES, BIOGRAPHIES AND BIBLIOGRAPHIES

# *The* LITERARY SPOTLIGHT

## PART ONE

# *The* LITERARY SPOTLIGHT

## *I: Brander Matthews*

THE year 1922 was an *annus mirabilis* in many ways. One of the most unexpected occurrences was the inexplicable departure of Professor James Brander Matthews from the weekly book review of our largest daily newspaper. Professor Matthews had been like death and taxes in one respect. He was always with us. Fifty-two times a year his name was to be discerned appended to printed matter in the New York "Times Book Review." This matter took various forms. Sometimes it seemed to be a review of a current publication. At other times it wasn't. Professor Matthews's article could often be identified by certain phrases. One of them was "Forty years ago, etc." Another was the quotation of Jules Lemaître's fallacious but epigrammatic, "Criticism of our contemporaries is not criticism, it is only conversation." No epigram, of course, can be more than partially true; its very neatness defeats its own logic. But for Professor Matthews this statement by a distinguished Frenchman was the text of his life. He made his literary existence a long sermon in defence of it.

When Professor Matthews was not writing a review (he insists, quite rightly, that he does not write criticism) he was enlarging upon M. Lemaître's epigram. When he was not doing this he was rewriting himself. He made quaint admissions. He affirmed that he did not have time to read the younger men, but nevertheless he could not sleep for the horrendous tocsin of revolt that re-echoed in the streets adjacent to his mossy tower. Because of his attitude toward the younger men Professor Matthews is an important figure in current letters. His humanity is charming. He is so much what one would expect a representative of the older order to be that most of the younger generation experience a warming of the cockles of the heart when they think of him. It is true that they do not think of him very often, not so often, for instance, as they think of Stuart P. Sherman, but this is mainly because of Professor Matthews's repetitiousness. He scrapes away on the same old fiddle at the same old tune, and the younger generation (not barbarians really but rather nice young men who are mostly guilty of the attempt to think for themselves) know it by heart.

Professor Matthews was the Jeremiah of the New York "Times Book Review." He did not criticize; he judged. His weekly articles were the dumplings in the stew. About them gathered the beefy chunks of Dr. Maurice Francis Egan, the carrots of Professor William Lyon Phelps, the parsnips of Austin Hay, the Irish potatoes of Herbert S. Gorman, and the thin gravy of Richard Le Gallienne. Now and again the concoction was enlivened by a dash of paprika from Benjamin De Casseres, who ate the mystics and was mad. The dish was quaint and one can but note with some consternation that it exists no longer.

Professor Matthews as the dumpling in the stew was naturally in a position of some importance. It is to be suspected that he had merely to nod his head toward a certain book and that book leaped toward him on the wings of the parcel post. His range of enthusiasms extended from Gelett Burgess's idea of "Æsop's Fables" to Gilbert Murray's Greek theories. Poetry of the lighter

BRANDER MATTHEWS

sort (vers de société) titillated him. Now this was but natural, for is not Professor Matthews himself the author of that deathless panegyric to the young Yankee maiden? Lest any of the younger generation have failed to memorize this effort it is drawn from its obscurity and set down here.

AN AMERICAN GIRL

She's had a Vassar education,
  And points with pride to her degrees;
She's studied household decoration;
  She knows a dado from a frieze,
  And tells Corots from Boldonis;
A Jacquemart etching, or a Haden,
  A Whistler, too, perchance might please
A free and frank young Yankee maiden.

She does not care for meditation;
  Within her bonnet are no bees;
She has a gentle animation,
  She joins in singing simple glees.
  She tries no trills, no rivalries
With Lucca (now Baronin Raden),
  With Nilsson or with Gerster; she's
A frank and free young Yankee maiden.

I'm blessed above the whole creation,
  Far, far above all other he's;
I ask you for congratulation
  On this the best of jubilees:
  I go with her across the seas
Unto what Poe would call an Aiden,—
  I hope no serpent's there to tease
A frank and free young Yankee maiden.

*Envoy*

Princes, to you the western breeze
  Bears many a ship and heavy laden.
What is the best we send in these?
  A free and frank young Yankee maiden.

Can one read this without affection for Professor Matthews? One wonders if he was not the F. Scott Fitzgerald of his day, and yet there is a certain naïveté that precludes any such opinion. Professor Matthews was and is as naïve as Jackie Coogan. Yet behind his unsophisticated humanity is a sound and important intellect. He has written admirably about Molière and Shakespeare. His scholarship in certain lines must remain unchallenged. His naïveté rests in his inability to understand when it is time to stop and where he should pause. He protests, without much reason, when the younger generation fails to adapt its pace to his. He belongs to the Bunner school of letters (a school that played delightfully and superficially with life) but he does not quite accept the fact that that movement is a thing of the past. They were gentle scholars, sound and sunny and sometimes close to saccharinity. One can but note with regret that the sweetness once implicit in Professor Matthews's work has grown a bit acidulous. This is mainly because he insists upon concerning himself with a modern movement of mind and spirit with which he has nothing in common. His blood does not tingle to that tocsin which he hears so loudly ringing in the streets of his Little Old New York. A new race has sprung up about him with other dreams. They are not interested in the things about which Professor Matthews's mind revolves. They don't care about Jules Lemaître's epigrams. They can roll their own.

Professor Matthews has written more than one article (or rather he has rewritten the same article several times) striving doggedly to prove that book reviewing and criticism are two separate things. Very well. They are. Very well. They aren't. It is simple enough to grant that a book review is not necessarily criticism and it is equally simple to grant that criticism is not necessarily a book review. But when Professor Matthews asserts, as he does, that a book review may not be a criticism if it is concerned with a book by a contemporary author, he is merely expressing a personal opinion that other readers are not bound to accept. The idea that one may not criticize one's contemporaries because, presumably, of the nearness of the subject and the consequent lack of proper perspective, is a controversial subject with as much evidence on one side as on the other. Certainly Ben Jonson's opinion of Shakespeare (*his* contemporary, Professor Matthews will grant) has not been seriously destroyed as a piece of criticism by subsequent Shakespearian scholars. This is a subject assuredly in which one example will serve to destroy Professor Matthews's argument. If it has been done once it may be done again, and one does not need to search the archives of literature for an abundance of examples. So much has been written about this attitude of Professor Matthews that the foregoing statements are designed, not to destroy his attitude—for that would take an article in itself—but to illustrate one facet of his mind which is revelatory of his character. Professor Matthews is dogmatic, settled in his convictions, and not open to argument. He knows what he thinks; his opinions crystallized years ago; and the shiftings and fluctuations of the intellectual world have not moved him from his sturdy stand. He is in himself an epitome of that older order that grudgingly observes the younger generation and slams a ponderous fist upon it almost as soon as it opens its infant mouth.

It is futile for the older order to summon up a smile and assert that it does not deprecate the younger generation, that it likes youth and the thoughts that go with youth, and that it views with disapproval only the aberrations of the younger generation, the false experimentations and elaborate extravagances, etc. For the older order the younger generation itself is an aberration. The older order likes its own scheme of things and measures all movements accordingly. It is not qualified to judge either the merits or demerits of the experimentations of the younger generation, for it cannot enter into the spirit of them. It stands outside and observes objectively. The turmoil of the spirit, the urge to discovery and self-expression that lead the younger generation into such queer paths are meaningless gestures to the older order whose traveling days are done, whose roads have been made smooth in the days when its members were too young to realize that they themselves moved through the disadvantages and obstacles of a still older order. Castle after castle crashes down and the progress of art continues. No one generation can affirm that it has reached the appointed goal. The secret of great art is that the goal is never reached.

These are the things that Professor Matthews does not understand, and so clearly defined is his position that he is a welcome signpost for the younger generation. That much maligned group is glad to have him there, for he stands for the outworn things that have hardened, that have perished from a spiritual arteriosclerosis. It is futile for Professor Matthews or any representative of the older order to assert that the younger men are contemptuously flinging aside Shakespeare, Goethe, Dante, Shelley, and such divine constellations as squeezed oranges, for this has never been the case. The younger generation is as reverend as any where genius is concerned and past achievements are still past achievements. The difference between the older order and the younger generation is that the youthful group is not content to retravel roads that long ago were exhausted, to bask itself in an old tradition which indubitably has its place in the whole perspective of world literature but which is nothing more than a starting point for younger feet. The younger generation cannot think Professor Matthews's thoughts and exist; it would automatically destroy itself in the attempt.

Various tales (which may not be true) have arisen from Professor Matthews's attitude toward life and letters. There is the one about the young student taking his father's notebooks to a class conducted by Professor Matthews and discovering that he need take no new notes. Even the jokes fell in the same places. There is also the tale regarding Professor Matthews's explanation that he could not lecture on Emerson to his class as he had neglected to bring his notes along. These stories are possibly mere apocrypha, jaunty dramatizations of an atmosphere by impertinent youths, but they serve to show what Professor Matthews and all that he stands for suggest to the younger men.

He is the essentially personal prophet of the older order. Anything that he considers derogatory to the fetishes of his youth (which have remained fetishes all his life) he takes as a personal matter. An insult to Emerson is an insult to him. One can but observe this militant oldster (born in 1852) with admiration as he sallies into the vexed arena of modern letters bearing his frayed gonfalon. He will die fighting and he will die with the respect of the younger generation, for his sincerity is undoubted and in spite of criticism the younger men revere sincerity. But he will not be taken seriously, since he never possessed any value as a constructive thinker. His literary animosities rather reveal this deficiency. The tocsin of revolt peals in his streets of the mind and he rushes forth; but he is neither trampled upon nor thrust aside by the impatient youngsters who follow the alarum of that bell. They merely dart past him and far up the street. Farther than Professor Matthews's eyesight carries, he may hear the shouting of the young warriors.

## *II: Booth Tarkington*

HE has been a "great man" longer than any other living American novelist.

There is a poignant story told of a young man who was ruined by living across the street from him, in the days when he was a romanticist—in life, as in his fiction. This youth got the idea that to be a famous writer it was necessary to keep two or three cabs chugging out in front all night, in case you might suddenly want to go out.

He has had a terrible time "growing up"—in fiction as in life. He managed this, in both respects, quite recently.

He looks to-day like an old actor. Probably you would not say precisely that he looks like a bad actor, but I doubt whether he would suggest to you a particularly good one. He looks like that kind of actor the menu of whose Thanksgiving dinner, at Oriole, Ohio (a one night stand), would wind up with bread pudding. He would use at that meal a crinkly tissue-paper napkin with Japanesque birds on it done in blue. He (the actor, that is) would figure everything in weeks. He might work fourteen weeks out of sixty weeks. If he ran an extra week he'd live throughout the summer on that extra week's salary. He would open at Stamford, Connecticut. He might speak the opening lines of the piece, which would likely be some such momentous words as "Why, hello, Alfred, old boy! Where have you been keeping yourself for so long?"

Tarkington's wardrobe inclines to emphasis in color, striking effects—pearl-gray soft hats, suits dashingly light in tone with high-power checks, ties with no faint stripes, that sort of thing. He could not appear on the street without a stick, generally a stocky canary-hued staff with

BOOTH TARKINGTON

a heavy silver top. His most humorous makeup is a black derby hat, wherein he seems to be very much nose, a Cyrano oddly got into sharply pressed modern tailoring.

His voice certainly ought to carry all over the house. It has timbre and moving volume. It has been spoken of as hoarse and has been said to boom. He himself describes it as a "rich contralto." Anyway, he may be said to be generally in very good voice.

Old, an old actor? And only in, as he puts it, the "infant fifties." Well, perhaps it's his stoop that goes far to produce the effect—a quaint blend of the amiable elderly with a spice of the debonair spirit of youth. I fancy he rather relishes his stoop, in a subconscious way. It's effective when you arrive anywhere late to stand for a moment somewhat stooped at the entrance. One does not want to seem too brash and forward, you know. Then, also, it is a good deal of trouble for one who never takes any regular exercise to sit up quite straight all the while. And, further, though you walk briskly enough, it is amusing to feel that you have known the world for a considerable length of time. *Vanitas vanitatum!*

It is gratifying to love many old-time things: the old buildings at Princeton; the old house of Edwin Booth on Gramercy Park, the home of The Players; and the old family homestead in Indianapolis. That club is now for him "full of ghosts," there is "a new population down there." It is mellowing to the spirit to contemplate that one's dancing days are in the past. It is an invigorating exercise for the mind to hate with a good rousing hatred many new-fangled things: a "forest" of telegraph poles before your door, street cars all about, burglars and burglars and burglars, the insane new dances, the rage for "bigness," the "boosting" spirit come to town, the hordes and hordes of new citizens of mongrel blood filling the streets.

Why, before his town became a city, when he was a boy, his father used to come home from business at three or four in the afternoon, with their shepherd dog which had gone downtown with him in the forenoon bounding about him. Those were days for living! And, above all, it was long before the time of the great and awful smoke.

It is well, too, exceedingly well, to have got over long ago the juvenile desire to write stories doctored up for theatrical effect. One woman reader was heard to speak of "Alice Adams" as a "flat" story. A mighty flat story, indeed, he thought it. Doubtless, it would not be quite correct to say that he now deliberately sets out to write a flat story, but an earnestness almost gruesome which has come to eat at his vitals in the matter of creating fiction, makes the sort of story which strikes this lady as flat the only kind of story he can continue to write.

His energy of expression, in speech, in correspondence, and in his fiction, has its spring in his saying things straight ahead as they come through an honest mind, clear and simple in its workings and close in feeling with everyday stuff. That critic wouldn't be so misguided who should declare that one of the finest lines in literature is that one somewhere in "Penrod" where one of the characters "let out a yell like a gin-maddened nigger."

It is possible to read his handwriting by the exercise of patience and with the aid of a fair amount of former experience with it. He begins at the top of the page with letters of generous size and good clear spaces between the lines, but generally as he nears the lower right-hand corner of his sheet of paper, cramps things up woefully. The very deftly drawn pen sketches with which he now and then adorns his letters have an amount of wit and go to them seldom found in magazine illustrations. He has probably never written out the word "them" in any letter; it is always " 'em"; as "I would" always is "I'd," and so on. His pounding earnestness leads him to underscore something every few words, with somewhat the resulting effect of his shouting it at you. He may write you three long letters within two weeks, and then not again for eight months—unless you call upon him to do something for you, when he responds at once.

The difficulties occasioned many by the activities of Mr. Volstead are quite without sting for him. He decided to duck, as he puts it, the allurements now prohibited, a round number of years ago. Indeed, on that tack he is mighty earnest, too: he will tell you it is "nasty stuff"; and tell it to you strong.

His dissipation is what he calls work sprees. And his closest friends confirm the idea that these affairs are chronic in their occurrence and in character extreme and protracted. He has come to be, like all sensible men keenly intent upon their jobs, very guarded against promiscuous intrusion. And to break in upon him, by telephone or in person, without warrant—you might as well try Buckingham Palace. But if you have honest need of him you'll find him.

At home you'll find him pouring glass after glass of ice water out of a tall silver pitcher and, as elsewhere, smoking an endless number of the mammoth cigarettes which he has made for him, a hundred to a tin box, and labelled "B. T."

An old-time friend of his, an actor (really an actor), has an amusing story of how he disported himself one evening by presenting twenty dollar bills to vagrants in Bryant Park, taking his reward in relish of their astonishment. But that was many years ago, before the business of being a serious novelist engrossed him completely. He derives amusement from surplus money to-day in another fashion, by buying bonds. He seems to have become something of an amateur of bonds, a collector. The bond habit he will strongly recommend, if you have inclined him to think that you are interested in the subject.

Though he has, as we all know, lived for lengthy periods in various parts of the world, the intensity of his Americanism perhaps would amuse a budding cosmopolite. He frequently refers to "foreigners" without malice in inflection but certainly as to those, as it were, of another faith.

He has owned a succession of dogs illustrious locally. Probably of no other living writer have so many different portraits appeared in the course of the past twenty years. He does not care to be long in great cities: a week or so once or twice a year in New York is enough for him. He spends the months between late fall and early spring at his home in Indianapolis, then migrates for the rest of the year to Kennebunkport, Maine, where a few years ago he built a very handsome new house. The child of a town far inland with no ships in his books and no seafarers among his forebears, he has called the new place "Seawood," and among the proudest interior decorations of the house are a number of very elaborate models of ships. He is very fond, he declares, of the country, and of being on the water.

By birth, inheritance, education, freedom from the necessity of engaging in business routine, and success in his own work, he has always been, you might say, on the inside. From "Beaucaire" to "Alice Adams" one outstanding circumstance has always attached to the character holding the center of his stage. Alice is again what he calls an outsider. At length, he had almost shaken off the lace and ruffles of chivalry. And then, at last, the most awful catastrophe overtook her which could befall a heroine of his: grim tragedy brought her to the door of a business college.

Many people have seen his plays, but dramatic critics almost never do.

How long will he continue to bottle the now old reliable "boy stuff" for popular drug store consumption?

His first editions fetch two dollars.

But he is brought out in the most sumptuous edition de luxe of any living American author.

## *III: Sinclair Lewis*

YOU and I know the kind of individual who happens to be blessed with a lowest common denominator among names—let us say "Smith," and who lives in so personal a world that he cannot hear the name "Smith" mentioned without asking, "Where's he from? I wonder if he's any relation of mine." If your own ego and the hub of the world you live in are sufficiently concentric, no Smith is too far out on the rim of existence for you to claim kinship with him, or for mention of his final syllable to fail to tickle, deep within you, a familiar and pleasant feeling, a homely blend of pride and recognition.

It is apparently the same way with authors. It must have been some years after he wrote it that Fielding began to think of "Tom Jones" as a common English name rather than as the name of the hero of his book. Weren't there times in Flaubert's life when, overhearing some one on the street say "Madame"—followed by an indistinguishable sound—he started slightly, and his own lips, audibly or inwardly, filled out the blank with "Bovary"? Didn't Dante often feel something in his own mind click when people about him referred to hell?

Say "Alice" or "Myrtle" suddenly to any mother, and she will think, not of the army of Alices or Myrtles of various shades of hair or length of limb, but of her own, her private, her universal child. Say "Main Street" suddenly to Sinclair Lewis, and he will at once think, not of drug stores and mangy trees and hitching posts and the boys loafing about at the corner, but of a best seller with a blue and orange cover. In his dictionary, "Main Street" is "the big book by Sinclair Lewis."

SINCLAIR LEWIS

Let's do him justice. Those two words meant something, besides a mere local address, before he came along. They meant something definite to a good many people, and probably a good many people had used those two words to express smallness and repetition and mediocrity, and the unutterable tyranny of the unseen chains that by the tens of thousands bound restless souls to small roosting places. But these meanings were scattered, and lurked underground, and festered in minds lacking the will or the knack for communicating them. Nobody had all the meanings of "Main Street" in his head and was ready to stand up on his hind legs and shout them at a country which was half aware of those meanings but was waiting for the big voice with the megaphone. Lewis did the job. He didn't think he had the big voice, and he had no way of knowing that the Main Streeters would stop, look, and listen to him as they only will for a megaphone. He had gone about the job with some humility, and little expectation of success. He had withdrawn from frothy potboiling for the Satevepost to speak, all by himself, the truth that he felt was in him. He spoke—he must have thought—in solitude, and to a blank wall, only to find that the blank wall was a stage curtain which lifted and showed him audiences in multitudes, frantically applauding.

We'll have to give Lewis the credit for this: no matter who its real parents were, no matter if it would have been born anyway, he was the midwife who brought into the American world an expression, a slogan which set a large part of that world talking about itself. He made America Main-Street-conscious. He rescued from that disconnected limbo of small towns which is America, a name by which America can call itself. He gave the two simple words, "Main Street," a whole set of echoes and savors which people will for a few years at any rate think of when they hear those words. There must be a lot of people, among those who read books at all, who used to see a vague picture of the only thoroughfare in town which boasted a car line and where shirts cost more than $2.49, when you said "Main Street" to them, who now think, if perhaps still as dimly, of Carol Kennicott or the Doctor. The dramatization of "Main Street," its translation into a symbol, is current even among the least literate. President Harding, explaining that he is just as good as any other man but no better, confessed himself "a plain citizen of Main Street." What's in a title? you ask. Lewis will tell you, if he felt like it, that there's enough in it to live on comfortably for the rest of your life.

What is there in "Main Street," for you and for me and for Lewis, besides the title? Call it "Gopher Prairie" and enough readers drop off to keep Lewis from enjoying a trip to Europe. Call it "The Life and Trials of Carol Kennicott" and the royalties dwindle till you can touch bottom with a foot rule. Call it anything else you like and it's a sure bet that Lewis goes back to potboiling short stories for the Satevepost. I'll admit, if you want to talk about things in the grand style, that Lewis had genius of a kind for hitting upon that title. So had the authors of "It Floats," "The Flavor Lasts," and "There's a Reason." If you'll let me talk about him in my own way, I'd prefer to say that Lewis was the small red catalytic atom which hustled along a reaction in the chemistry of the national mind—a reaction which had been under way for some time, was bound to happen eventually, and might just as well have been hustled along by some other lucky atom. Lewis was the train dispatcher for trains of thought which had been running on no schedule. Or, in a country which had been vaguely hunting about in the dark for something to hit itself on the head with, he stepped forward with a neat and ready brick. At the bedside of an inarticulate middle class suffering from a colic of autointoxication, he won fame by being the first doc to take the pills out of the bottle.

Of course he wasn't really the first. The truest thing ever said about Lewis—it was also the highest praise he ever deserved—was that "Main Street" was one of the milestones in the discovery of America. Yet what quantities of people, whose fold he seems irrevocably to have joined, thought it the discovery itself; as if Main Street, under some less conspicuous title, had not often before been found, and cherished, and described, with far more art, a wider humor, and a deeper understanding of bipeds. Can you read "Main Street" when you are not under the spell of the enthusiastic voices—ask Mr. Harcourt how many hundred thousand they were according to the latest returns—who pronounce it great, powerful, epoch making, eye opening, deafening, and true to life? You'll find it, in spite of some qualities, an ugly, repetitious, rather shrill and formless story about people—excepting here and there Dr. Kennicott—who were not so much people as the embodiments of the silly, trite, or cruel things Lewis had heard real people say in the Pullman smoker. Life, as the writer in him looks at it, is every day more and more of a circus parade of the things he hates. He doesn't try to understand these animals—if he did, they would cease to serve his ends. He is listening to their human, their foolish words, but he is always listening hardest when they make fools of themselves. For the bumptious and silly sides of them will fatten his soup—the other sides won't. So he goes on, until his world is one vast nauseous Pullman smoker full of Rotarians, Fraternians, Boomers, Realtors, and Baboons getting off one damn-fool remark after another. Their talk would be poison to you and me; it would be hateful to us to listen to it for long and realize that this is so great a part of what our fellows are like. Lewis hated it too, once, but then he began collecting this rubbish, and the more his collection grew the more he loved it and the more he went on collecting it. Lewis is sensitive in a way, and honest, and liberal minded, but the vindictive collector in him has pushed these other qualities aside, so that now, out of what used to poison him, he makes his bread. The first loaf was "Main Street"; the second, "Babbitt," is baked of the same dough. If he keeps on baking in the same way, and thinking and talking about it as he does, he'll wake up to find out that he's got back to the poison again.

Let's go back and look at the antediluvian Lewis—the Lewis who lived before "Main Street" flooded his world with gold. It's a familiar story, and a rather gallant one, showing us the best there was in him. He'd been writing for years breezy popular stuff which he didn't like. It paid fairly well, but not well enough to give him the leisure to unload what he thought he had in him. At last he had collected enough—about two thousand—so that he could do just as he pleased for a whole year. He sat back for that year and wrote "Main Street." He didn't think of it as a best seller. Not with the topside of his mind at all events; but all of us preserve on the little dark shelves of our hearts some prehensile and ridiculous longing to be president, or Captain Courageous, or the best poker player east of the Alleghenies. He didn't show openly any such longing for success, though I suspect he carried deep within him the seed of what later so astonishingly blossomed. He thought well of "Main Street" when it was finished; thought it a serious job well done. He didn't expect a golden shower, or even a silver one; he was ready for brief but passing favor, acknowledgment by the critics of an honest effort, then perhaps silence, all of which, together with poor sales, would mean a return to the popular rock pile of our greatest weekly advertiser. He had written about small and mean people in their millions: would they even so much as stir when he scratched them? Hardly. There was no hope for recognition from them. Walt Whitman, who sang in passionate praise of the common man, remained unread by all but a few who wore spectacles and were otherwise far from common. What hope then that Main Street would even turn over in its sleep just because Sinclair Lewis had spit in its face?

His friends all bought the book, then the cognoscenti, then the literati, then the literate. A paltry thousand or so. Then the sleeping beast turned over, rubbed its eyes, and woke up. Fifty thousand. It howled in an ecstasy of self-torture. One hundred thousand. It licked its tormentor's hand. Two hundred thousand. It cried for more. Three hundred thousand. His publishers estimate that it has beyond doubt reached two million readers. And people are still buying it and reading it for the first time this very day.

Not the small band of intelligent onlookers only, but the very people he was writing about were reading him. "How true!" they cried. "Oh, how very true to this dull life of ours!" For the moment Main Street was at his mercy. The scorpion was on its back with its legs in the air. It seemed to enjoy the flaying. Yet in its soul it was wounded; something of its pride and self-complacency had been trampled upon. And we mustn't forget that it is in the nature of scorpions to sting.

Perhaps I impute too much reason to the amorphous mass that is Main Street in thinking that it planned to get even with Sinclair Lewis. Yet Main Street has an organism of its own—as nature's blind but powerful, and, like nature, it will have its revenge.

How did Lewis take it when his shoddy Main Street

was suddenly paved with gold? Did he take it, as one might who was more of an artist, a little shyly, and wonder if perhaps something was a little wrong when stones he had thrown came flatteringly back to him all wrapped in gold leaf? He did not take it questioningly, or lightly. He took, and now takes it, as sublimely natural, and also the most important thing in the world. If you wake him up in the middle of the night, you will find him pondering the latest high water mark of his book's sales, and if you point out to him that the town of Zenobia, Iowa, has not bought the book to the extent of the quota that might have been expected of it, he will forevermore have an unfriendly feeling for that town. For him all streets not Main Street are now side streets. I imagine him picturing to himself, in the form of one of those colored statistical pies, what parts of the United States have been reading him most faithfully. He is always running to the barometer which indicates the sales, and which determines the weather of his existence. Say "Main Street" to him, and it is as if a coin went down the slot; as with those machines into which we drop casual pennies while waiting for the ferry, he begins to pour forth, like a mechanical record, the latest news about "Main Street," and who was the last person to compliment him upon it, and what it means and will continue to mean for the world. If he died suddenly, you would find written on his heart, in blinking electric bulbs of letters, those two magic words. He goes abroad, and brings back little but more news of "Main Street" and the ripples from it that have met him over there. He eats it three times a day, and expects his friends, who are beginning to have their misgivings, to enjoy this personal fare as much as he. If he were to receive a dime every time he said "Main Street" or the words crossed his mind, he would have as much money again as he got in royalties. I don't mean that he is thinking always of dollars, for he is not—or at any rate was not—mercenary, but he is human enough to crave fame insatiably, and looks to the dollar barometer as to that by which fame is most reliably measurable. Fame, success, prestige, being talked about, being photographed as he sails with wife and child for Europe, hearing the gathering surf of comment about "Babbitt" as it heads in from sea toward the critical shore—this is his life, his joy, the all for which he gets up in the morning. He doesn't as yet see how he is disquieting and annoying the people nearest to him, who had a right to expect more humility.

Lewis always was, and still is, an admirable mimic. His reproduction of the salesmen telling the world about their automobiles in the Pullman smoker makes you rock with laughter. You know how the patter runs; it is the raw material of "Main Street" and, in a slightly different way, of "Babbitt" also: "I have a little Buick—say, boy, that machine can sure go. Why, Saturday we went from Parson's Landing to Felchville—eighty-three miles—and from there to—you know the town with the tough turn on the top of the hill. Well, we did that on high, and by the time we reached Pipp Centre I didn't need to put in but only a half pint of new oil. Now I want to tell you . . ." I can see a smoker full of writers—in so many of whom the salesman predominates—talking of what hills their novels make on high, through a blue haze of cigar smoke. Lewis's is the clearest and most emphatic voice of all: "I want to tell you that there's nothing like that little twelve-cylinder Main Street. You don't need any gas—it's all there, go as far as you like. She skids, but she won't turn turtle. Why, my wife and I went all the way to Europe and back on that car. Next year we're going to have a new one. A Babbitt. I've tried it out. Speed—say! and endurance. Watch out for that bus. It's a knockout. I'll bet it beats all the records. . . ."

So Main Street, the insulted and injured, has won out after all. It has taken Lewis into its materialistic camp. It has made him worship, against his surface will, perhaps, its own kind of success. He "belongs" now, does Sinclair Lewis. The "bigger and better" bug has bitten him. Is he strong enough to overcome it, or will Main Street's revenge be lasting?

Meredith has a few lines which apply extremely well to the Sinclair Lewis of to-day, the slayer caught in his own mesh, the tamer tamed:

> O Raphael! when men the Fiend do fight,
> They conquer not upon such easy terms.
> Half serpent in the struggle grow these worms . . .
> . . . While mind is mastering clay,
> Gross clay invades it.

## *IV: Mary Johnston*

THE case of Mary Johnston is not exactly that of Herman Melville; but neither is it that of Margaret Cameron. And yet there are, or seem to be, similarities to the author of "Moby Dick" and to the author of "The Seven Purposes." Melville's mysticism led to the production of books which his generation found incomprehensible; and Miss Johnston's mysticism may yet lead to the writing of a book based on personal experiences, as Margaret Cameron's is.

Let these comparisons stop here; they are too easily misleading. The plain facts regarding Miss Johnston are as follows: she is over fifty years old and an absolutely human sort of person. You see a markedly oval face with a small and pointed chin. Her manner is serene and friendly and welcoming—she is very hospitable to you at her large and comfortable house near Warm Springs, Virginia. The tangible world, its people and affairs, interest her markedly. Living with her sister and brother, who really keep the house and look after the place, she is more isolated than one need be these years in Arizona or Teheran. But this condition seems to be largely accidental; she shuns nobody, is indifferent to nothing that amuses or vexes others living other lives.

She will tell you that of late years she has had access to the superconscious. This, of course, has nothing whatever to do with the usual varieties of spiritualism. Miss Johnston has not, so far as I am aware, any tales to relate of communication with the dead. In the beginning, the thing simply happened. I think the details are her affair, as well as her own philosophy concerning the whole business, since she has actually written what may be the first chapter of a book dealing with the subject. But anyway: she felt this surprising and unprecedented extension of her consciousness into that region so many have tried to explore. In this state I suppose she saw, or more particularly felt, certain things which can only be dimly expressed by some one else. Unquestionably she felt that this everyday world was a series of adumbrations of the Reality that had touched her. The conviction of an underlying Unity, Oneness, became henceforth her great certitude and her active faith.

She waited for the renewal of that first experience. It came. Again and again it came. Finally she thought that some control might come too; and I think it has. By "control" I mean an apparent power or privilege of access when she wanted it—access to the superconscious as one might open the wicket gate of heaven. This would not be to gain a glimpse of heaven, but to look forth upon the earth from a vantage quite immeasurable.

I believe the first experience followed illness, somewhat in the fashion of those "Twenty Minutes of Reality" with which Ellery Sedgwick stirred up his hornet's nest of "Atlantic" readers some few years ago. Miss Johnston has had a great deal of illness in her life. There were about ten years during which she must have been frequently hard to get along with or live with—but that's past for good. She traveled up and down the earth extensively, but principally between Egypt and Scotland, in the search for health, achieving a semi-permanency which made possible the home, "Three Hills." I don't know that living there has been quite the best thing for her, but it seems logical enough. Any influences powerful enough to change her personality would have had to come much earlier; the introversion of her nature must have

MARY JOHNSTON

begun when she was a mere girl, perhaps when the death of her mother left her in charge of a household at the age of sixteen. There are so many kinds of self-fulfillment and the kinds are all so valuable to the race, that to wish for one kind, in a given instance, is mostly foolishness. The sensible, of whom at stray moments I have the honor to be one, wish only for self-fulfillment by the many and not merely and perpetually by the pitiful few.

For this one a husband, for that one a brother; for a third one the chance to think unhurriedly.

Now we come to this point: having had her wonderful personal experience, Miss Johnston couldn't just go on writing historical novels. So she wrote "Foes."

"Foes" is a dramatic story of eighteenth century Scotland with a lasting feud, a long chase, and a crescendo of hatred and peril. The hero, a fairly dour and hard-headed Scot of the Culloden era, is pictured lying in the grass of the Roman Campagna and comprehending, all of a sudden, that Everything is One. Christ and Buddha are One. "There swam before him in the light, Oneness, Unity." The critic could correctly say: "This is an historical anachronism. Miss Johnston has no excuse for imputing to an eighteenth century Scot the concepts of a Hegel or an Emerson." And the reader who cherished the memory of "To Have and To Hold," or even the later memory of "The Long Roll" and "Cease Firing," was heard to exclaim: "This stuff about Oneness and Unity! I don't get it."

"Foes" was followed by "Michael Forth," and that mystical welter was succeeded by a metaphysical maze called "Sweet Rocket." "The waves of transcendentalism," wrote one young man sadly, "are fast closing over Mary Johnston's head as they closed over Herman Melville's." Perhaps pardonably, he failed to foresee that two years later the submerged Melville would again be riding the surface, as much of a portent as his own great Whale.

The whole situation, from any but a transcendental viewpoint, was unfortunate and becoming more so. Consider that Miss Johnston had made a marked popular success with her first novel, "Prisoners of Hope," back in 1898; and had multiplied that success with her second book, "To Have and to Hold." These books are still read. She added "Audrey" and "Sir Mortimer" and "Lewis Rand"—not counting a poetic drama, "The Goddess of Reason"—and by 1911, when the first of her two Civil War novels was ready, the preceding books had passed the million mark in sales. Phenomenal, in those days! The Civil War novels, "The Long Roll" and "Cease Firing," did not lessen her huge and loyal following. The vogue of the purely romantic historical novel had gone, but the day of the soberly historical novel does not go by. Through a succession of stories, one or two, like "The Wanderers," plainly experimental, Mary Johnston's large audience kept reasonably well with her or within hailing distance. But "Foes" staggered the loyalists, "Michael Forth" frightened them away, and "Sweet Rocket" was exploded, a graceful gesture, with no one to see. Gone, gone, all gone.

The manuscript next handed to the publisher was "Silver Cross," a tale of the England of Henry VII, and of rivalry between two religious establishments. Written in a clipped sort of prose stripped of "a" and "an" and "the" and other particles as well as articles, the text is a highly mannered English replete with cadenced sentences and animated by nervous rhythms. The very diction bears poetic surcharges, and the whole effect on the reader is to distil in his soul a delicate enchantment or else to exasperate him to death. When I say so much, however, I have really said nothing, not even of the story or its constant spiritual "implications"; the truth, I am sure, is that "Silver Cross" is either a vision or an abortion. But the same thing could be said of much modern art—so perhaps it *is* art.

This, I think, can be said determinately: in "Silver Cross" Miss Johnston preserves something that was in "Michael Forth" and "Sweet Rocket" and expresses it, more or less effectively, through the historical medium of which she has always been mistress. Reynolds (wasn't it?) answered the inquiry as to what he mixed his paints with by saying pompously: "With brains, sir!" But in "Silver Cross" the significance is that Mary Johnston has begun to mix paint with her brains. She has told a story. She has not imposed her metaphysical idea upon her story, as she did in "Foes." She has not lost her story, as she did in "Michael Forth" and "Sweet Rocket." Her story has sprung out of her idea, a child well begotten, perfectly formed.

As to beauty . . . but the perception of beauty is too subjective, too altogether personal to the beholder, for me to decide. And I sometimes wonder if the true appeal of a metaphysical idea is to anything more rational than the emotions, after all. Where we recognize the appeal to be preponderantly emotional we say "mystical"; but the notion of the appeal ever being to anything else (to "reason," for example), may be mere human flattery and self-deception.

On all counts, I have been glad to see "Silver Cross" getting off to an excellent start; for that should mean the acquisition and retention of a moderately large public for "1492," which is to appear this fall. This, of course, is a narrative of the discovery of America by Columbus. Miss Johnston employs a narrator, a Jew who has suffered the persecutions usual at that period for his faith. Banished from Spain under the decree of Jewish exile promulgated by Ferdinand and Isabella, this obscure Spinoza sails on the expedition from Palos. What he sees is sufficiently worth while, but his apperceptions are the essence of Miss Johnston's story. The Genoese commander, perhaps, sees around the curve of the hemisphere, but this exile has glimpses along a larger arc than that.

Mary Johnston, in a loose cloak, with a stout stick, walking the Virginia hills, sees with him, and meditates. Sitting quietly in the liberal house, where sister Eloise passes to and fro on errands between the linen closet and the cedar room, Mary Johnston is deeply contemplative. Or, comfortably established before a mahogany desk in a room walled with books and containing two globes, one terrestrial, the other astronomical, she labors to put her vision on paper, her free hand reaching out now and again for bites of a red apple that lies within easy reach. She is a pacifist, but perfectly ready to describe a battle up to the hilt; her description will shirk nothing but will be free from such hopeless embitterment as Barbusse's. She is a mystic bent upon the expressive embodiment of what eye hath not seen and ear hath not heard until she saw and heard it; but she is absolutely without the proselyting zeal and spirit. She is a tolerant dissenter from many men's thoughts and ideals; yet to know her is to respect her work, however much you dislike it . . . and to honor her purpose and admire her courage in a difficult adherence.

## V: *Amy Lowell*

AMY LOWELL towers above most contemporary versifiers like a sort of nineteenth century Savonarola, exhorting them to beware the pitfalls of sin and the ways of the devil. She is the sternest of Puritans; but over her gray sense of duty she wears a multitude of jewels. She wreathes herself in flowers, exotic colors flame from her hair, and while she consigns lust to the bonfire she makes sure that both lust and the bonfire are attractively tricked out with pretty words. Probably no great woman ever so successfully concealed herself by elaborate trappings. The poetical Miss Lowell reminds me occasionally of a wholehearted and beautiful dowager who, afraid that her own person will fail to charm, hedges herself about with silks and satins, perfumes, flowers, jewels, and clanking metals, until she seems a veritable museum of *objets d'art,* and the real woman beneath, fine and true as she is, becomes discernible only to those who are patient enough to look and to wait. The genius of Miss Lowell is based on a conflict—it is the quarrel of New England conservatism with an almost pagan love of the beautiful—and the result is, naturally enough, a firm code of denial, of duty in the strictest sense.

I do not purpose to ridicule Amy Lowell in these paragraphs, nor to belittle her literary powers. Any one so vital as she is, so tremendously active, gives broad chance for the cheap journalist and punster to indulge himself in comic regard. All her life she has been subject for such attacks; but those who have attacked her have not retired unscathed. In 1914 she was limned by "Town Topics" which said, among other vicious things: "It is reported that the Macmillans will publish a book of Miss Lowell's verses. Poor Old Boston." F.P.A., from his scornful heights of columny, parodied her again and again and even resorted to personal jibes. It was not the real poets, however, nor the real critics who bombarded her with criticism. It was the little versifiers and wits, who found the marching cadences of Miss Lowell's verses and the virile rush of her imagination easy to parody and to criticize. The firm quality of her work can be judged easily from the list of her critics. Radicals like Max Eastman attacked her, yet in 1915 W. D. Howells gave her high praise. Professor John Erskine and J. C. Squire still look askance at her, yet in 1921 even H. L. Mencken admitted grudgingly that she had "undoubted talents." Clement Shorter compared her to Dr. Johnson as the "unacknowledged head of Literary America." In 1913 Louis Untermeyer referred to her slightingly, but he has since paid her many glowing tributes. Her championship of the imagists brought down showers of controversy about her, which she weathered with little apparent effort. That she actually likes a good argument there is no doubt; but her hates are more intellectual than personal, and her raillery is most often leveled at dunderheads and dodos. She is forever sweeping out dusty minds, and her broom is more vigorous than cruel.

Miss Lowell has published six volumes of her own poetry. Two critical books, adaptations of Chinese translations and of two French operettas, critical pieces, and essays form the enormous body of her work. Before me now, in uniform size and with bright gemlike bindings, lies the complete set of her poems. After rereading them all I confess myself thoroughly humbled. There has never lived a woman poet of such range, versatility, and power. She reminds one of Byron or Browning. I am convinced that future time will find in her one of the literary giants

AMY LOWELL

of our time, and that, in spite of her overpowering personality, she will be known for her *poetry*. I know of only one way of phrasing my belief. She is a great poet.

Consider the poems. They range from the delicate, sometimes trite lyrics of "A Dome of Many-Coloured Glass" to the passionate virtuosity of "Can Grande's Castle" and the more closely knit dramas of "Legends." There are pieces as fragile and as finely wrought as Italian glass. Pieces like the serene and musical "Patience" or "Madonna of the Evening Flowers" or "White and Green":

> Hey! My daffodil-crowned;
> Slim and without sandals!
> As the sudden spurt of flame upon darkness
> So my eyeballs are startled with you,
> Supple-limbed youth among the fruit-trees,
> Light runner through tasselled orchards.
> You are an almond flower unsheathed,
> Leaping and flickering between the budding branches.

There are pieces of atmospheric description that startle by their trueness and glow with imagery. Turn to "Motor Lights on a Hill Road," or "Before the Storm." There is humor, even in such grim New England tragedies as those Yankee dialect poems in "The Overgrown Pasture." There is the perhaps more characteristic drama of "Patterns," of "The Cremona Violin," or "The Cross-Roads"; and, most important of all, Miss Lowell's imaginative grasp of historical events, her linking of them to human passion as in the epical "Bronze Horses" or that great portrait of Lady Hamilton, "Sea-Blue and Blood-Red." She sees often not one country but several, and their contrasted events of the same epoch.

Are these six books, these hundreds of poems, and the many others known to be in existence but still unpublished, the unrelated effusions of a vigorous mind and a prolific pen, or are they related by some deep philosophy of life? To me Miss Lowell, in even firmer accents than Robert Frost or than Stuart Pratt Sherman, is preaching the philosophy of Puritanism and is at the same time, especially in her earlier volumes, longing to escape from it. This regard for morality, this stern preaching of duty, this conviction that moral laws infringed lead only to punishment by nature or by God, is evident in every one of her books. I do not think that she has been unaware of her doctrines; but I fancy she has not realized how much of a propagandist for them she is. In her early work she was quite unashamed. She spoke occasionally almost with the accents of Gipsy Smith or Billy Sunday. In "Azure and Gold" we find a trite stanza that might come almost from a Y. M. C. A. hymn book:

> Centre Stone of the Crown of the World,
> "Sincerity" graved on your youth!
> And your eyes hold the blue-bird flash,
> The sapphire shaft, which is truth.

Here is philosophy concealed by no Maeterlinckian gauzes. Again we have it in "Fatigue":

> Dower me with strength and curb all foolish eagerness—
> The law exacts obedience. Instruct, I will conform.

She doesn't particularly wish to conform, mind you; but *she will!*

Over and over in the dramatic poems the story reiterates this idea of retribution for sin or dalliance. "The Great Adventure of Max Breuck" has it—Max loses all that is best to him in life because he tarries a moment by the way. Paul Jannes in "The Shadow" is turned from the pathway of sanity by his absorption in a shadow on his wall, the image of his own desire, the image from which he cannot escape. Lady Hamilton and Nelson are victims of their passion. Their tragedy is the most moving in "Can Grande's Castle." In "Guns as Keys: and the Great Gate Swings" Admiral Perry seizes on and opens to the world the mysteries of Japan—but what will be the consequences, Miss Lowell asks:

> Occident—Orient—after fifty years.

In "A Tale of Starvation" the old man gives up life in his quest for the beautiful and, as he finds, the foolish. Napoleon is a figure which appeals to Miss Lowell as a symbol of lofty ambition brought low. In "Hammers" she paints him magnificently.

Unfaithfulness, adultery, she again and again uses as the theme for grim tragedy: in "Pickthorn Manor," in "The Cremona Violin," in "Reaping," in "The Ring and the Castle," and others. Along with this is the other motif, the longing for escape, the desire to flee from the standards that life imposes. In the early books she feels this more keenly. Twice, she compares this mood to a pathway, leading somewhere. Where? In "The Way" she sees

> . . . spanning the river a bridge, frail promise to
> longing desire

and in "A Coloured Print by Shokei"—

> For it must lead to a happy land,
> This little path by a waterfall spanned.

Even more definitely personal she repeats this longing for change in "The Starling."

> I weary for desires never guessed,
> For alien passions, strange imaginings,
> To be some other person for a day.

In her latest volumes her philosophy of retributive justice is thoroughly crystallized. With the exception of two pieces of purely descriptive writing, all of the verses in "Legends" are on the one theme. "Memorandum Confided by a Yucca to a Passion-Vine" is the story of the fox who was desirous of the moon, and the consequences of his fearful quest. Says the fox:

> "And I have come here to drink this poison and die."

"A Legend of Porcelain" is the story of expiation for sin—

> Snared by beauty, she permitted her august father's house to go unguarded.

"Many Swans," an Indian variant of the Prometheus story, tells how "Many Swans" desired the possession of a gift of Heaven against which fate had warned him and which, then, accomplished the destruction of himself and his people.

> "The thing I wanted is bad," but he had the thing and he could not part from it.

"Witch-Woman" is the bizarre story of evil love—

> These kisses shot with poison,
> These thoughts cutting me like red knives.

"The Ring and the Castle" is a terrifying study of insanity and murder resulting from adulterous love:

> "Benjamin Bailey, Benjamin Bailey, sinners repent when they come to die."

"The Statue in the Garden" is not unlike "The Shadow" in its symbolism—a man is again absorbed in a concrete image of ideal beauty or love, and is pursued by this image.

In the vivid and almost brutal "Dried Marjoram," a mother tries to expiate her son's sin. "Before the Storm" is the legend of old Peter Rugg who is trying to find his destination through the ages—it is perhaps humorous that the object of the search is in this case not love nor beauty—but Boston! "Four Sides to a House" is a story of revenge, and of the ultimate disaster which a murdered man brings upon his murderers. There it is! Take it for what you will—obsession or philosophy—it is the secret of Miss Lowell's work; and yet, and yet, though she shrinks from seizing the object of desire, though she shows the retribution that inevitably follows, she admires those who seize it.

There is not so much of the prude in Miss Lowell as I may appear to think. She does not say, "Don't! Don't! Don't!" She simply sees with terrible clarity what is likely to happen to you if you do. She cannot bring herself to believe that happiness ever follows fulfilled desire. It is destruction to "follow your instincts." Napoleon fires her imagination. "Impudent! Audacious! But, by Jove, he blinds the eyes!" And for John Keats, who is almost her greatest hero, she has a wistful regard—he found beauty and seized it, in spite of all.

> Now comes a sprig little gentleman,
> And turns over your manuscript with his mincing fingers,
> And tabulates places and dates.
> He says your moon was a copy-book maxim,
> And talks about the spirit of solitude,
> And the salvation of genius through the social order.
> I wish you were here to damn him
> With a good, round, agreeable oath, John Keats,
> But just snap your fingers,
> You and the moon will still love,
> When he and his papers have slithered away
> In the bodies of innumerable worms.

Miss Lowell's own life has been fulfilled by the most rigorous discipline. Ever since she undertook to write poetry, she has made its creation, its entertainment, and its criticism her entire existence. She spends at least half her days in one of the most beautiful private libraries in the world—her own. Her life is organized for literature and is arranged to meet the demands made of it by the instinct to create! She understands *life* thoroughly; but she is afraid of it. She has spent her whole poetical career in disciplining her emotions. It is her mind only that wanders far afield. She has more intellectual curiosity than any other woman I have ever known. If she were a man, she would probably employ the best athletic trainer in the country to keep her in shape for her greatly varied tasks, tasks which she imposes on herself, like "The Life of John Keats." These tasks are exacting and worth while, and in accomplishing them she never pauses midway. She has been known to read hundreds of reference books to obtain the atmosphere for one poem. If you should tell her that she could have achieved the same effect with less use of accurate detail, she would give you the retort courteous that a poem, to be a poem to her, must be intellectually satisfying; that half-truths do not satisfy her.

Although she is constantly picturing the downfall of arrogant power, she is herself an aristocrat of no mean positivity. While she recognizes the worth of democracy, beauty, to her, is possible only through the refinements of life. She is intolerant; but, in the main, of one thing only —stupidity. Her mind works with almost miraculous rapidity. Those who arrive at conclusions more slowly, often find themselves lost in the maze of her questioning. She occasionally forgets that conclusions reached more slowly may be quite as sound.

Her thirst for constructive thinking has made necessary

her critical writings and her interest in the spread of enthusiasm for poetics. It is the same interest that prompts her to devour practically all of the new detective novels. It is the same instinct which led her to undertake the writing of a biography—which is, after all, the detection and reconstruction of a series of facts grouped around a working theory, then a proof of that theory by a proper presentation of the facts.

Her enemies—and she has many—are mostly those who resent her intolerance of intellectual sloppiness and her strong sense of moral values. She attends many banquets and her presence is often the cause of a torrent of disagreement.

What are her critical opinions of her contemporaries? You may find them in "Tendencies in Modern American Poetry" or, better still, in the anonymous "A Critical Fable," a pamphlet written in the tradition of Miss Lowell's greatuncle's "A Fable for Critics." In this are recorded her latest critical ideas. She denies that she wrote the screed, and for present purposes I accept the denial.[1] Nevertheless, its dicta are from the oracle of Brookline—her sibylline accents breathe through its pages. It is thoroughly in the Amy Lowell tradition. Its author has sat before the Lowell hearth and has heard the flow of brittle wisdom that greets the crackling flames and assaults the orchids from the Lowell greenhouses. Yes—it is as much in the Lowell tradition as are the family heirlooms and the orchids.

Her imagery, careful, direct, vivid, according to the imagist creed, occasionally takes the breath away by its strangeness. She tends to choose a hard image for representing soft things. She is forever comparing people to flowers, natural objects to jewels—

[1] She has now acknowledged the authorship of this poetical pamphlet.

. . . and one Rubens dame,
A peony just burst out,
With flaunting crimson flesh.

or

The notes rose into the wild sun-mote
Which slanted through the window.
They lay like coloured beads a-row,
They knocked together and parted,
And started to dance . . .

Her style is varied and practically always musical. For one who has been noted for her championship of free rhythms, she is remarkably devoted to form. Even her poems which at first reading seem chaotic gain in structural roundness as they are studied. She has molded her mind carefully to the pattern she desires, and it is according to this pattern that her poetry is made. Her rhythms vary from the boom and surge of polyphonic prose such as we find in the memorable close of "The Bronze Horses"—

The boat draws away from the Riva. The great bronze horses mingle their outlines with the distant mountains. Dim gold, subdued green-gold, flashing faintly to the faint, bright peaks above them. Granite and metal, earth over water. Down the canal, old, beautiful horses, pride of Venice, of Constantinople, of Rome. Wars bite you with their little flames and pass away, but roses and oleanders strew their petals before your going, and you move like a constellation in a space of crimson stars.

So the horses float along the canal, between barred and shuttered palaces, splendid against marble walls in the fire of the sun.

—to lilting delicacies such as the following:

It is Chou-Kiou who paints the fighting crickets
On the egg-shell cups;
Who covers the Wa-Wa cups

With little bully boys;
Who sketches Manchu ladies, Tartar ladies,
Chasing crimson butterflies with faint silk fans,
On the slim teapots of young bamboo.
Chou-Kiou,
Bustling all day between the kilns and the warehouses.
A breath of peach-bloom silk
Turning a pathway—
Puff! She is gone,
As a peach-blossom painted on paper
Caught in a corner of the wind.

This suiting of mood and story to rhythm is characteristic of Miss Lowell and is one of her greatest gifts as a poet.

Her best work is her latest. In a certain sense she will probably never surpass the vision and the execution of "Can Grande's Castle," but in "Legends" and in new poems not yet gathered in book form, she exhibits a smoothness and a dramatic fervor greater than in any previous work. She gives way with infrequency to the sharp, muted, and sometimes inept phrases which marred many early poems. She has not written so thoroughly prosaic a piece as "The Forsaken" in many years—nor do we now find such unfortunate couplets as

And fragrant as fir-trees are
When breezes in their needles jar.

Her later style is fluid and gracile, the thought deeper, the dream clearer. She deals with life more directly, as if she had suddenly come to understand both herself and the world better and was no longer afraid to speak boldly and truly. She puts down the veil. She comes out from her harem of fretwork and jewels, from her passionate absorption in gardens, from her wayward habit of being distracted from the point by the sudden sight and smell of flowers. She speaks with accents which are at the same time firm and beautiful. So great is the vitality possessed by her, that this progress has been possible. Heaven grant that she will use all her energy from now on in creating poetry and criticisms and in delivering her fervid lectures, that she may not again feel that literature and life require her to propagate a "school" of poetry or nourish another flock of poets. No matter how great her influence may have been in producing the new poetry in America, she has never furthered a poet greater than herself; and to herself, rather than to Johnny Jones or even John Keats, she should turn the efforts of what should prove her most productive years—the next ten!

## *VI: Floyd Dell*

BERGSON has pictured the life of humanity as a sort of wave, rushing ahead, over or through every obstacle. It is a cheering picture, and whenever I visualize it strongly I seem to see Floyd Dell riding on the topmost crest.

Or, if you prefer, you may think of him as a small boy running ahead of the parade—and always knowing intuitively which corner the parade is going to turn.

His own early life is more or less given to us in his first novel. He was born, in fact, near Davenport, Iowa, he did work in a candy factory, then on a newspaper—from which he was discharged not for his own shortcomings but because the house which the proprietor gave his daughter for a wedding present cost more than the estimate and necessitated retrenchment—and he did leave Davenport for Chicago, where he obtained a job as a reporter on the "Evening Post."

Intellectually, the Dell of those days is pretty much the Dell of to-day. In other ways—in emotional attitudes and what we may roughly call ethics—there has been a vast change. Soon after he joined the "Post," Francis Hackett became editor of the "Friday Literary Review" and Dell became his associate. That was in 1909 and I met him soon after. I had read some of his reviews, and imagined their author as a leisurely, rather elderly and very wise gentleman writing them in a quiet room in his club. Dell personally gave anything but that impression. He was exceedingly young looking, shy looking—but that vanished when he began to speak—thin, fair, with hair rather long in front, and a slight stoop. In short, he looked appealing rather than distinguished.

In a sense it is, doubtless, beside the point to write about his earlier days—for has he not recently confessed that he has been psychoanalyzed and that it has made a new person of him? That should mean, of course, that his past is dead—and it would be rather ungracious to dig it up and confront his new self with it. At least the reader may be warned not to try to interpret the present Floyd Dell in the light of such ancient history as I may resuscitate. That past seems to have been actually forgotten by the new Floyd Dell—when I recounted to him some anecdotes of his old Chicago life he was bewildered and incredulous. "Was I really like that?" he asked. And when I assured him it was so, he remarked: "No wonder people hated me."

To say that people "hated" him would not quite be true. Some of them liked him loyally enough; but they were the ones who had an opportunity of knowing him intimately, and were aware that he did not deliberately seek—as some others supposed—to make himself disagreeable. But, though he did not try, the fact is that he succeeded. He came to Chicago at a time when that city—and all America—was still under the régime of a polite reticence about all sorts of facts which have since then forced their way even into parlor conversation. Dell seemed unaware of these conventions—and he continually shattered them, in speech and in writing. Times have changed, and perhaps Floyd Dell would not seem so terrible a young man to Chicago to-day. But terrible he did seem then. He had, as his friends knew, a deep regard for truth—for truth as he saw it—and a youthful insensitiveness to other people's feelings. Perhaps he was unaware that other people had feelings—he was frequently accused of having none of his own. Perhaps he

FLOYD DELL

gave other people credit for the same kind of impersonal enthusiasm for truth that he himself possessed. At any rate, the combination was sometimes devastating, and it is not to be wondered at that in some quarters he was regarded as a highly offensive personage whose brilliancy only increased his objectionableness. It is possible that, immersed in his own world of ideas and surrounded by a few friends of his own sort, he was never quite conscious that he was living in a provincial and prudish middle western town: it is sufficient to say, in this connection, that he not only talked and wrote but lived as though he were a denizen of the Abbey of Thélème whose rule is "Do what you will."

How, in view of these circumstances, he ever gained a journalistic position which enabled him to annoy, shock, and outrage the sensibilities of his respectable fellow citizens, is somewhat of a mystery. It may have been that his journalistic abilities were of the sort that inevitably command recognition. Just how good a reporter he was, I really do not know. The only story of his I remember seeing was one he wrote on a birthday of John Milton. He looked up all the contemporary John Miltons in the telephone directory and went out and interviewed them—with especial reference to their occupations, which were usually quite non-poetic.

But his personality began to emerge and his popularity and unpopularity to grow when he became associate editor of the "Friday Literary Review" of the "Post"—and then its editor, when Francis Hackett left to write that novel for which we are still waiting. Dell had a flat in a suburb and he used to invite us out there to hear his friend Arthur Davison Ficke read his poems. Later I introduced him to the late George Burman Foster, who taught comparative religion in the University of Chicago, and who was indeed the greatest theological scholar in the country. But behind the theological scholar was a rebel, and Foster and Dell got on splendidly—even when Floyd's tendency to *épater le bourgeois* shocked all Foster's other guests.

On one occasion one of the guests was a local artist who painted landscapes of a very sentimental quality and liked to talk about "art." This artist had been asked to give a little talk to his fellow guests on art—and he had complied, with some abysmally silly remarks. Floyd Dell had come in late, and sat inconspicuously by the door. The artist ended his talk by offering to answer any questions. Dell, in dulcet tones, said he would like to ask one. The artist with a benevolent gesture signified that he might.

Dell: "What is the difference between art and apple butter?"

It may seem strange, to any one who has never known the Chicago of that date, that this disrespectful question should have created so much consternation. Dell might as well deliberately have taken a vase from the mantelpiece, said "I don't like this," and smashed it on the hearth. It was a thing that was positively *not done.* It established Dell as rude, insulting, egotistic, unprincipled, and dangerous. And it may be imagined what an innocent remark on the subject of sex—such as would pass fairly unnoted even in conservative circles in these Freudian days—it may be imagined, I say, what social havoc such a remark would create, with what a gasp it would be greeted, with what an embarrassing silence it would be followed, and how it would be whispered afterward into a multitude of horrified ears!

Dell seems to have forgotten, but he must have enjoyed these situations. At all events, he created them. But it is probably true that his intention was not so much to shock the bourgeoisie as to let the bourgeoisie know that its ideas profoundly shocked him. He was, in fact, quite natural and simple in all his social contacts. And he was in those days still naïve enough to think that he could show the bourgeoisie by a little cold logic just how shocking it was.

His naturalness irritated even Professor Foster on one occasion. He and Dell were both on an ambitious program designed to celebrate something in connection with Robert Browning—his centenary, I think. Anyway it was a very boring occasion, until it was very unexpectedly enlivened by Dell. Professor Foster, being a philosopher by trade, had to speak of Browning as a philosopher—and he made out a good case. But making the best of a bad job was too pragmatic a concept to find lodgment in Dell's mind. When he was called upon—his subject being Browning as a dramatist—he impetuously launched an attack upon Foster's argument: "I disagree utterly with Professor Foster. Browning was not a philosopher at all. There is more philosophy in one page of Shaw than there is in all of Browning . . ." and so forth, with some ridicule for the philosophy of "God's in his heaven; all's right with the world." But Dell made up to the Browningites present, if not to the Fosterites—for there were more people there who came to hear Foster than there were readers of Browning—by his excellent defence of Browning as a dramatic poet.

Although some people are now affecting to think of Chicago as the literary capital of America, there seems —to an occasional visitor at least—nothing in the city to-day quite like that little society which grouped itself around Floyd Dell. There was George Cram Cook, now the director of the Provincetown Players, who was then known to a small circle as a novelist.[1] Dell had met him in Davenport and for a year or so had been in partnership

[1] Mr. Cook has died since this paper was written.

with him in a truck farm. They had had a terrible struggle. Their vision of living from the farm and having leisure for literary work faded very soon. They tried to fight insects and frosts but their methods were inadequate. If it is true, as Cook's friends say, that he is the laziest man in America, that truck farm is to blame for it. And even Floyd was never able to finish his first novel until after being psychoanalyzed, although whether memories of the truck farm showed up at all in the analysis he has never told me. Then Charles Hallinan, an editorial writer on the "Post," was a member of the group, as were Lucian and Augusta Cary—who succeeded Dell as literary editors of the "Post"—and Llewellyn Jones, then a contributor to the "Friday Review" and now its editor. There was Margaret Anderson, too, then literary editor of the "Continent," a Presbyterian paper not at all like "The Little Review" which she now so ably captains. Sherwood Anderson was, toward the last, one of this group, and it may be said—in fact, Sherwood Anderson does say it—that Floyd Dell was his "discoverer"; at least, Dell was the first person who knew what literature is who recognized and hailed him as a writer. In fact, when Dell left Chicago for New York he took with him the manuscript of Anderson's first novel, "Windy McPherson's Son," and tried vainly for several months to find a publisher for it—and at last found one in England, who made arrangements for its publication by the American branch of the house. Theodore Dreiser, on his visits to Chicago, was a familiar in the group; and so was Vachel Lindsay, as yet unknown to fame, on his visits from Springfield. Carl Sandburg, also as yet unknown as a poet, was occasionally present. And the Little Theatre company, and their director, Maurice Browne, were part of the group as well.

This group, held together by their common love of art

and ideas, gradually disintegrated as one after another left town. The émigrés outnumber those who have remained. Dell was among those who went to New York. He became one of the editors of "The Masses," a radical and art magazine, lived in Greenwich Village, and for several years devoted his leisure to writing and producing one act plays. They were first presented at the Liberal Club in Greenwich Village, and in a sense these plays initiated the contemporary little theatre movement in New York. For one of the offshoots of the Liberal Club theatre was the Washington Square Players organization, which gave birth in turn to the Provincetown Players company and the Theatre Guild. Besides writing and producing plays, Dell amused himself by organizing the earliest of those Greenwich Village balls which, together with other Greenwich Village activities in which he had his due share, presently advertised the Village so thoroughly to all America that the sons and daughters of the bourgeoisie flocked in by the thousands seeking "freedom," and the original inhabitants of the Village fled to the suburbs—Dell among them. It was a time of play, brought to an end by the war and perhaps also by the fact that after a time nothing becomes so tiresome as pleasure. It was at this period that Dell simultaneously discovered that life is real, life is earnest, and that Freud is its prophet. He was "psyched," became the husband of B. Marie Gage, settled down, and wrote his first novel.

Just how much he has changed as a result of his psychoanalytic conversion is a question. His intellectual passions and curiosities remain the same—on the one hand a disinterested devotion to pure (and hence useless) beauty, and on the other hand a strangely utilitarian kind of social idealism. He is ready to uphold Prohibition, or even to have smoking (he smokes cigarettes continuously) abolished by law, on grounds of efficiency. But his emotional nature has apparently undergone some real change, not entirely for the worse. What his complexes were I have not asked him, but psychoanalysis seems to have straightened out the kinks, and made it possible not only for him to write his novels but to find happiness in life. And because Freud has been accused so often of breaking up homes, it may be of interest to note that its effect in this instance seems to be in the direction of a more conservative attitude toward sex. Indeed, Dell seems to some of his friends unduly sensitive to—or perhaps he is merely bored by—jokes on the subject; at any rate he fails to find any amusement in the kind of Rabelaisian anecdotes for which most of his fellow human beings have a genial weakness. If that is the result of psychoanalysis, it seems rather a pity!

Since some of his acquaintances of earlier days have looked upon him as an idle jester, and still others as a dangerous social radical, it would be desirable, if it were possible, to explain in just what ways he has changed. He is still some kind of Socialist, and might perhaps be called a conservative Bolshevik. During the war both aspects of this conservative radicalism were in evidence. He was an editor of "The Masses," a magazine which opposed the war, but in another Socialist magazine, "The New Review," he wrote attacking German imperialism in terms which left nothing to be desired by the most ardent patriot. He was indicted, along with the other editors of "The Masses," for criticizing the government. The specific crime charged against him was writing an article in defense of conscientious objectors; and yet when he was himself drafted for military service he did not become a conscientious objector. He was actually sent back from a training camp to be tried a second time for his defense of conscientious objectors! Dell himself explains that he was "a little muddled." But I think he has a genuine streak of conservatism and an equally genuine streak of radicalism in his nature, and that his actions were perfectly consonant with this mixed temperament. He has a real passion for freedom of utterance, and would see nothing absurd in going to jail in behalf of the right to praise conduct which he himself had no desire to emulate. The puzzled jury found itself unable, in two trials, to decide that he was a menace to the Republic. Then the armistice came, and the indictment was dismissed—and he was left at peace to devote himself to his real work, the writing of novels.

With the publication of his first novel, "Moon-Calf," some of his friends were surprised to find no trace of the ardent rebel, the stringent social critic that they knew, in its pages. The rebel, the social critic, appears it is true in the person of the hero, Felix Fay—but the novel seemed to be rather a criticism of him than a justification. This impression was strengthened by the second novel, "The Briary-Bush," in which the same hero, after trying out various modern experiments in conduct, comes at last to accept certain established conventions—particularly the convention of marriage in its most old-fashioned sense.

This impression, taken together with the fact that the author, after (or so it is rumored) a somewhat hectic and ultramodern emotional career, is now enjoying an old-fashioned happy domesticity at Croton-on-Hudson, with his wife and son Anthony—plus the fact that he is said to appear on social occasions in conventional dinner clothes —has caused some of his acquaintances (especially some of that younger generation to whom his name was, along with those of Dreiser and Mencken, a shibboleth of radicalism) to mourn for him as a lost soul. They would not be surprised to hear that he had voted for Harding and joined the local Rotary Club. His old friend Dreiser, meeting him recently, gave expression to these current notions, saying sardonically, "I hear you have become reconciled to Church and State." Dell merely grinned in reply.

When an author has the good fortune to be damned as conservative, it is rather too bad to spoil the illusion. But Dell's novels really do not justify the notion that he has gone over to the Old Guard. They are not propaganda, it is true; they are written from a point of view from which ideas of any sort, modern or old-fashioned, are in themselves of no fundamental significance, representing as they do merely some of the outward guises of human emotion. It is with these human emotions, as contemporary life serves to illustrate them, that the novels deal; and perhaps the author of them has done a real, if unappreciated, service to the cause of modernism by showing how very powerful indeed are the impulses with which that modernism must contend, and how frail are the intellectual plans of young modernists in comparison with the immemorial instincts of the human herd—of which they are, as they sooner or later find, themselves a part.

## *VII: Edna St. Vincent Millay*

EDNA ST. VINCENT MILLAY is a slim young person with chestnut-brown hair shot with glints of bronze and copper, so that sometimes it seems auburn and sometimes golden; a slightly snub nose, and freckles; a child mouth; a cool, grave voice; and grey-green eyes.

With these materials, she achieves a startling variety of appearances. When she is reading her poetry, she will seem to the awed spectator a fragile little girl with apple blossom face. When she is picnicking in the country she will be, with her snub nose, freckles, carroty hair, and boyish grin, an Irish "newsy." When she is meeting the bourgeoisie in its lairs, she is likely to be a highly artificial and very affected young lady with an exaggerated Vassar accent and abominably overdone manners. In the basement of the Brevoort, or in the Café de la Rotonde in Paris, or the Café Royal in London, she will appear a languid creature of a decadent civilization, looking wearily out of ambiguous eyes and smiling faintly with her doll's mouth, exquisite and morbid. A New England nun; a chorus girl on a holiday; the Botticelli Venus of the Uffizi gallery. . . .

She is all of these and more. A contradictory young person! And the real Edna St. Vincent Millay, beneath all these disguises? That is hard to say. She does not give you any help by what she tells you of herself. Her speech is another series of disguises—of fictions, if you will. In the last few years there has grown up an Edna St. Vincent Millay legend, a sort of Byronic legend, which the younger generation is pleased to believe in. She accepts it; doubtless she is flattered by it—as any of us would be, the more flattered, the more untrue it was!—and perhaps she may have tried after a fashion to live up to it. She is certainly not the person to spoil a good story, especially if it is about herself, by prudish denials. As to that, she has a proud maxim: "I am that I am." Yes, she is what she is. Which leaves the matter where, doubtless, she prefers it to remain—in mystery.

The Edna St. Vincent Millay legend is based on her poems—or, to speak more exactly, upon one particular book of poems, the one entitled "A Few Figs from Thistles." Its title gives an indication of its cynical optimism. Previous to this volume she had been known as the author of "Renascence," and had gained the devout admiration of a few poetry lovers, but no popular audience. With the publication of "Figs from Thistles," she became the poet laureate of the younger generation. The first poem in the volume is as follows:

> My candle burns at both ends;
>   It will not last the night;
> But ah, my foes, and oh, my friends—
>   It gives a lovely light!

The second poem utters the same gospel of impulse:

> Safe upon the solid rock the ugly houses stand:
> Come and see my shining palace built upon the sand!

To the younger generation beauty must come speaking some such gospel if it is to be acclaimed. The state of the young mind is individualistic, egocentric, passionately rebellious against authority. If these boys and girls hail Edna St. Vincent Millay as their poet, it is because she seems to be writing about them. The youth of to-day, cherishing no illusions as to its own stability or fidelity, and the girl of to-day, practically confronted by the prob-

EDNA ST. VINCENT MILLAY

lems of association with such youth, are alike happy to find it celebrated in such a comparison as this:

Oh, Prue, she has a patient man,
  And Joan a gentle lover,
But Agatha's Arth' is a hug-the-hearth,—
  But my true love's a rover!

Mig, her man's as good as cheese
  And honest as a briar,
Sue tells her love what he's thinking of,—
  But my dear lad's a liar!

. . . . . . .

Cold he slants his eyes about,
  And few enough's his choice,—
Though he'd slip me clean for a nun, or a queen,
  Or a beggar with knots in her voice,—

. . . . . . .

Joan is paired with a putterer
  That bastes and tastes and salts,
And Agatha's Arth' is a hug-the-hearth,—
  But my true love is false!

The newer mood of girlhood, that mood of freedom which is dramatized outwardly by bobbed hair, finds itself pleasantly expressed in this volume:

And if I loved you Wednesday,
  Well, what is that to you?
I do not love you Thursday—
  So much is true.

It is a mood of freedom gaily maintained even in the midst of what might seem an emotional bondage:

Now it may be the flower for me
  Is this beneath my nose;
How shall I tell, unless I smell
  The Carthaginian rose?

Or, as it is earnestly but not less gracefully put in another poem:

> Oh, think not I am faithful to a vow!
> Faithless am I save to love's self alone.
> Were you not lovely I would leave you now:
> After the feet of beauty fly my own.

This attitude toward life is summed up in the sonnet with which the volume appropriately ends:

> If you entreat me with your loveliest lie,
> I shall protest you with my favorite vow.

Not every poet can have a legend. There must be something in his personality, as well as in his poetry, to stimulate the imaginations of his fellows and make them project their own wishes upon his image. That is not always his fault; and it may be his misfortune. The Edna St. Vincent Millay legend, so agreeable to the fancies of the younger generation, has distracted attention from work of hers that is more beautiful and more deeply sincere than these graceful and impudent little lyrics, with their suggestion at once of the Cavaliers and of Calverley. Yes, Calverley—for are not some of these things after all a kind of *vers de société,* not less so because the society with whose emotions these poems politely and playfully deal is the bohemian society of fellow artists? These are the ratiocinations of a creative artist at odds with life and love, half fearful of some desperate and fatal trap, half proud of his escape. But this light mockery has a forced note in it. Love is dealt with more honestly, even though more cruelly, in another poem, the concluding sonnet of "Second April"—in which the poet repudiates with cold anger the lover's "mouth of clay, these mortal bones against my body set," and "all the puny fever and frail sweat of human love."

In this fierce Manichæan denunciation of the body and the poor joys it has to offer, we find the real attitude that underlies these frivolities—and it is far from being a frank acceptance of the facts of life. It is not modern, it is something very ancient—an austere religious idealism, none the less austere and none the less a religion because it now has artists for its priests. It is a belief in something beyond this mortal life—the immortality, in this instance, of art. And it is not as a woman that the poet speaks here, but as a human being and a creative artist. Her mortal lover, with his dream of a warm earthly happiness to which she as woman must minister, is pushed aside. "You shall awake," he is told,

> from dreams of me, that at your side,
> So many nights, a lover and a bride,
> But stern in my soul's chastity, have lain,
> To walk the world forever, for my sake,
> And in each chamber find me gone again!

In a sense it is a rebellion against sex, and—since women are by social custom more the servants of their sex than men—against being a woman: a triumphant escape into an impersonal realm of art, which resembles heaven in that there is no marrying nor giving in marriage. Another woman poet, Anna Wickham, has expressed quaintly the same rebellion:

> I hide my breast in a workman's shirt,
> And hunt the perfect phrase.

But it is, as found in real life, not so austere a state of mind as might be imagined. In these feminist days it is not unusual to talk to a girl in forgetfulness of the fact that she belongs to the other half of the human race; but it is nevertheless not yet so commonplace that one does not feel a thrill to discover in a girl the capacity for such a broadly human relationship. Edna Millay is, eminently, such a person, the most delightful of companions—a gay and whimsical comrade, heartfree if not carefree, keen, generous, and braveminded.

The poetic scorn of mere human nature has its origin, of course, in the fact of the transiency of life. Life is pitiful because—as poets more than other people are given to reminding themselves—it comes inevitably to an end. "This flawless vital hand, this perfect head, this body of flame and steel"—shall die like any other: "it mattering not how beautiful you were."

Meanwhile, awaiting death, the poet has brave things to say: "the sands of such a life as mine run red and gold even to the ultimate sifting dust" . . .

> In me no lenten wicks watch out the night;
> I am the booth where Folly holds her fair,
> Impious no less in ruin than in strength. . . .

But still the thought of death recurs. Therefore—

> Suffer me to take your hand.
> Suffer me to cherish you
> Till the dawn is in the sky.
> Whether I be false or true,
> Death comes in a day or two.

And again, for a more sufficient solace against the thought of death, comes the hope of that immortality which art offers to those who serve her well:

> Ah, when the thawed winter splashes
> Over these chance dust and ashes,
> Weep not me, my friend!

Me, by no means dead
    In that hour, but surely
When this book, unread,
    Rots to earth obscurely,
And no more to any breast,
    Close against the clamorous swelling
    Of the thing there is no telling,
Are these pages pressed!

It is in such poems as these, in which the thought of death makes life more sweet, more beautiful, and more to be cherished moment by moment, that Edna Millay is at her best and loveliest. She has the gift of seeing things as though with her last living look. Her poem "Renascence" embodies the strange fantasy of one dying and coming alive again to look once more upon the earth. Another poem, "The Blue Flag in the Bog," relates a still stranger fantasy—the destruction of the earth, and of one sadly watching it burn, from heaven. "Now forevermore good-bye, all the gardens of the world!" In both poems it is a child who sees the beauty of earth so poignantly; and it is thus that Edna Millay sees it, always, with the eyes of a child—and thus that she salutes it, as one who is about to take leave of it forever.

All her early life was spent on the coast of Maine, and her young mind seems to have been filled with an infinity of impressions of the sea: "The sticky, salty sweetness of the strong wind and shattered spray"; "the loud sound and the soft sound of the big surf that breaks all day." She began to write poetry as a child, encouraged by her mother, who is a poet of real if unfulfilled talent, and a woman besides of vivid, humorous, and tolerant personality. But it wasn't of these familiar scenes that Edna as a child wrote; it was, as in a poem to be found in the files of "St. Nicholas," of "the road to romance"! It was only, perhaps, when she had trodden the road away from childhood that she looked back and found it so beautiful:

> Always I climbed the wave at morning,
> Shook the sand from my shoes at night,
> That now am caught beneath great buildings,
> Stricken with noise, confused with light.

It was the child who climbed the wave at morning, and not the adult wearied with city noise, who wrote "Renascence." That poem, comparable in its power and vision to "The Hound of Heaven," was written during her eighteenth and nineteenth years. It was submitted in a prize poem contest and published among other poems in "The Lyric Year," in 1912. It is now generally remembered as having won the prize; the fact is that it was passed over altogether in the awards.

This strange, lovely, mystical poem aroused in literary circles curious speculations as to its author, who was imagined as a child mystic. A poet, now better acquainted with her, wrote a solemnly congratulatory letter such as he might have written to young Christina Rossetti, or to Santa Teresa herself. He was much puzzled by the irrelevant and frivolous missive he received in return—dealing chiefly with the elated purchase of a pair of red dancing slippers. She was, it seemed, a real nineteen year old girl!

The year following she entered Vassar. She graduated in 1917 with an A.B. and a reputation for brilliant scholarship. She had written two plays at college and acted in them—"The Princess Marries the Page" and "Two Slatterns and a King." And now her first volume of poems appeared.

The volume, "Renascence," included together with the title poem some quietly notable new ones. These showed no signs of influence by any of the jazzy contemporary movements in poetry; they were not cubistic nor post-impressionistic, they were not in free verse, nor intended to be chanted to revival tunes; the lines were chiseled, the rhythms classical—she was so old-fashioned, even, as to write sonnets. The new poems contained nothing so astonishing as "Renascence," but they showed a marked individual talent, and they maintained for her the respect of lovers of poetry.

She came from college, ambitiously, to New York, and settled in Greenwich Village, where rents were—in those days—low; in a very tiny room on Waverly Place, hardly large enough for a bed and a typewriter and some cups and saucers; a room, however, with the luxury of a fire-place, for which Joe the Italian brought, every few days, staggering up the stairs, a load of firewood at ten cents a precious stick. Here, on the floor, hugging the fire, she sat, remembering the coast of Maine: "the green piles groaning under the windy wooden piers"; "robins in the stubble," and "brown sheep upon the warm green hill" . . . remembering these, and making of such images poignant poems, only, as always happens with young poets, to get them back again from magazine editors who were "already overstocked with poetry."

A poet can, of course, live almost exclusively upon tea and coffee. But one must have cigarettes once in a while. Also, it is pleasant to have real cream, instead of condensed milk, in one's coffee. So, remembering her acting experience at Vassar, she went to the theatrical agencies, seeking a job. She was sent to the Provincetown Theatre on Macdougal Street, and acted in a number of comedies, and presently had some of her own plays put on. But the Provincetown Theatre, at that time, was very much an art-for-art's sake institution, paying neither actors' salaries nor authors' royalties. It was a happy moment when she was given a small "part" in one of the Theatre Guild productions and a salary.

But there were no more "parts," and no more salary; and meantime she lived on bread and coffee, or, for a change, bread and tea; except when, according to the happy bohemian custom of the Village, some one dropped into her tiny room on Waverly Place with a delicatessen dinner of pickles, olives, cold roast beef, potato salad, and, if he were a true friend, a bottle of cream—honest-to-God cream!—or on those other exceptional occasions when somebody had the money to pay for a dinner in the basement of the Brevoort.

When they dropped in, laden with packages from the delicatessen, or with the elate air of one who is going Brevoorting, they might find her crouched brooding on the floor of an unswept and disorderly room. She was not brooding over some shattered romance—for romances are always shattered, so why trouble about a thing like that?—but over a batch of manuscripts just come back from some magazine. . . . She *ought,* no doubt, to make use of her knowledge of shorthand and get a job as a stenographer; or even go to work at the ribbon counter of a department store. If people didn't want beautiful poetry why should she starve writing it? A fair question! . . . But to go to work, in that dull mechanical sense, would be a final surrender of her pride as a creator; it meant giving up being a poet. It would be spiritual suicide; and if it came to that, why accept the ignominy of doing drudgery for people who don't care for poetry? Why live in such a world at all?

On the other hand, why not? She had had no illusions about the world. It was an ugly and absurd place. She had never supposed otherwise, nor had any serious hope of its ever being made much better by her revolutionary friends. But, ugly and absurd as it was, the poet could find beauty in it. That was what poets, apparently, were for—to squeeze this toad of a world with unflinching fingers until it gave up the jewel, of which—as all children who read fairy tales know—it is the venomous guardian! Perhaps she had better stick it out—which, upon further consideration, she decided to do.

In this tiny room might be seen, at times, her charming younger sisters, Norma, who had also come to New York, and Kathleen, on her vacation from Vassar—and sometimes the three of them could be persuaded to "harmonize" an old song of their own, Edna taking a throaty baritone:

Oh, men! Men! Men!
Oh, men alluring,
Waste not your hour
(Sweet hour!)
In vain assuring.
For love, though sweet,
(*Oh, tho thweet!*)
Is not enduring.
Ti-di-dee and ti-di-da!
We must take you as you are,
Etc.

—A pleasant scene to remember. . . .

"Aria da Capo," a very beautiful and impressive little play, first produced by the Provincetown Players, was published in 1920; "A Few Figs from Thistles," "The Lamp and the Bell" (which was the Vassar play for the year), "Two Slatterns and a King," and "Second April" all in 1921. In "Second April" her poetry came to full bloom—the poem of that volume called "The Poet and His Book" seems destined to be recognized as among the great lyrics of the language.

Her later career includes a year of European travel, the award to her in 1922 of the Pulitzer prize for poetry, significant of the general recognition of her genius, and the publication in 1923 of "The Ballad of the Harp-Weaver and Other Poems." In this latest volume the gay mockery of the "Figs from Thistles" period becomes magnificently candid and poignant utterance. "What sets Miss Millay's poems apart from all those written in English by women," as Carl Van Doren has said, "is the full pulse which . . . beats through them. . . . Rarely since Sappho has a woman written as outspokenly as this."

## *VIII: Stuart P. Sherman*

AS Gargantua, according to the record, the moment he was born cried out in a masterful voice demanding liquor, so Stuart P. Sherman, according to a record equally authentic, asked physician, midwife, nurse, neighbor, and all the other bystanders what the devil "these young people" were doing there. He was, it is true, as young as any within hearing, but he had come into the world with one element of his technique already perfected. Ever since, he has been forcing "these young people" to stand and deliver him some reason why they should exist and why they should be so little like the classics.

Let it not be thought that he is actually the snow-bearded Rhadamanthus he is sometimes thought to be. Though he is older than the younger generation, he is—to put it in round numbers—a year younger than H. L. Mencken and Joseph Hergesheimer and Ernest Poole and Carl Van Vechten; two years younger than James Branch Cabell and Vachel Lindsay; three years younger than Upton Sinclair and Henry Seidel Canby and Carl Sandburg; five years younger than Willa Cather and Sherwood Anderson; six years younger than Robert Frost, seven than Amy Lowell and Clarence Day, ten than Theodore Dreiser, and twelve than Edgar Lee Masters. He is the senior by only one year of Ludwig Lewisohn and George Jean Nathan and James Oppenheim; by only two years of Francis Hackett; by only three years of Sara Teasdale; by only four years of Sinclair Lewis and Carl Van Doren and Louis Untermeyer; by only five of Van Wyck Brooks, and six of Floyd Dell, and seven of Heywood Broun. He has used less critical muscle in spanking his juniors than in skinning his contemporaries.

Sherman seems older than he is for the reason that he was nearly the earliest of his generation to achieve any solid fame. He took the road by which it is always easiest for a young man to arrive at a reputation for subtlety and wisdom: he allied himself with his elders in discontent with the turbulence of youth. In 1908 there was no "New Republic," no "Freeman," no open-columned "Literary Review," no BOOKMAN sensitive to the latest movement, no new "Dial," and no new "Nation." Only the old "Nation," with Paul Elmer More as literary editor, gave serious criticism half a chance. More discovered Sherman and Sherman justified his editor's confidence. How he eviscerated poor George Moore! How he decorated his barn door with the hide of Dreiser! How he ranked H. G. Wells among the windy angels of Utopia and denied that the man was talking about the real world at all! How, one after another, Sherman punctured humanitarianism and dissected sentimentalism and slit the gullet of naturalism! He was witty, he could be eloquent, he had dramatic force, he wrote like a cynical seraph. Many people began to look up, and several began to look up to him.

Then something happened. The war tumbled the established structure of opinion about the ears of young and old, and it was the young who first poked their heads out of the tangle of laths and the heaps of plaster. All of a sudden there were new poets and new critics and new novelists in every quarter. They founded organs and got a hearing and took revenges. Not entirely by accident did they choose Sherman to be their special target for anathema. He was the wit among their rivals. He had himself started the vendetta and he had spared no one. He had planted exploding darts in the sturdy neck of Mencken. He had disturbed the fastidious steps of Van Wyck Brooks. He had raised the lily-white banner of

STUART P. SHERMAN

Anglo-Saxonism and had vexed, besides Francis Hackett, Jew and German and Scandinavian and cosmopolitan and pagan. He had swallowed Woodrow Wilson whole.

Yet it is not fair to single him out as the uncritical choragus of the Old Guard. He has always despised Brander Matthews; he has traveled far from his early satisfaction with Irving Babbitt; he would cross bayonets any day with Paul Elmer More on the topic of democracy. Remember how he comprehends and praises Mark Twain and how gorgeously he mocked the complacent toryism of Alfred Austin. He knows he talked and wrote a good deal of nonsense during the war. Though he seems so essentially a midwesterner that a writer in the Richmond "Reviewer" lately undertook to reconstruct Urbana, Illinois from the mere fact that Sherman lives and works there, he thought "Main Street" the best novel of 1920 and still thinks so. He has recently come to have a positive reverence for Whitman. In his newest book, a selection from the prose and verse of Emerson, he uses for a motto that radical dictum of his author: "Man is a fagot of thunderbolts." It troubles Sherman, no doubt, to be forever regarded as a conservative. It must sadden him. It may even make him, in certain introspective moments, bewail his fate.

It has not yet, however, taught him to stop his incessant digs at "these young people"—a mannerism which enrages the young, with whom he is not nearly so much out of sympathy as he forces them to think, and which bores many of his coevals and his elders who sicken of that tiresome sport. It happens that this mannerism of his has been encouraged by almost all the facts of his career. Peep behind the scenes. He was a prize boy at Williams College; academic hands applauded him through the Harvard graduate school; there were many academic gates wide for him when he came out. In the University of

Illinois he climbed the hard steps of promotion so fast that at thirty he was a full professor and had already begun to reap the crop of invitations by which envious universities have sought to tempt him to other learned groves. From the first, responsibility has sat upon his shoulders. He has been a pillar, an arbiter, a last resort, a throne. He has had to walk cautiously among the elder statesmen of his bailiwick; he has had to assume maturity to match his power over his numerous subordinates. Compelled to administer and to account for his administration, he has been too busy ever to have the fling which his years deserved. Is it any wonder that he seems immemorially four-square? Is it any wonder that he has come to be curt with the irresponsible, to be cool toward the impassioned, to be the challenger of experiment, to be the upholder of the true and tried? Is it too much a wonder that, shaped in New England and the middle west, and innocent of travel in any country where English is not spoken, he remains unawakened to the cultures of racial stocks besides his own?

No, responsibility has cut him off from many of his kind and age, as if he were a crown prince somewhere and had to live in the broad eye of noon. But let no one think that Sherman has always been a pillar of his state. In his Harvard days, grubbing among the grammars into which the system forced him, he swore dreadfully. There he discovered the austerity of Pater and the softness of Thoreau; there he ransacked the decadents, from purple Rome to yellow Nineties, and specialized in the more immoral Elizabethans; once done with Harvard, he bludgeoned its manner of literary study till the welkin shook. The philologers then hated him like vulgar poison. The recalcitrant among the scholars then rallied round him. So, too, when he first went to Illinois from Massachusetts, he was full of brash irreverences, an æsthete stranded in a village, homesick Ovid among the honest Goths. Where another man would have flown the coop in irritation, Sherman buried himself in Boswell's "Johnson" and learned how to rule a clucking roost. He buried himself in Burke and learned how, while distrusting revolutions, to fit his stride to the progress of a race. He buried himself in Matthew Arnold and learned how to test all things by the best. Yet beneath these crusts of discipline there were—and are—hot fires in him. He has a gusto, an insolence, a rage of his own, for all he so unmercifully knifes cruder gustos, insolences, rages. If only he would feel a little less of that damned responsibility! If only he would act a little less as if every new author were some raw sophomore badly in need of a perspiring session on the diaconal carpet!

Well, any critic good enough to be worth criticizing is this sort of man or that, but not all sorts or no human sort at all. If Sherman is far from being a William Lyon Phelps, a literary tea-taster greeting each new spoonful with uncensored approbation, so is he far from being a Paul Elmer More, sulking perpetually in his tent with Plato and Racine and such large deer. Sherman shudders at the hilarious Rabelais but he understands the intelligent Montaigne; he hates the expansive humanitarian but he loves the essential democrat; he grins at aristocracies but he stands for excellence; he asks for form in art but he responds to various colors which leave the formalist cold; he craves order but he is not wholly comfortable in a cemetery. Were he a little more alive to current literature he might lack his gift of studying the transitory under a learned light; were he a little further sunk in learning, he might forget the living altogether. This stark position of his isolates him. Imagine what Brander Matthews thinks of him for his public praise of Ludwig Lewisohn's account of the unmaking of an American.

Guess what Katharine Fullerton Gerould thinks of him for his pillorying of her snobbishness. See what Burton Rascoe thinks of him for his Puritan enthusiasms and proprieties. Inquire of the younger poets what they think of his attitude toward their novel practices in verse. There he sits in his midwestern study and swings the lash, while innumerable lions, big and little, snap back at him.[1] He could not do that effectively if he were not a personage as well as a scholar and a critic. And he is a personage. He is one of the finest and strongest the country has.

It is a lamentable thing that he should have become a legend through being so long a voice of which so few have seen the body. His victims fancy that his temper is querulous, when in reality it is eminent and profound and packed with laughter. He fancies wrong things about his victims from seeing them solely in their books or in their piqued replies to him. It would do everybody good if he and Mencken could swap confidences about the tastes they have in common for careful linen and superior cigars and bitter ale: thereafter fur and feathers might fly less superfluously from their controversies. It would do Sherman good to have a flyting with Edna St. Vincent Millay: thereafter he might not bully women quite so recklessly. It would do Van Wyck Brooks good to learn from Sherman how much generous suspectibility to abundance of life can go with a temper as classical as his own. It would do conservatives and radicals alike, of all hues, tendencies, and degrees, good to see Sherman and, say, J. E. Spingarn or Maxwell Bodenheim quarreling in candid language. For want of such relieving frays, exasperation multiplies and the Sherman legend grows.

[1] Since this paper was written Mr. Sherman has resigned from the University of Illinois to become literary editor of the New York *Herald-Tribune*.

## *IX: Frederick O'Brien*

ONE recalls an anecdote that went the rounds several years ago, when starting in to write of Frederick O'Brien—that debonair, devil-may-care explorer and *bon vivant.*

It seems that there was in New York, long since, a newspaper woman who, after years of potboiling, suddenly burst into print with a remarkable short story in one of the better-class magazines. Two of her friends met on Fifth Avenue one day. Said the first, "Why, I didn't know that Miss M—— wrote fiction." Whereupon the other smiled. "My boy," he said, "didn't you ever read any of her interviews?"

Now, how much of O'Brien is truth, and how much is fiction? That is a question which has been asked from the first. He claims that it is all true—those white shadows in the South Seas really fell upon him and enveloped him; yet some of us, hoping we are still blessed with brains, have wondered late and long just what "white shadows" may be. We never found out in that fascinating volume. We are still in the dark, so to speak. The style is charming—just as the man is; but where does fact end, and fiction begin?

In every travel book that O'Brien has given to a waiting world one has the sense that there is a devilish lot of hokum mixed in with the essential truth. The temptation to rhapsodize was too great to resist. His name would of course lead one to believe that he is part Irish; and we know the Irishman's love of twisting things which concern himself so that they bear a resemblance to the truth, yet are magically and adroitly made to appear highly romantic. In other words, if there wasn't a love affair, there *should* have been one; therefore throw it in. If the girl was ugly, she became pretty; if pretty, she was turned into the most beautiful of women. And finally, the romanticist gets to believe in his heart of hearts that what he has set down is gospel truth, and it would be hard to persuade him, particularly after three or four editions, that the initial plainness of his dusky adored one ever existed. Mythical loves are easily turned into shining realities; and then creeps in, naturally enough, the provocative line that hints of other happenings which cannot be told. Ah, how wicked this fellow has been, 'way off there in the South Seas, with no one to watch his philandering, no one to whisper of his boyish shortcomings! A roistering, hard-drinking, amorous cut-up—that's what he is. And more power to him.

O'Brien has reveled in the reputation for rakishness which he has achieved—through his own efforts. He has seen life through rose-hued glasses, and he has painted glamorous pictures of existence as it should be in far off places. *Dolce far niente* is his middle name. Do not his photographs, displayed like those of a matinée idol, convince his readers—and his publishers—of that? Naughty boy! Oh, fie! But how profitable it has been to this robust grown-up, with hair just turning silver and a profile that any sculptor would be happy to perpetuate on a medallion. All the youth of the happy-go-lucky Eighteen Nineties rolled into one could not compete with his desperate love making. He is the Lothario of middle age; he is the Don Juan of the present century; he is the king of lovers in a materialistic world. He represents, in his own sad, mischievous eyes, a type of loving which puts Pelleas in a back seat, makes Shelley seem even a cruder boy than he was, convinces us that Aucassin was not what

FREDERICK O'BRIEN

he was cracked up to be, and that Dante, though a poet, was certainly an amateur when it came to women—as indeed he was.

That is why, when O'Brien was paid the tribute of being satirized, he proved such a shining mark. The author of "White Shadows" may have counted upon a rival in the field of adventuring forth to little-known lands; he never could have counted upon a Dr. Traprock who would pounce, not upon the South Seas, but upon O'Brien himself, and make us roar with delight at his lampooning.

For a while, things looked dark for Freddie O'Brien. The veil was lifted—yes, and rent, just a little; the papier-mâché scenery he had painted so well was stripped of its colors; the gold was exposed as mere tinsel; the glamour as mostly make-believe. This was terrifying. This was awful. This was unthinkable. How could one overcome, in the future, this sort of treacherous showing up? A gullible public was no longer to be fooled. How nerve-racking to be considered another Dr. Cook, instead of a stalwart Ulysses come home from joyful wanderings!

O'Brien tore his beautiful hair. He paced his sunny porch at Sausalito, stopped in his rapid dictation of another delectable volume. If the truth must be known, and in the jargon of the day, he was scared stiff. He would come on to the east—that wretched east where he had been exposed—and settle matters.

Forthwith he took a train—and with loud trumpet blasts gave a dinner in honor of Dr. Walter E. Traprock at the Coffee House. *He'd* show 'em he wasn't to be crushed by such trumped up charges. *He'd* tell the world that he was O. K., Number One, the Alpha and Omega of all that embraces integrity, good sportsmanship, and sturdy manhood. He would put this humorous pretender in his place. He would be valiantly unafraid. That, he reasoned wisely and craftily, was the only thing to do. Disarm one's critics and vilifiers with human kindness, and they wouldn't have a leg to stand on.

The trick was done. To the credit of Freddie O'Brien, let it be said at once that it worked like a charm. How could one resist such naïve methods of self-defense? The fun-poking of Traprock acted as a boomerang. Every one was for O'Brien, forthwith. There were good-natured recriminations on the well-set stage where this memorable banquet was given, and finally, in a frenzy of feeling, the two protagonists embraced and wept on each other's shoulders; and all was well.

Clever? Very. But O'Brien is a clever boy. Did any still suspect that he was wounded by this erstwhile friend's betrayal? Not one, I fancy. It was the most convincing piece of histrionic art that we have witnessed in many a moon. Perhaps, a few cynics thought, it might have been a case of the lady protesting too much; for there was a lot of speech-making and clasping of hands, and many jovial pattings on the back. And Freddie said too often, maybe, that he didn't care a tuppenny damn. But his tears, though ready, were genuine, and—his own books still sell. Wasn't it worth a lot of weeping to regain those temporarily lost sales? Indeed it was.

You will notice, if you will take the pains to look in "Who's Who," that Lothario O'Brien does not give the date of his birth. He was born in Baltimore, the incomplete record tells us, and educated at a Jesuit College and at the University of Maryland. He married Gertrude Frye, of Paris. They have no children. He has been a newspaper man on New York, San Francisco, and Paris journals; and he has lived much in Manila and in Honolulu. He can tell rattling good yarns of those years when he was a correspondent in the Philippines—yarns that may or may not be true, but are none the less vivid and interesting on that account. For Freddie has the gift of gab to a marked degree. He loves to talk, for he is conscious that he talks well—and so few people do.

He is a thorough pagan—another reputation that he delights in—who of us wouldn't? He likes to be made a fuss over—show me the man who doesn't—for he is the eternal boy. And after all, it is something to have risen, in the twinkling of an eye, from the obscurities of newspaperdom to a celebrity such as he now indubitably enjoys. Editors are clamoring on all sides for his work; but it must be said of Freddie that he doesn't care very much about money. He appreciates and knows his own value as a writer, but he does not hold a battle-ax over a publisher's head and make demands which he is aware he could enforce. One of his best and oldest friends is Morgan Shuster, president of the Century Company; and I think he would honestly dislike to take one dollar from Shuster that he felt he hadn't earned by the sweat of his brow. He is fair and square; and though he has recently made a contract which will net him a goodly sum for several years, he does not boast of it. He is strangely humble, youthfully amazed at his sudden ascension in the literary heavens, looking upon it as a phenomenon apart from himself.

He has a dashing way with him; and men like him quite as much as women do. His humor and his appreciation of the humor of others—which is quite another gift, and far more unique—cause him to be sought on all occasions. The present writer was once invited to that delightful oasis in the desert of the metropolis, the Coffee House Club; and there he observed, among only a dozen or so photographs, one of the handsome O'Brien. For when Freddie first came east after his meteoric success, he was given a dinner in this exclusive club of intellectuals—a rare honor; and now, in the gallery of distinguished guests, his picture will remain forever. He has since achieved membership—how could his name be omitted from the roster of the great? And he is a popular member—not, as somebody once observed of a certain other out-of-town member, because he seldom attends the luncheons, but because when he does appear he is witty and wise.

Yet here is a curious thing about this dapper and urbane Irish-American: he talks amazingly well, but when one comes to quote from his running monologue there is little that is in the nature of a *bon mot*. The charm of the man is undeniable; but it is impossible to lay one's finger on any distinguishing grace. "He is too long-winded," some one said of his speeches. "If he only understood the gentle art of sitting down!" But when one is alone with him or traveling with him in a small crowd, then one discovers the rare loveliness of soul behind the too verbose public orator. His smile would encourage and justify all followers of Pollyanna; and the shape of his head has attracted the eye of many feminine admirers. He is lionized wherever he goes, and, humanly enough, he revels when he is elevated to a pedestal and the multitude bows before him.

Now let us see what O'Brien, as an artist, has brought to American literature. Not every one can relate his travels entertainingly. A mere flat statement of what one has seen would make mighty dull reading. Maiden aunts who visit St. Peter's in Rome for the first time send back statistical tables and think they are "literary." One's own point of view must enter largely into any record of a jaunt. The personality of the writer must illuminate every page—yes, every paragraph. That is why, when we first picked up "White Shadows in the South Seas," we were thrilled; for behind the printed pages we discerned a definite being; out of the cold type there emerged a man; and whether or not it was all truth was of little account, since here we had found an essayist as well as a traveler—a writer who knew his craft, and glorified the scenes he had observed with so enthusiastic an eye.

It was sheer magic. He got away from the cut and dried methods of his predecessors; he adventured not only into the South Seas, where many had been before him, but into a realm of fancy and dream. The result was an outpouring of beautiful words, lovely images; and we realized again, what we had almost forgotten in the rush of our days, that prose *per se* may become an exquisite tapestry, if it is woven by hands that deftly and tenderly touch each thread of sound.

Frederick O'Brien may not be a faultless master of style; but he is surely a weaver of delicate fancies. At the same time he has brought to us a robust music, out of the fulness of a ripe experience; and his old newspaper training has taught him, as it has taught many another, a nice economy of words. For all the brilliant color that he slashes on, he does not overwrite. And though Dr. Traprock frightened him once, he can never do that again. For O'Brien's gifts are immeasurable; he has a substantial and devoted following—readers who will avidly await his next volume, whatever it may be, and forget those who basely travesty him.

## *X: H. L. Mencken*

PICTURE a butcher's boy with apple cheeks, who parts his hair in the middle and laughs out of the side of his mouth, and you have a fair idea of the facial aspect of Heinie Mencken. He is forty-three, but there are moments when he looks fifteen. These moments are frequent when he is with George Jean Nathan. He never knows when Nathan is kidding him and, although he has been associated with Nathan for over twelve years, Nathan remains to him an enigma past resolving.

Nathan has been trying to get him to dress like an Algonquin ham ever since the day they met. At the present rate of progress he will have achieved success about the time Mencken becomes professor of English literature at Western Reserve University. Nathan got him to discard suspenders in favor of a belt and after years of persuasion prevailed upon him to carry a cane. Heinie backslid on the cane after tripping himself on the thing for weeks and catching it between his bowlegs every time he boarded a street car. During the interlude he used to carry the cane with an anguished air of affected jauntiness. In Baltimore he always left it at home until after nightfall, when he could practice carrying it without braving the guffaws of the yokelry. . . . And last August Nathan badgered him into buying a new hat in place of the battered relic he had been having annually renovated by a Greek bootblack. Nathan has yet to persuade him to turn over to the Salvation Army the faded cravenette which hangs from his champagne-bottle shoulders in folds like the skin on McAdoo's cheek.

H. L. MENCKEN

It would be a mistake to assume from this that Mencken is a sloppy dresser. To the contrary, he is one of the best dressed men I have ever seen. He learned early that the secret of dressing well is to wear nothing which will attract attention either by its smartness or its shabbiness. In a word, to quote Stuart P. Sherman's memorable phrase, he has risen above his tailor. He would no more wear yellow gloves than he would wear a rubber collar. His clothes fit him; they are of excellent material; and they are always in subdued colors. When Belmont collars first came into style, he discovered that they effectively covered up his Adam's apple and felt all right on his neck, so he has worn them ever since. When he was in school, it was the style for youths to part their hair in the middle. He parted his hair thus, and, being a creature of habit, he never changed it.

A relentless opponent of Christianity, Mencken is the most Christian of men. A verbal flouter of the bourgeois virtues, he practices them all. He is thoroughly honest; he discharges his obligations promptly; he keeps his appointments; he is a man of his word; and he is a dutiful and affectionate son. I have never seen a man who is so ridden by relatives. He has scores of them, and to them all he is obliging and courteous. He is always doing something for them: assisting at weddings, arranging for proper hospital service, meeting them at trains, taking them for automobile rides, or minding their babies when they are off to the theatre. He lives with his mother and sister in the old family home in Baltimore and he is a model householder. He built a garden wall of which he is proud and boastful. He sees that the bin is full of coal and he can mend a leak in the plumbing.

He used to belong to a club in Baltimore which met every Saturday night in the back room of a dealer in musical instruments. The club had to be abandoned after

Prohibition because two members died of the ill effects of near-beer. Expenses for floral horse-shoes and Rocks of Ages exhausted the club funds. But during brighter days than these it was a happy gathering. For exactly one hour every Saturday night they made an awful din with two violins, a cello, piccolo, and bass tuba, with Mencken at the piano, pressing with might and main on the loud pedal and pounding like Percy Grainger. "Sweet noises," was Mencken's invariable comment after each debauch, "I'm as thirsty as a bishop." Then they would bundle away a few blocks to the top floor of a restaurant whereat a long table was ready with filled steins and a patent meat chopper. Mention of that meat chopper is important, for it was the instrument used in preparing the weirdest victual ever devised by the human mind. Into it went raw meat, onions, and other ingredients which no stomach not made of cast iron could hold longer than five seconds. Just as a guest of the evening would get the first mouthful down, Mencken would lean over and impart this jolly little bit of information: "That fellow there at the meat chopper is a surgeon at Johns Hopkins. He discovered that the rump and loin of unembalmed cadavers is both highly nutritious and palatable. He has been able to obtain some choice cuts without expense to the club, through his hospital connections." . . . I succeeded in forking three helpings into my vest and two into my hat without being detected and earned thereby hearty commendation as a gentleman and an epicure. It wasn't for long. It was, by mistake, Mencken's hat.

He is an inveterate practical joker, and in this he is not always the soul of honor that he might be. He and Nathan once engaged to write some sweet and bitter facts about each other to be printed in a pamphlet. Mencken got Nathan pickled and wrote both of them, handing himself all the berries in the world and libeling Nathan scurrilously. He has stolen, to date, fifty-eight Bibles, and presented them to friends. He collects religious leaflets and tracts, especially those announcing the second coming of the Lord, and passes them on to his correspondents, urging them to repent of their sins.

He has his house cluttered up with prints of funny looking fellows he calls his ancestors. He bought the lot of them at curio shops in Germany.

The erroneous notion sometimes obtains that Mencken is a Jew. His physiognomy belies it. He has the blond, broad features of a typical Saxon. One trait, though, suggests that some remote ancestor was Semitic: he washes his hands fifteen or twenty times a day. That is a Jewish trait which probably had its origin in the days when—but it is best not to go into that here.

The healthiest individual you could possibly imagine, he is always complaining of ills in such a manner that you would think he was dying. Probably this comes from reading too much medical literature. His technical knowledge of anatomy and therapy is amazingly large; probably no man living has a vaster vocabulary of medical jargon. He reads all the medical journals, quack and legitimate, from table of contents to lost-vigor ads. As a residuum of so much reading, he has come to believe that all doctors are quacks. Still, he has tried sixty-seven "cures" for hay fever and confidently announces every spring that he is rid of it. Just as regularly he begins to sneeze about the middle of August. He satirizes prophylaxis in an amusing play but he is a bug on bacteria. He is tidy and clean. When he has a stag party at his house, he sends his mother and sister away. After the fellows have gone, he sweeps the floors, dusts the furniture, washes and dries the dishes, puts everything in place, and leaves the rooms orderly and immaculate.

Once he engaged in a book-length debate, in the form of

letters, with Robert Rives La Monte on the subject "Men vs. the Man." Mencken argued fiercely for individualism, *les droits de seigneur,* aristocracy, and the right of the few to exploit the weak. La Monte argued with equal heat for the rights of the proletariat, the need for socialism, and the blessings of altruism and the equal chance. The joke of it is that Mencken at the time was sweating away in his shirt sleeves at a newspaper job while La Monte was taking his ease on a beautiful country estate in Connecticut.

All this only goes to show that the Freudians are right and that all literary expression is merely a projection of subconscious wishes. For all that Mencken disparages American civilization, he would be profoundly uncomfortable if the sort of society he presents as desirable should happen to exist. Burton Rascoe is right when he says that Mencken in any other country would be unthinkable and is right again when he says that Mencken is America's most ardent patriot. Nine-tenths of his life is given over to denunciation, and were there nothing to denounce he would be profoundly unhappy. As it is he is as happy as Pollyanna. No one gets more fun out of living. Indeed, such a jolly time does he have dancing about "with arms and legs," goosing solemn and serious people and playing ribald jokes, that for six years he has been repeating himself, progressing far too little, developing almost not at all. For two years he has not bothered to vary his startling vocabulary and it is becoming a little stale. This is, perhaps, the penalty of getting a reputation based upon a manner. An audience is created by it and an audience demands repetition. It is hard to imagine cynical Ecclesiastes writing the Psalms of David or Jeremiah singing another Song of Songs.

But whatever Mencken's destiny or place may become in American literature he will always remain, you may be sure, a warmly human figure. All women, without exception, like him. And all men do too, who have ever met him—scholars, pedants, boozers, preachers, teamsters, politicians, highbrows, lowbrows, and medium brows. That is a test and an achievement. The secret of this is that he is frank and unaffected, courteous, gentle, amiable, wise, jovial, and a gentleman.

## XI: *Edwin Arlington Robinson*

THE simplicity of Edwin Arlington Robinson baffles so many people that it occasionally disturbs the poet himself. "Why cannot they read one word after another?" he once exclaimed when the charge of obscurity was hurled at him. In fact the one obscure thing about Robinson is Robinson—his personality, in other words. He has never seated himself in the middle of the market-place and permitted the curious public to stroll about him. A reticence, that may be the result of a New England heritage, has restrained him from venturing into the whirl of modern letters, although it should be pointed out that he is in no sense of the word a hermit. It is rather from critical conflicts, cliques, back-slapping dinners (although of late *his* back has been strenuously slapped, much to his bewilderment), public readings, and the like that he carefully absents himself. He does not live in a cave; neither does he eke out a precarious existence in a hall bedroom, staring at the wall for inspiration all day. He has his own circle of friends and he is a welcome adjunct to their gatherings, although he much prefers to sit and listen rather than talk. The outward manifestation of Robinson's life may be divided into two phases, and from them the visible aspects of the poet may be constructed. Therefore let his existence be for once portrayed under captions A and B, with a prologue describing the single character of a play in which all other personages are merely lay figures and background. The phase under caption A has its locale in New York, "The Town Down the River"; that under caption B is centered in the midst

EDWIN ARLINGTON ROBINSON

of the pleasant greenery of the MacDowell Colony at Peterboro, New Hampshire. And so to our

PROLOGUE

A tall, slender man. A high forehead with dark thinning hair. Quiet contemplative eyes which peer through spectacles. A short dark mustache (English fashion) barely concealing a thin secretive mouth. A gravity of demeanor that often breaks into a smile which trembles curiously about the mouth. He dresses quietly, generally in dark clothes, and always carries a cane. When he walks he stoops slightly, the droop of the scholar who is an inveterate reader. He hates to walk. He wears a soft hat. He never talks about his own poetry. He never criticizes other people's poetry. He wouldn't read in public for a million dollars. He is anti-Prohibition.

CAPTION A

He lives in New York during the winter. Just where he lives is his own secret, although it may be stated that he moved from Brooklyn last spring after three years' residence there. Most of his winter days are passed in visiting his small group of friends and attending the theater, a pastime for which he has a genuine passion. He does not write much poetry during the cold months, reserving that for his long summers at Peterboro. He reads all the magazines and follows closely the various trends of American letters. And now, perhaps, some history may be mingled with description.

Contrary to several statements, he was born in Head Tide, Maine, and his first interest in letters, he once said, manifested itself in reciting "Lochiel's Warning" to his mother, while seated on the kitchen floor. He did not state how his mother received it. He passed some years at Harvard but he did not stay to graduate. At that time he made certain friends who noted the unique character of his work and have remained faithful to him during the years that followed. His first book, a small green-covered paper-bound volume entitled "The Torrent and the Night Before," established his style and he has not deviated from that method since, except in developing a richness, a mellowness, and a profound depth that is untouched in modern poetry. That style is established upon a relinquishment of so-called "poetical" words, a finished technique, and an analytic incision that cuts like a scalpel. Many of the poems contained in "The Torrent and the Night Before," which later were transferred to his second book, "The Children of the Night," were written in the barn of his home at Gardiner, Maine, to which place he moved while a small boy. In those years he was a radical, a peculiar phenomenon in a land that adored "purple passages." The saffron Nineties did not influence him, for he had discovered his own métier and had resolved to stick to it. The years that followed "The Children of the Night" remain for his biographer. They are marked by residences in Boston and New York. He even dwelt in Yonkers for a short time. The struggles that marked his first years in New York were the struggles of all unknown, penniless, determined poets. Even the flattering article written about him by Theodore Roosevelt, then President, which appeared in "The Outlook" in 1905, did not aid him materially. True, the President placed him in the New York Customs House after seriously considering sending him to Mexico, and Robinson remained there for several years. But he was a born poet and it was inevitable that he should go back to his chosen life-work.

He was, and is, a shy man. He is easily terrorized, especially by women, although of late years he has rather acclimated himself to society. He works with a furious intensity that is the blessed virtue of few writers; although his volumes have been appearing with a fair regularity of late, he is very slow in his composition. He once affirmed that his hardest job in life was to make the non-spontaneous portions of his poetry read like the really spontaneous sections. His prime interest is humanity and this has manifested itself in the series of remarkable character portraits that star his books. The long neglect which was his portion does not seem to have soured his nature. He is naturally serious, yet while he may regard life as an uphill climb he does not despair of humanity. The war troubled him greatly, although its influence upon his poetry was slight. That brief influence may be discerned in portions of "Merlin" and such pieces as "The Path of Glory."

CAPTION B

The scene is the large room in Colony Hall at the MacDowell Colony in Peterboro. The immediate property is a pool table. A tall gentleman in a light gray suit and a yellow tie makes a shot and ingloriously scratches. He observes the cue ball with the utmost bewilderment and a shout of amusement goes up from the side lines. The tall gentleman smiles and twinkles through his glasses. It comes his turn to shoot again and he studies the positions of the balls with meticulous caution.

"Kiss it in," suggests somebody. "Kiss it gently. Kiss it as you would your sister."

A quick smile animates the tall gentleman's face.

"You never saw me kiss my sister," he retorts. Then quite calmly he achieves a difficult shot and beams with honest delight at the result. This is Robinson in his own element at Peterboro. Whoso has not seen him in that delectable corner of New Hampshire barely knows him. William Rose Benét hit him off perfectly when he described him as Merlin playing pool.

Robinson leads the ideal artist's life at the MacDowell Colony. He rises early and, after breakfast, tramps to his studio which is hidden among trees but from whose door he can see the blue crown of Mt. Monadnock rising in the distance. With that vision before him he sits and composes his best work. Luncheon is brought to him, as it is to all the other colonists, and placed upon his doorstep where he may get it when he pleases. He lives uninterrupted days in what is perhaps the most charming environment for a writer in the United States.

And he changes and glows at Peterboro. He emanates a jovialness that is unhampered by city cares. Practically all of his evenings are passed at the pool table, where with such companions as Arthur Nevin, the composer, Jules Bois, the French writer, William Rose Benét, the poet, and others, time flies. Robinson has developed into an excellent pool player, for it is his one mode of relaxation. And right here Caption B may end.

Now what manner of man is Robinson? Is it possible to set down the personality of a man who has become great because of his personality? At the beginning of this article it was stated that his simplicity baffles many people. The writer has discovered himself in the awkward situation of those very people at whose vain attempts at understanding he had planned to smile. The laugh is on himself. Certain threads of information exist, certain suggestions, which may point toward the influences that formed Robinson, but it is quite impossible to set him down on paper. He once stated that he descended from good New England yeoman stock. This is suggestion number one. His boyhood was a rather lonely one.

This is suggestion number two. He loves to be exact in his reasoning and to settle questions to his own satisfaction. Suggestion number three. He once said that if he were placed on a desert island and permitted but three books for the remainder of his life he should choose the Bible, Shakespeare, and the dictionary. There is suggestion number four. He has never married and has no intention of marrying. Suggestion number five. His favorite writer of fiction is Charles Dickens. He possesses a profound admiration for the poetry of William Wordsworth. He takes off his soft hat to Thomas Hardy. In New York he rises late and generally goes to bed long after midnight. He adores detective stories and Sherlock Holmes is one of his heroes. He is absolutely immune to cults, 'isms, and movements. Surely these scattered facts are straws pointing to the personality of the man.

Then there is his absolute modesty. The last few years have witnessed a great number of honors which have fallen to Robinson, but the poet remains unchanged. When Yale gave him a Lit.D. he surreptitiously disappeared from Peterboro and returned silent and confused. He couldn't get away from the excited comments of his friends soon enough. He likes to be let alone when he is working, although he is never unsociable. His courtesy is too innate for that.

So there he is—tall, quiet, silent, unassuming, unconcerned, deliberate, careful, and withal extraordinary. And the extraordinary part of the man is something that must be beyond words. It reveals itself fleetingly in a sense of mighty reservoirs that are meticulously controlled. Like all true geniuses he suggests that he still possesses more than he gives, that his source is inexhaustible, that subterranean rivers flow beneath the surface with which he calmly meets the world. He is more than a dreamer although he is a great dreamer. Life passes before him in a rich show and he possesses the capability of viewing it in an objective manner. He assimilates and digests life and draws memorable conclusions. He ferrets out the soul of humanity and turns it over and over with analytic interest, making his acute deductions, and stabbing truths home to his readers with a phrase. His simplicity consists in resolving things to their original elements, of disdaining mawkishness, sentimentality, preconceived theories, and propaganda. He is an alchemist refining gold out of the chaos of modern life.

## *XII: F. Scott Fitzgerald*

IT has been said by a celebrated person that to meet F. Scott Fitzgerald is to think of a stupid old woman with whom some one has left a diamond; she is extremely proud of the diamond and shows it to every one who comes by, and everybody is surprised that such an ignorant old woman should possess so valuable a jewel; for in nothing does she appear so stupid as in the remarks she makes about the diamond.

The person who invented this simile did not know Scott Fitzgerald very well and can have seen him only, I think, in particularly uninteresting moods. The reader must not suppose that there is any literal truth in the image. Scott Fitzgerald, as anybody will recognize almost immediately upon meeting him, is not a stupid old woman but a good-looking young man of not undistinguished appearance and ingenuous charm, who far from being stupid is extremely entertaining. But there is, none the less, a symbolic truth in the description quoted above: it is true that Fitzgerald has been left with a jewel which he doesn't know quite what to do with. For he has been given imagination without intellectual control of it; he has been given a desire for beauty without an æsthetic ideal; and he has been given a gift for expression without many ideas to express.

Consider, for example, the novel with which he founded his reputation, "This Side of Paradise." It has almost every fault and deficiency that a novel can possibly have. It is not only highly imitative but it is imitated from a bad novel. Fitzgerald, when he wrote it, was drunk with Compton Mackenzie, and the book sounds like an American attempt to rewrite "Sinister Street." Now Mackenzie, despite his extraordinary gift for picturesque and comic invention and the capacity for pretty writing which he says that he learned from Keats, lacks both the intellectual force and the emotional imagination to give body and outline to the material which he secretes in such enormous abundance. With the seeds he took from Keats's garden (one of the best kept gardens in the world) he exfloreated so profusely that he blotted out the path of his own. Michael Fane, the hero of "Sinister Street," was swamped in the forest of description; he was smothered by columbine. From the time he went up to Oxford, his personality disappeared and when last seen (at Belgrade) he was no longer recognizable as anybody in particular. As a consequence, Amory Blaine, the hero of "This Side of Paradise," had a very poor chance of coherence: he had more emotional life, it is true, than the phantom Michael Fane, who, like most of Mackenzie's creations, had practically none at all; but he was quite as much an uncertain quantity in a phantasmagoria of incident which had no dominating intention to endow it with unity and force. In short, one of the chief weaknesses of "This Side of Paradise" is that it is really not *about* anything: intellectually it amounts to little more than a gesture—a gesture of indefinite revolt. For another thing, "This Side of Paradise" is very immaturely imagined: it is always just verging on the ludicrous. And, finally, it is one of the most illiterate books of any merit ever published (a fault which the publisher's proof-reader apparently made no effort to correct). It is not only ornamented with bogus ideas and faked literary references but it is full of English words misused with the most reckless abandon.

I have said that "This Side of Paradise" commits almost every sin that a novel can possibly commit: it is true

F. SCOTT FITZGERALD

that it does commit every sin except the unpardonable sin: it does not fail to live. The whole preposterous farrago is animated with life. It is, to be sure, rather a fluttering and mercurial sort of life: its emotions do not move you profoundly; its drama does not make you hold your breath; but its gaiety and color and movement gave it a distinction for a literary criticism long accustomed to heaviness and dinginess in serious American fiction. If one recalls the sort of gritty fodder of which Ernest Poole's "The Harbor" is an example, one understands the extravagant enthusiasm with which "This Side of Paradise" was hailed.

For another thing, it was well written—well written, *quand même*. It is true, as I have said above, that Fitzgerald misuses words; his works are full of malapropisms of the most disconcerting kind: you will find—"Whatever your flare (*sic*) proves to be—religion, architecture, literature," "the Juvenalia of my collected editions," "There were nice things in it (the room) . . . offsprings of a vicarious (vagarious?), impatient taste acting in stray moments," "a mind like his, lucrative in intelligence, intuition, and lightning decision," etc., etc. It reminds one rather of

> Agib, who could readily, at sight,
> Strum a march upon the loud Theodolite.
> He would diligently play
> On the Zoetrope all day,
> And blow the gay Pantechnicon all night.

It is true that Fitzgerald plays the language entirely by ear. But, for all that, his flute is no mean one. He has an instinct for graceful and vivid prose which some of his more serious fellows might envy.

In regard to the man himself, there are perhaps two things worth knowing for the influence they have had on his work. In the first place, he comes from the middle west—from St. Paul, Minnesota. Fitzgerald is as much of the middle west of large cities and country clubs as Lewis is of the middle west of the prairies and little towns. What we find in him is much what we find in the prosperous strata of these cities: sensitivity and eagerness for life without a sound base of culture and taste; a brilliant structure of hotels and exhilarating social activities built not on the eighteenth century but simply on the prairie. And it seems to me a great pity that he has not written more of the west: it is perhaps the only milieu that he thoroughly understands; when he approaches the east, he brings to it the standards of the wealthy west—the preoccupation with display, the love of magnificence and jazz, the vigorous social atmosphere of amiable flappers and youths comparatively unpoisoned as yet by the snobbery of the east. In "The Beautiful and Damned," for example, we feel that he is moving in a vacuum; the characters have no convincing connection with the background to which they are assigned; they are not part of the organism of New York as the characters in, say, "Bernice Bobs Her Hair" are a part of the organism of St. Paul. Surely Fitzgerald should do for Summit Avenue what Lewis has done for Main Street.

But you are not to suppose from all this that Fitzgerald is merely a typical middle westerner, with correct clothes and clear skin, who has been sent east to college. The second thing one should understand about him is the fact that he is part Irish and that he brings to the writing of fiction some qualities rarely found in America. For, like the Irish, he is romantic, but is also cynical about romance; he is ecstatic and bitter; lyrical and sharp. He is bound to represent himself as a playboy, yet he mocks incessantly at the playboy. He is vain, a little malicious, of quick intelligence and wit and with a gift for turning language into something iridescent and surprising. In fact, he often reminds one of the description which a great Irishman has written of the Irish:

> An Irishman's imagination never lets him alone, never convinces him, never satisfies him; but it makes him that he can't face reality nor deal with it nor handle it nor conquer it: he can only sneer at them that do . . . and imagination's such a torture that you can't bear it without whisky. . . . And all the while there goes on a horrible, senseless, mischievous laughter.

For the rest, he is a rather childlike fellow, very much wrapped up in his dream of himself and his projection of it on paper. For a person of his intellectual nimbleness he is extraordinarily little occupied with the general affairs of the world: like a woman, he is not much given to abstract or impersonal thought. Conversations about politics or criticism have a way of snapping back to Fitzgerald. But he seldom makes you angry in this way; he does it usually without pompousness or airs. He is utterly devoid of affectation and takes the curse off his relentless egoism by his readiness to laugh at himself and his boyish uncertainty of his abilities. And he possesses, both personally and in his writings, a quality exceedingly rare among even the young American writers of the day: he is almost the only one among them who has any real light-hearted gayety. Where Sinclair Lewis would stew "the Problem of Salesmanship" in acrid rancorous fumes, Fitzgerald, in "The Beautiful and Damned," has turned it into hilarious farce. His characters—and himself—are actors in an elfin harlequinade; they are as nimble, as gay and as lovely—and as hard-hearted—as fairies: Columbine elopes with Harlequin on a rope ladder from the Ritz and both go morris-dancing amuck on a case of bootleg liquor; Pantaloon is pinked with an epigram that withers him up like a leaf; the Policeman is tripped by Harlequin and falls into the Pulitzer Fountain. In the end, Harlequin puts on false whiskers and pretends he is Bernard Shaw; he gives an elaborate interview to the newspapers on politics, history, and religion; a hundred thousand readers read it and are enormously impressed; Columbine nearly dies laughing; Harlequin buys another case of gin.

Let me quote a characteristic incident in connection with "The Beautiful and Damned," which will give a better idea of Fitzgerald than any number of adjectives could do.

Since writing "This Side of Paradise"—on the inspiration of Wells and Mackenzie—Fitzgerald has become acquainted with another school of fiction: the ironical-pessimistic. In college, he had supposed that the thing to do was to write biographical novels with a burst of ideas toward the close; since his advent into the literary world, he has discovered that there is another genre in favor: the kind which makes much of the tragedy and "the meaninglessness of life." Hitherto, he had supposed that the thing to do was to discover a meaning in life; but he now set bravely about to produce a sufficiently desolating tragedy which should be, also, 100 per cent. meaningless. As a result of this determination, the first version of "The Beautiful and Damned" culminated in a carnival of disaster for which the reader was imperfectly prepared: Fitzgerald ruined his characters wholesale with a set of catastrophes so arbitrary that beside them, the worst perversities of Hardy were like the working of natural laws. The heroine loses her beauty at a prematurely early age and her character, though it is hard to see why, goes incontinently with it; Richard Caramel, a writer of promise, loses all his literary ideals and becomes a prostitute of popular taste; and the hero, Anthony Patch, who has formerly been very rich, not only loses all his money but, unable to make a living by himself, succumbs to inertia and drink, and eventually goes mad. But the bitterest moment of the story comes at the very end, when Anthony is wandering the streets of New York in an attempt to borrow some money. After several humiliating failures, he finally approaches an old friend whom he sees with an elegant lady just getting into a cab. It is Maury Noble, the most brilliant of all his friends, a cynic, an intellectual, and a man of genuine parts. But Maury fails to recognize Anthony; he cuts him dead; and drives away in the taxi. "But," the author explains, "he really had not seen Anthony. For Maury had indulged his appetite for alcoholic beverage once too often: he was now stone-blind!"

But the point of my story is this: though he had written the passage in all seriousness, as soon as he heard other people laughing at it, he began laughing at it himself, and with as much gayety and surprise as if he had just read it in Max Beerbohm. And he began to improvise a burlesque which ran somewhat as follows: "It seemed to Anthony that Maury's eyes had a fixed glassy stare; his legs moved stiffly as he walked and when he spoke his voice seemed to have no life in it. When Anthony came nearer, he saw that Maury was dead!"

To conclude, it would be unfair to submit Fitgerald already to a rigorous critical overhauling while he is still only in his twenties and has presumably most of his work before him. His restless imagination may yet precipitate something durably brilliant. For the present, however, this imagination is certainly not seen to very good advantage: it suffers badly from lack of discipline and poverty of æsthetic ideas. Fitzgerald is a dazzling extemporizer but his stories have a way of petering out: he seems never to have planned them thoroughly or to have thought them out from the beginning. This is true even of some of his most successful fantasies, such as "The Diamond as Big as the Ritz" or his comedy, "The Vegetable." On the other hand, "The Beautiful and Damned," imperfect as it was, marked an advance over "This Side of Paradise": the style is more nearly mature and the subject more solidly unified, and certain scenes in it are probably the most convincing he has ever invented.

And in any case, in spite of all I have said, Fitzgerald has his intellectual importance. In his very moral anarchy, in the very confusion of his revolt, he is typical of the generation of the war—the generation described on the last page of "This Side of Paradise" as "grown up to find all gods dead, all wars fought, all faiths in men shaken." There is a profounder truth in "The Beautiful and Damned" than the author perhaps intended to convey: the hero and heroine are strange creatures without purpose or method, who give themselves up to wild debaucheries and do not, from beginning to end of the book, perform a single serious act; but you somehow get the impression that, in spite of their madness, they are the most rational people in the book: wherever they touch the common life, the institutions of men are made to appear a contemptible farce of the futile and the absurd; the world of finance, the army, and, finally, the world of business are successively and casually exposed as completely without dignity or point. The inference is that, in such a civilization, the sanest and most creditable thing is to live for the jazz of the moment and forget the activities of men. And it is not altogether a personal confusion which has produced the confusion of such a book. It may be that we must not expect too much intellectual balance of young men who write books in the year 1921: we must remember that their environment and their chief source of stimulation have been the wars, the society, and the commerce of the Age of Confusion itself.

## *XIII: Edna Ferber*

AT one time, Edna Ferber was in the gravest danger of letting her cleverness run away with her. It might have been her artistic undoing. She would start a short story so brilliantly that one gasped, fearful for the climax of anything so sparklingly begun. But she got over that, and she got over the O. Henry influence. There may be many who will contradict this; certainly there is justification for the opinion that she was an imitator. But she has learned to write her stories backward. She once told an editor who had praised a certain piece of work of hers, that she was certain it was going to turn out a good story because she was able to put down the last sentence before she wrote the first.

I imagine she writes all her stories that way. Turn to "The Maternal Feminine" in a recent collection. I would wager anything that the process she employed was the one I have uncovered. But don't spoil a great short story by reading it backward. Then look up "The Gay Old Dog," if you are a man, and wince at the knowledge Edna Ferber has of the male species. How has she learned so much about us? What divination is hers, that she can read the man heart so clearly, understand the loneliness of the old bachelor, the while she also reveals the truth about the unmarried woman in one piercing sentence? It is little short of genius to put these things on paper. If Emma McChesney leaped from the page, and grasped your hand, and lived at your house all the while you read of her, there are likewise dozens of Miss Ferber's characters since those happy days who will always hold a place in your fiction friendships.

Edna Ferber came from a small town. She worked on newspapers in small towns in the middle west; and she has absorbed the people of small towns as few writers since George Ade have done. Indeed, she seems to me quite as important as that great philosopher-humorist, even though she lacks his profound observation.

It is little more than ten years since her first story appeared in "Everybody's Magazine"—one of the best bits of character drawing she has ever done, by the way. It was called "The Homely Heroine," and I think it runs to not over 2,300 words. For it she received the munificent sum of $62.50. She was tickled to death—particularly with the extra fifty cents. She had broken in. The little Kalamazoo girl had arrived. What matter that the check was small? She'd show 'em.

Those who imagine editors are always trying to find ways of keeping young authors in their place, should note what followed in the case of the utterly unknown Edna Ferber. People talked of that yarn. It was passed around in editorial offices, spoken of as the most promising short story since O. Henry's earliest work. There was a mad rush to get Miss Ferber's next product. I think importunate telegrams were sent to her. But her head was not turned. She was too wise, too poised, too sensible, even at that early age. You see, when you have knocked about on newspapers in Appleton, Wisconsin, in Milwaukee and Chicago, you take flattery lightly. There are bound to be bumps ahead, for all the momentary clear sailing. But Edna Ferber was not a flash in the pan. Her next story was equally good; and "The American Magazine" got hold of her—one of the editors went west to call upon her, to see who she was, find out what she looked like, after the manner of the modern progressive hunter after fiction. He found a slip of a girl, alert, with brown eyes that glowed like live coals, an abundance of

EDNA FERBER

black hair which she slashed right back from a well molded forehead, and a skin like velvet on which cream has been poured. He heard a vibrant voice, that uttered terse, sharp sentences. Sometimes they were too sharp and terse; for Miss Ferber likes her own way, deny it as she will, and never hesitates to say just what she thinks, regardless of whether or not it is wise to do so. Here was a keenness of mind that was refreshing. Edna Ferber exuded health and energy; her answers were apropos, discriminating, final. There was little pose about her. She was just a normal girl with a wild ambition—though she confessed even then that she would rather be an actress than an author. I have seen her give an imitation of Bernhardt that was uncanny—she can even look like the great French tragedienne by the simple process of putting a feather boa around her neck and pulling her hair over her eyes, from which the glasses have been removed.

But the stage was not for her. She took to the pen—or the typewriter, as they all do nowadays—as a Salvation Army lassie to a tambourine; and she sailed in bravely and wrote a novel. It was called "Dawn O'Hara." Miss Ferber herself would tell you not to read it now, she has gone so far beyond it. It was crude and forced and jerky. She was, in those days, essentially a worker in miniatures, and after the near-failure of this maiden effort, she was wise enough to revert to the writing of brief short stories on the order of "The Homely Heroine." They seemed to flow from her pen—typewriter, I mean; but they didn't do anything of the sort. They were the result of most assiduous work. She plugs away every morning of her life, whether she feels like it or not. When she is living in New York, at an uptown hotel, she hurries out before breakfast and gets a brisk walk around the Reservoir in Central Park, to freshen her brain, and think over what she shall do that day. When she is in

Chicago, it is the shore of Lake Michigan that feels the patter of her rapid feet as she takes a constitutional around Jackson Park. She divides her time now between these two great cities, and has never been able to say which she likes the better.

Though she lives in hotels, with her mother, she is the most domestic person you can imagine, and she almost resents the prepared food she eats. For she loves to cook, and knows all sorts of tempting recipes. But she says she and her mother cannot be bothered with servant problems; and so they go on living at comfortable apartment hotels, free to come and go as they wish.

For Miss Ferber likes to travel; but she doesn't like to pack her bags without an object in view. Therefore, whenever she decides that she wants a trip to the coast, she arranges a neat little reading tour for herself. In this way she appeases that never dormant desire to express herself histrionically. And how she does read her own stories! Women's clubs who have been lucky enough to capture her, have always felt more than rewarded. She knows "The Gay Old Dog" practically by heart. She merely puts the book on a table near her, as an orator places his notes by his plate for occasional reference, and then plunges into the story, like the true artiste she is, and gets her effects through dramatic pauses which many a professional actress might do well to study and emulate. She can imitate almost any dialect; and shop-girl slang is heaven to her. I really think that the stage lost a great character actress when literature claimed Edna Ferber.

After the immense vogue of the McChesney stories, it was inevitable that they would be dramatized. George V. Hobart collaborated with their creator; and Ethel Barrymore played the leading rôle for two years, with enormous success. Since then, Miss Ferber has written but one play, and that again in collaboration. Newman Levy and she got an idea-of-the-moment in the small salaries paid to college professors in American universities; under the title of "$1,200 a Year" they tore off a comedy that was tried out and came to grief on the road; but it lives within the pages of a volume, and is well worth looking up. Parts of it are astonishingly clever. I think the trouble with it was that too few people, immersed as they all were in their own tragic financial difficulties, gave a hang what salaries college professors were paid. It is not what might be called a burning question. And it was not an altogether actable play. Maybe it was written too hastily. It is curious how many fiction writers think that a play is an easy method of expression.

There are those who abominate Miss Ferber's cock-sureness, her too-scintillating phrases, her measured determination always to be apt and smart. I can see perfectly how certain of her stories would grate on certain people; but beyond that surface glitter and shine there is always, to me at least, a realization of her understanding of, and sympathy for, the plain folk she writes about. She loves humanity, and is unafraid to reveal her love. A waiter, a manicure, a tired Cook's tourist, an ex-convict, a seamstress, a milliner—all these claim her heart; and she can put them on paper in blinding, vivid paragraphs, and cause you to exclaim, "Why, I know a person just like that!" Sometimes she is too photographic; and then again often she slurs over some character in whom you have become greatly interested. For some reason he or she has not held Miss Ferber, and so it's out of the story for that unfortunate. I am thinking particularly of the poet, in "The Girls." There was not nearly enough of him.

And speaking of that flaming novel of Chicago, how Miss Ferber must be chuckling at those critics of hers who have insistently reiterated that she was not big enough to write anything sustained. Oh yes, they were prompt to praise her collections under such titles as "Buttered Side Down," "Half Portions," "Roast Beef Medium," and "Personality Plus"—a goodly showing, when you come to think of it, even though the titles might be found fault with by the discriminating and over-sensitive. Is there a little cheapness in such names of books? I have heard critics deplore her tendency to be downright common. She has played to the gallery, they contend; she is too fond of the newspaper method, too anxious to seem to know it all. "She's fresh"—and I use the word in its double sense—was the way one critic put it. All her books have gone into several editions, and there is no doubt that Miss Ferber could go on indefinitely reaching a loyal public through her short stories alone. But she is not content to remain in a groove. "The Girls" formed in her active brain as a cameo; but it got away from her, swept her off her feet after she began it, and she found page after page rustling from her machine. Then one day, having shut off the telephone for weeks, she discovered on her desk a full-fledged novel, which "The Woman's Home Companion" wanted as a serial, at a most gratifying price. And later the astute reviewers of the land hailed it as one of the finest novels of the year—Heywood Broun, F. P. A., Percy Hammond, and a host of others were loud in their praise of it.

It is so far ahead of "Fanny Herself" that one wonders where Miss Ferber will go in the next ten years.[1] If she can travel that fast, there's no telling what broad highway she may take. For her art has ripened; and in depicting the manless household of the Thrift girls, on Chicago's South Side, she has torn down not only one wall, but all four, and allowed the whole world not to peep

[1] This paper was written before the publication of *"So Big."*

but to see openly those three generations of lonely women. The story mounts with every chapter; and Miss Ferber's clean-cut style, held beautifully in check, exactly suits the material at her hand. She pounds in her effects, makes these "girls" walk down the streets with you, turn windy corners with you; and she causes the old Chicago to pass in a panorama before your eyes. The scene wherein the soldiers of the Civil War march away from the Lake City is tremendous—a whirlwind of action. And all the threads are finally gathered up—as the critics all said a mere short-story writer couldn't gather them. They are not only gathered, they are tied in a deft knot, and one is left with a feeling of complete satisfaction. It is Miss Ferber's triumph that she has accomplished this *tour de force.* Yet was it artistic to cover so long a period of time in so short a compass? There are moments in "The Girls" when you feel the nervous desire of the short story writer to whittle to the bone. It might have been a greater book if she had expanded more and compressed with less anxiety.

Edna Ferber is known for her reliability in her dealings with editors. If she is asked to finish a certain piece of work by four o'clock on a Tuesday afternoon, at four o'clock on the Tuesday afternoon the completed product is on the editorial desk. She says it is just as easy to be businesslike as not. Her newspaper training, no doubt. Her letters accompanying her manuscripts are often as clever as the manuscripts themselves. Her abrupt beginnings and endings are a joy. There's never a wasted word.

She motors in Chicago as if she had done it all her life—loops around the puzzling Loop with ease and grace; and her passenger doesn't even hold his breath when she swings into throbbing Michigan Avenue and darts out to the South Side or over toward Evanston.

Like all successful authors, Miss Ferber has had innumerable offers to write directly for the screen. What captions she could do! She spent a few months in Hollywood, wrote a fine article about her impressions of that mad little colony, and incidentally sold the motion picture rights to two or three of her books. But her mother was almost killed in a motor accident on one of the boulevards, and they experienced a definite trembling of the earth; and altogether Miss Ferber felt she would be more at home in the middle west; so they packed up and shipped back to Chicago. Then they packed up and shipped on to New York, where, Miss Ferber claims, she misses Chicago. She says, very wisely, that if any of her material is suitable for screen production, there it is to purchase; but she hasn't the time nor the inclination to spend her energy on scenarios. It is the right attitude to take; when every author realizes that it is foolish to try to serve two masters, both books and motion pictures will be all the better.

Miss Ferber has many friends. I heard her say, with her usual frankness, to a good-looking young man, "You're handsome, yes—but you're stupid." Afterward he told me that he was afraid of her, but found such candor refreshing. She will dance, when she is seeking copy, in the lowest of Chicago "dives," with Carl Sandburg or Ben Hecht or Harry Hansen or young Gene Markey; and the next evening she will be at the smartest dinner, talking brilliantly with these same men, enjoying each party with equal gusto. She likes Fanny Butcher's Book Shop, and all the people in it; and when she comes east she hobnobs with Franklin P. Adams, William Gillette, Rutger Jewett, Albert A. Boyden (when he isn't in Poland), Julian Street, Charles Hanson Towne, Alexander Woollcott, and many others who make New York the shining spot it is. But much as she cares for social life, she cares more for good honest hard work. That is why she is one of the highest priced short-story writers in the whole country to-day. She refuses to produce too much, believing that the best one is capable of cannot be written hastily to meet the needs of waiting markets. I know of one editor who, eager for her work, left a signed blank contract with her. She had but to fill in the figures and return it to him. She confesses that the temptation was great; but she did not feel that she could do her best under such conditions and so the contract went back—unsigned by her.

Do you get a picture of Edna Ferber from that little story?

## *XIV: Henry Blake Fuller*

IN a brilliant sentence wherein he gives us the character and temperament of the hero of his "Chevalier of Pensieri-Vani" Henry Blake Fuller also thus partly describes himself: "He was sufficient unto himself, exempt from the burdens of wealth, the chafings of domestic relations, the chains of affairs, the martyrdom of great ambitions and the dwarfing provincialism that comes from a settled home."

So sufficient is he unto himself that it is only with the greatest difficulty that one can unearth anything about him. Those who have known him for a great number of years as intimately as Mr. Fuller can be known, can tell you very little except that he is a charming gentleman. He is exempt from the burdens of wealth, though he has an income from some property in Chicago which suffices amply for his needs. Far from being chafed by domestic relations, he hasn't even a permanent residence. His address is set down in "Who's Who" simply as "Chicago." He is constantly changing his lodgings, whose location he keeps not only from acquaintances he would avoid but from his closest associates. He receives his mail ordinarily at the office of "Poetry: A Magazine of Verse." That he does not suffer the martyrdom of great ambition is evidenced by the dilettante character of his whole career. He spent a great part of his youth abroad and seems rather to have yearned wistfully for Italy all his life. That he is utterly lacking in the provincialism that comes from a settled home is perhaps one reason why his excellent novels shoot over the hearts and heads of the public: he is in life but not of it, and that aloof-

HENRY BLAKE FULLER

ness of the author which gives so great an air of artistic detachment to his work is, in the last analysis, the elusiveness of personality in a man whose zest is very tepid.

It is all very well to declaim bitterly against the general reader's neglect of an artist, but it is an eminently sensible procedure now and then to take pains to discover to what extent the artist himself is responsible for this neglect. Mr. Fuller's first great literary master, Stendhal, is hard put to it even at this late day to muster that handful of appreciative readers who, he said, would not only understand his work but would cherish it as being unique. Irony and satire, especially if they are refined over-subtly, have never a general appeal; and the irony and satire of Mr. Fuller's novels are not ensanguined by any passion whatever. Stendhal, literary caviar as he is, had animated and driving emotions: he worshiped Napoleon, and his Julien Sorel is the first great avatar of the Nietzschean superman. Mr. Fuller has, apparently, not even any inclinations, to say nothing of worship, concerning any person or thing. There is no palpable idea in his work; there is only a pervading and gentlemanly diffidence. And diffidence is the last thing in the world to excite the general reader. What it all comes down to, I am afraid, is that Mr. Fuller is deficient in vitality, that vitality which makes pages glow with human warmth and animates the reader with sympathy or distaste. Critics will never quarrel over Mr. Fuller's merits; they will either acknowledge them without passion or remain indifferent to them. And the public, I suspect, will continue to exist in happy ignorance of the dozen books with which he has honored American literature.

Within the last year I have observed a phenomenon which gives credence to my impression that Mr. Fuller's shyness and self-isolation is that of a disappointed man. He has begun of a sudden to appear as a prolific reviewer;

his analyses and estimates of books appear simultaneously in a half-dozen publications; at sixty-four years of age he seems to have decided belatedly to impress his name, if only by repetition, upon the minds of American readers. Throughout his career as a writer he has been an occasional contributor of reviews and papers to the literary magazines; but these appearances were so few and far between that the cumulative effect was never great enough to keep an audience aware of his existence. Every once in a while he would be referred to by some critic as the "late H. B. Fuller": and his achievements were somehow thought of as belonging to the last century, even though his last novel, "Bertram Cope's Year," was published as late as 1919.

I believe that if Mr. Fuller had had his present urge to be useful in the literary scene when he was a younger man he would not only have been much better known as a writer but would have endowed his novels with just that animation which they lack. He had no need ever to struggle for a living; he prepared himself for a profession only in a dilettante way by studying music and architecture and wrote his first novel without any bread-and-butter urgency. He has never held any job except that as an honorary advisory editor of "Poetry: A Magazine of Verse." In this capacity, Harriet Monroe tells me, he is faithful, punctual, and efficient: he is at his desk several mornings out of a week, reading poetry in manuscript, dictating letters of rejection, discussing with the other editors the verse which is to be used in the forthcoming issue of the magazine. But this again is a sort of make-believe employment; there is no suggestion of professionalism in his editing, his journalism, his criticism, or, indeed, in his fiction-making. He has had, in fine, no real work to do in his life. Possessed, like his Chevalier, of a temperament opposed to all restrictions upon his freedom, scouting the obligations imposed by great ambition, domestic life, augmented wealth, and a permanent home, he practically cut himself free from life altogether. He has not even had his Chevalier's flair for adventurous activity. His career in the flesh no less than in fiction seems to be characterized entirely by an austerely passionless curiosity.

In person Mr. Fuller is a furtive little fellow with a neatly trimmed white beard and white hair; his skin is smooth and white; his voice is soft and hesitant; his eyes gleam with amused inquisitiveness; and he is always perfectly shod and tailored. He is neat, gracious, charming, excessively quiet. At any gathering, at tea or dinner, he never takes part in general discussion; at best, if he says anything, it is to one or two people whom he has withdrawn or who have withdrawn him into a corner. He chuckles, rather one suspects from nervousness and shyness than from actual mirth; he chuckles a great deal when there is nothing particularly to chuckle about. In any discussion he is much more concerned with drawing out the other fellow than with expressing any opinion himself. When he does express an opinion orally he circumscribes it with reservations and puts it forth, as it were, tentatively, as though ready to withdraw it on second thought.

He is deeply interested in young people, and for a bachelor and recluse he has an extraordinary habit of keeping in touch with the children and grandchildren of his friends. If there is a boy or girl in the family of his circle of acquaintances who is being graduated at high school or college, Mr. Fuller somehow learns of it and, on graduation night, is always to be found in the first row, beaming in a sort of proprietary or parental pride. He follows the activities of the literary youngsters with a sympathy and understanding which is unusual among men past middle age. He has, so far as I know, never uttered a deprecatory, admonitory, or shocked word against the younger generation. So alive is he to what is being done by the younger men that not long ago he wrote a highly appreciative article pointing out the peculiar merits of a dozen or so of the most eccentric and revolutionary of the young modern poets.

II

Mr. Fuller's first novel, "The Chevalier of Pensieri-Vani," was written as long ago as 1886. It did not find a publisher until 1890, when it came out anonymously. When the second edition of the book was issued he attached his name to it. A year later appeared his "Chatelaine of La Trinité," which, like the first novel, was a romantic comedy, with a touch of the gentlest raillery, the scene laid in Italy. In his next two novels, "The Cliff Dwellers" (1893) and "With the Procession" (1895), he took up the realistic manner and applied it to stories of contemporary life in Chicago. In these books no less than in his earlier ones, however, a tincture of Stendhalian irony, heightened perhaps by Mr. Fuller's instinctive repugnance for the crudeness and garishness of the Chicago of those days, gave his books, if not a bite, at least a nip. In the books he published between 1895 and the advent of the world war—"From the Other Side," "The Last Refuge," "Under the Skylights," and "Waldo Trench and Others"—there is the same exquisite design, the same polished style, the same quiet humor and delicate irony which distinguish all his work, and the same absence of any glow that would give his work force and character. Then there was a period of nine years when nothing, except a few articles here and there, appeared under his name. In 1917 he brought out a book of humorous and experimental verse, parodies and adaptations of the manner of the free-verse writers. The book, many items of which had already appeared in Bert Leston Taylor's "Line-o-Type" column in the Chicago "Tribune," was called "Lines Long and Short." Then in 1918 he wrote a novel in strict conformity to his theory that no novel should exceed 60,000 words in length, wherein he developed two contrasting figures of equal importance to his story, one of them the vital and successful, though crude, man of action and the other an artist in temperament, unassertive, withdrawn from life. In this novel there seems to have dawned upon him the first realization of what I believe to be the failure of his own career—the failure to make a choice between two roads. If he was to stay in Chicago and use the fiction material at hand in such a way as to give it great significance and meaning, it would have been necessary for him to accept Chicago with fewer regrets that it was not Florence or Milan. If he was to expatriate himself it would have been necessary to do it as thoroughly as did Henry James. In "On the Stairs" he showed for the first time his understanding that vitality and driving purpose, however crude, is naturally more admirable than ineffectiveness, however cultured and beautifully mannered.

It may be said that "Bertram Cope's Year," in so far as it was read and understood at all, shocked Mr. Fuller's friends so painfully that they silenced it into limbo. It is a story, delicately done with the most exquisite taste, of a sublimated irregular affection. It received scant and unintelligent notice from the reviewers and, though it was filled with dynamite scrupulously packed, it fell as harmless as a dud, only to be whispered about here and there by grave people who wondered why Mr. Fuller should choose such a theme. Since then he has written no novels or, if he has written some, he has not published them. Diffidence again and disappointment have conspired to keep his name only a name in our contemporary literature. He has the sensibility and intelligence, the subtlety and delicacy, to produce artistic masterpieces but he lacks temper and gusto—vitality. This is all the more lamentable in that we have in our American literature an abundance of vitality, but not enough of the qualities which Mr. Fuller possesses in a high degree.

## *XV: Owen Johnson*

IT is Owen Johnson's triumph that every boy who has gone to college since he wrote his young-lad books, looks upon him as the dean of the authors of that type of fiction. It is his tragedy that, after a round dozen or more of years wherein he has compressed much literary work, he is still referred to as "the author of the Lawrenceville stories." All his later books are passed over, with the exception of "The Salamander," and one goes inevitably back to that first thrilling success, that time when he depicted the boy mind, the boy heart, as few writers since Mark Twain have done it. "The Tennessee Shad" and "Stover at Yale" are also always spoken of, in any summing up of his achievement, as well as that fine little golf story in one of his earlier collections—I think it's called "Par 3." Yet since those days of glory, those days of vigorous production—he was hailed as a boy wonder when he brought out "Arrows of the Almighty"—he has written "The Woman Gives," "Making Money," "The Wasted Generation," "Skippy Bedelle," and "Blue Blood."

He is but forty-six years of age—at that period of his life when he should be on the forward march. One thinks of his "Stover at Yale," with its truth and humor, and sighs over the stuff that followed it—with the exception of one. It is true that many of the most astute reviewers found much to praise in "The Wasted Generation"; and it is significant that they are of the older school, who first acclaimed him loudly. They speak of it as a fine interpretation of certain phases of the world war.

One remembers Johnson's golden opportunities. No young man ever started out so propitiously. A good fairy must have watched over his cradle. His father was a distinguished literary figure of what might be called the mid-Victorian era of American letters, and has since become our Ambassador to Italy. His mother is a splendid, cultured woman. Young Johnson had chances hurled at his door, and with the common sense of the astute youth he was, as well as with no small equipment of talent, he seized them as they came his way—made the most, for a time, of his growing popularity, certainly coined money, married and reared a family, was a good fellow at The Players and other clubs—in short, became highly considered in the tumult and passion of New York life.

During the war he produced little. One slender volume about France came from his hitherto prolific pen—that was about all. Hearst had gobbled him up, had seen the great possibilities in him; and it was rumored that he had signed a five years' contract for all his literary output, at a fabulous salary. He was to be free and untrammeled; there were to be no demands whatever made upon him for "sex stuff"; he would simply sit comfortably at home, a pad upon his knee, and let the words flow, or not, as it suited his whim.

Johnson is, when all is said and done, an artist of no mean parts. And artists cannot be tied down to contracts, cannot have life run for them on too-smooth wheels. There must be conflict, always, a bit of worry, if the true man of letters is to accomplish what he was ordained to accomplish. One novel a year —or less—would mean only a few hours' work a day; then golf in the afternoon, a bit of reading, and a dinner party, followed by a theater or the opera. An ideal life for an American gentleman of letters, still in his robust thirties! It sounded glorious—and it *was* glorious, for a

OWEN JOHNSON

time. But not glorious for Johnson's art. He did not care to keep the contract, and it was broken, I believe, by mutual consent.

At any rate, his next serial appeared in his first love, "McClure's." They ran "The Wasted Generation," spoken of above, in 1921.

Johnson has changed publishers, as he has changed editors, several times. He has had Bobbs-Merrill, Stokes, and now Little, Brown and Company; and I think one or two others, maybe Macmillan in those distant days when he was writing boy stories. In between he made a dramatization of "The Salamander," and Carroll McComas, if I remember correctly, played the part of the girl who kept herself from being scorched. It ran about two weeks on Broadway; but people had not forgotten his splendid adaptation of "The Return from Jerusalem" for the wonderful Madame Simone, and an original play for Nazimova called "The Comet," which ran for two years in and out of New York; and Arnold Daly in Johnson's delicate one-act bit, "A Comedy for Wives."

It has been said of Johnson that no one loves a harmless practical joke more than he. There are lots of his friends who know that he will never give his correct name when he calls them on the telephone: it is always the Federal Income Tax Collector, or some such dreadful ogre; and he loves to leave strange cards at editorial offices and then run away like a schoolboy. It is this spirit in him, perhaps, which has caused his stories of youngsters to be so popular. You see, he is still a boy at heart; he will never grow up, never be spoiled by success—and he has had his goodly share of it. Socially, too, he is popular, much in demand, though he is strong in his likes and dislikes, and never wastes much time on people he does not care for. He can order a good dinner; and how he does love the gastronomidal side of life! He is extravagant, sometimes to the point of foolishness. It's always a taxi or a hansom for him, when he isn't riding in his own limousine; but, unlike many writers, he does not bore even his best friends, when he dines with them, with long monologues concerning what he is doing or is about to do. Indeed, he is very modest about his work. He has often said that a man's books should speak for him; that all one has to say should be embodied in one's fiction. He certainly practices what he preaches. He is, in many ways, the most unliterary literary man I ever knew. But he does love the great books of all time, and he has read deeply, drunk deeply of those fountainheads of prose which have been his inspiration. He prefers the French writers to the English; and though his father is a poet of some distinction, the son has not inherited his taste for verse. Yet in his prose one will often encounter the singing phrase that proclaims a poetic inheritance.

He has had many charming and stirring friendships. He admired Theodore Roosevelt, and often made pilgrimages to Oyster Bay to lunch with the former President. During the war he was bitterly anti-German, and used whatever influence he had to spread the gospel of France. As a child, he had been to school in the country of Balzac; and after he had published "The Spirit of France" the French government decorated him with the ribbon of the Legion of Honor. He is genuinely and openly proud of that decoration, and always wears it.

If he is not a profound philosopher, he has a penetrating, incisive mind, though sometimes he appraises people unjustly, and is intolerant of their human shortcomings. What he needs is discipline. His novels always, to me, run to verbosity. Yet he has never, since the days of "The Varmint," joined that group of overwriters who grind out columns for the turnover of magazines at so much per word. The legend is that Johnson was piqued when his one and only serial in a certain publication brought him so much fame but very little money; for in those days he was not highly paid. But to jump in a few years out of the $3,000 class into the $25,000 class is an achievement of which any young author might well be proud.

Johnson once got mixed up in politics. He wanted to see General Leonard Wood made President, and he worked hard and unselfishly and untiringly to that end. He was honest, too, in his purpose. He had no ax to grind; though there were unkind lookers-on who said that he had his eye on an ambassadorship. Nothing, I think, was further from his thoughts; for he knew how much wealth an ambassador needs these days. He was content to see his father appointed by Wilson. As a matter of fact, young Johnson would make an almost ideal envoy at any foreign court; for he is thoroughly cosmopolitan, speaks French and Italian fluently, and has the necessary savoir-faire to make him a credit to the United States. When he is fifty who knows but that he may go abroad in some such capacity? But now, he seems to be quite content in his native land, with his wife and family about him. His political adventurings were short-lived. With his colorful and honest temperament, he could not cope with hard-boiled senators and charlatans in the ring at Washington, and he came back greatly disillusioned, and bravely said so. Enough of that sort of thing for him! Never again! A little of it went a long way. But he should have written some political stories—they might have been good stuff.

Johnson, above all things, is charming. A man is known by the company he keeps. Perhaps, then, it would be illuminating to give a list of those men with whom the novelist has always been more or less intimate. For years he was adored by, and adored in turn, Arthur Bartlett

Maurice; and it was while the latter was editing The Bookman that young Johnson's series of questions for college students, which had formed a passage in "Stover at Yale," was reprinted by Maurice—a literary interrogation list that stumped us all, and was exceedingly clever. He probably set the fashion for Edison and others; for he *is* a bit of a pioneer. Witness "The Salamander." It came five years before its time; now we realize its bitter truth. There is no doubt that his questions set the literati talking—and squirming; and it was all great fun. It may have been that Owen was at his old business of playing a practical joke. Nevertheless, the thing he did created a storm, a veritable upheaval. Not in years had ignorance been more plainly shown up; and many a college man hung his head and ran to cover, with a pathetic percentage of twelve or so in his favor.

Maurice and Johnson are as thick as ever; but the author of the Lawrenceville stories has kept other friends over a long period of years; and he has been catholic in his tastes. "The Wasted Generation" is dedicated to Hugh Walpole—a more or less recent spiritual tie, one imagines. He likes Frank Crowninshield very much indeed; but his great David and Jonathan attachment was with the late Walter Hale. That was a fine, solid, enduring friendship; and Johnson felt the artist's death keenly. Christian Brinton, the art critic, has always been close to him, the recipient of many confidences; and so have Gari Melchers, Austin Strong, Charles Hanson Towne, Harry Lindeberg, the architect, who was his best man at his last wedding. Then there are several actors and painters and singers of note with whom he has been on intimate terms. He is very fond of all interpreters of the arts, and when he gives a reception or a dinner he never makes a mistake. He likes things to be right—he is almost

Teutonic in his passion for precedents and form. He never takes chances, socially.

What does he look like? James Montgomery Flagg has made, a splendid, slashing drawing of him, though Johnson now has even less hair than when that likeness was made. He has a rather florid complexion, dreamy eyes, and lips that curl and reveal a certain worldliness. Yet there is a fine spiritual side to Owen Johnson. He loves the stillness of the country, though he is also city-mad. He exudes physical health, and though it would be better for him if he took off ten or fifteen pounds, he cannot be called too stout. There is a roguish look about him, a daredevil gleam in his eye when he is not working too hard. No one enjoys a banquet more than he. Then all his inhibitions vanish, all his dignity goes —particularly when it is a stag affair—and he becomes almost the court jester, as fond as Charles Lamb of atrocious puns, and is the ribald, flaming, delightful companion that he loves to be and knows so well how to be. For he can talk brilliantly, insert the almost Oliver Herfordlike bon mot into his conversation, make memorable phrases—when he is in the mood.

Like most professional writers, Johnson is delightful and tractable—unless his copy is tampered with. There is that memorable episode of his run-in with "Everybody's Magazine" when that periodical was publishing his novel "Making Money." It seems that the serialization of it began long before the manuscript was completed; and the final instalment reached the office at the very last moment. It was felt that certain knots in the plot had not been untied. But Johnson had sailed for Europe. One of the assistant editors volunteered, in the emergency, to wind things up satisfactorily.

When Johnson returned from his trip abroad he read

a curious distortion of his last chapter. He could not believe his eyes. It was as though some one had taken his child and amputated one of its arms, a toe or two, and chipped a bit off the left ear. He was a distracted parent. A totally changed brain-child stood before him. He was furious; and it is said that he threatened all sorts of damages unless his own version was printed in the next number, so that he could be artistically justified.

The editors, of course, consented. The files of "Everybody's" offer interesting proof of one of the most amazing contretemps between editor and author in the history of magazine-making. There is no doubt that Johnson won out; he has many letters from admiring readers to prove that his own version was the better of the two.

Owen Johnson may still write a novel that will atone for many old transgressions. He is capable of big ideas, and of putting those ideas upon paper. He is still very definitely in the literary ring, and he has a tremendous following. One of these days—let us hope it will be with his next book—he may beautifully record some of the captured magic from Olympus.

## *XVI: Mary Austin*

THE areas of the world which most completely possess and direct and mold the spirits of the peoples which inhabit them are not its easy places. Few of them have any obvious happiness to impart or much accessible inspiration of beauty. Their strength of influence lies rather in a sober and unyielding heroism implicit in the weather and the land and in a visual impersonality of the face of nature. No exactitude of skull measurement, no idiosyncrasy of religious observance can so vividly exteriorize this possession and this molding process as the study of the power which such areas wield over the formation and the quality of their literatures.

This is not merely to say that Wessex enthralls Thomas Hardy but that in no reach of his imagination can Hardy ever escape Wessex. The few serious thoughts which occasionally crossed the rate-per-word intelligence of Jack London had their roots between the round horizons of Alaska. The earth spoke to Conrad, once and forever, in "the senseless and mournful delusion" of the tropical seaboard and so, malignantly and permanently, assumed for him the tremendous insistence of destiny.

Once this miracle has befallen a writer he can afterward know other lands only through his own that has asserted itself upon him. He has no voice, no sight, no will, no point of view which is not colored with its glare and darkness and shaped to its own purposes. His philosophy, above all, is imposed upon him by the strange, invincible, and inanimate contact. All his force depends upon his fidelity to its domination. He may, from time to time, evade it, but he is almost certain to come off futile if he does. His track is laid for him and if he steps aside he flounders in shifting sands and amid trivial irrelevancies.

"I was transplanted," Mary Austin says, "from a middle western college town to that portion of the American desert which I have described in 'The Land of Little Rain' and 'Lost Borders.'" Such a transplantation considered, those two exquisite and beautiful books (and "The Flock," too, for that matter) assume the significance of confessions. Mary Austin went into the southwest and the desert made her life articulate. It has never failed her since nor freed her. She has never fruitfully forsaken its mastery and she never can. "A land of lost rivers with little in it to love; yet a land which once visited must be come back to inevitably."

Hers is, to be sure, a mind made to the desert's order. It has the classic rigor to cope with austerity and desolation and the precise delicacy of perception which sees intimacy and loveliness where they are most subtly and terribly concealed. It has the high emotional violence of romance to which no natural phenomenon is either indefinite or unimportant. It has the incessant curiosity which serves the amateur in lieu of the scientific attitude and it looks into the eyes of deity with the level gaze of the mystic.

All this seems normal enough of great minds, for great minds are singularly standardized. They have the same acquisitive impulse, by and large, and the same matter-of-factness and the same perceived and unperceived shortcomings and the same fundamental ruthlessness. Mary Austin is, by most standards, of the company of great minds. Her one essential lack is the comic sense. But there is no cruelty in her, and without cruelty humor offers but a meager refuge; a refuge moreover, to which she would never voluntarily go, for

MARY AUSTIN

she takes life too seriously and with too consistent kindliness.

She is deeply concerned with both deity and the universe. She is little interested by anything of less consequence. Desert and sea and timber-line furnish man with the three mirrors in which the will of the universe is most clearly discernible. Of the three, the desert seems the truest mirror of the mind of deity. Mary Austin found many things to her liking in the desert—small life amid desperate privation, vast amplifications of color, limitless space of clean air, and the feel of a country coordinated to the movement of gigantic rhythms. More than all this, however, she found in the desert a universe in which, by degrees, she became thoroughly at home, and a deity with whom she struck up the honest relationship of frank understanding and unabashed eagerness to serve. These two were the things she most needed. She read the desert's riddles and solved its domestic difficulties and set them down in her early books which are among literature's supreme interpretations of country. She took from the desert an emotional philosophy and a concept of God.

Her God is very evidently created to her requirements and the desert's by the union between the desert's spirit and her own. He seems a sort of combination between the Great Spirit of the Indian and the Smithsonian Institute. In his honor she founded an ethnological faith in which she is herself the perfect worshiper and which follows the observances of a special creed made up of physical geography and political liberalism and colored by a strong predilection for natural history museums. She did this in all seriousness, as her books attest. She deified her interpretation of the desert and she waits now for the prophet who shall come out of the southwest.

Her God taught her the mysticism of desert sage and blue distance and the appreciation of the problems of natural life which so engross her attention, and they, in their turn, invested her with their own pantheism. It is a specialized and a highly individualized doctrine—the idealism of a sublime detachment from all concrete human problems and most human thought. It disregards mankind and concerns itself alone and apart with those natural matters which are naturally irremediable. Beyond a doubt she was born to be a great and self-constituted defender. But the desert motivated her too spaciously. Though she is self-dedicated to the disinterested defense of human lost causes, the desert leaves her scant patience with humanity. It has, one suspects, fomented in her a recognizable discontent with having been born in human form and persuaded her that she would have been far better off as a goddess or a physical law. It seems likely even that, failing godhead, she would have chosen for herself a small furry shape and spent her lifetime scampering along desert water trails between stalks of sage and mesquite. She might have felt divinity the more surely and so come more perfectly into the natural scheme in which the southwest has enveloped all her intellectual and spiritual reactions.

Humanity is either too strong for Mary Austin's taste or not quite feeble enough. She can take such downtrodden creatures as the Pueblo Indians and Jesus of Nazareth and defend the one against Congress and the other against Christianity. This she can do because the plight of each is readily transformed into large emotional abstraction. For smaller injustice the wise, wide energy of the desert forever unfitted her. Her long assertion of the rights of womankind, the least successful of all her works, is the clearest proof of this. However arduously she may have pressed it, it is an enterprise impelled by conscience and by little else. She felt, it is quite evident, that she must do something for her sisters and she has done her utmost. But her comprehension of them is curiously at sea. Her philosophy holds no place for those who will not be abstracted. You cannot abstract women; you succeed merely in offending them if you try and set them on a tangent of vituperative contradiction. Mary Austin has offered them all the most grandiose pigeon-holes of her scheme of things and they have rioted in every one. Her sense of justice drove her into the woman problem; her really convinced non-humanity betrayed her. Let her deny this hotly as she will, it is none the less true. Woman is not colossal nor is she small, furred, and squeaking. Wherefore womankind does not abide in Mary Austin's alley and the sooner she has done with it the better.

You may call this spirit proud, but her humility is only the more genuine for its impressive stature. The lowliness with which she bows to the unalterable is without affectation and wholly unafraid. Her danger is that she too often credits with importance to herself matters which, in reality, neither interest nor involve her. From the first day of her transplantation she has been committed to the inevitable and to nothing else.

All of this that is here said of her is clear in her books, above all, in the most important of them—"The Man Jesus." There her imagination and her philosophy came together with their one real embodiment. The two forces met and, emotionally and spiritually, fitted one into the other as light fits into form. She brought to Jesus what the desert had given her and that is a nobler thing than theology. "The Man Jesus" is, by that, a stauncher book than Renan's "Vie de Jésus." The credulous platitudes of Papini shrivel beside it.

Mary Austin achieves a very perfection of courageous

understanding whenever Jesus speaks. The errors of her historical scholarship do not matter. Her Holy Land is none the less holy for being in her re-creation of its atmosphere mostly western and American. She knows the man and his disciples and the countryside through which they wandered because they were desert folk, bred in small and primitive communities, who had, in their time, looked upon her salty desolations and her verdant settlements and condoned the same small lives and great. She knows them for the fact that she and Jesus are both desert-taught and live both by a kindred humility and a kindred awe and by the same ignorance of the human formula.

What is so fine in the best of her writing, suffers whenever she follows conscience or the guidance of the momentary into more personable ways. What has the desert to do with theatric silliness? Her plays brought fine emotion and fine truth to the stage, but emotion and truth alike turn to empty gesticulation in the mouths of the puppet characters which she draws to be their spokesmen. Her novels will be read always for the serene elegance of her writing. The best of them is not their personnel but the feeling they have for the land, by some character or feature, her own land always, whatever exterior change she sets upon it. The everlasting best of her is that widespread simplicity and straightness, at once so kind and so impersonal, which she attained when she went away from her middle western college town into the "land of lost borders." Her tales are good tales, especially of westerners and the west, but her eyes in them again are far sharper for the land and its meaning than for the businesses of men and women.

She is herself true to her teaching and direct. She likes people best when she can question them. She likes scientists best of all. She will, on occasion, let down her hair and tell ghost stories to freeze your blood. The compromise she effects between Arizona and Gramercy Park is a good deal less than successful. She is better off in her California house on the coast of Monterey, though she seems, there, to live more outside her walls than within them. London troubles her less than New York because she feels less conscientiously responsible for it. She seems happiest in the west and on the open sea. That will be the outcome of her mysticism which conceives the chief duty of man to be a process of lonely waiting for the day when the hand of deity shall make use of him, and she feels herself more near (and more apparent, too) where mystery and the sky alone limit her vision.

She is greatly American by the chance that took her into her southwest and she reads her desert rhythms and symbols into all American institutions. American institutions do not always fit very precisely into the rhythms with which she clothes them but this disconcerts her very little. A sculptor must throw away a good deal of marble to make a statue; a thinker of Mary Austin's cast does not hesitate with the rebellious institution. She can, you may be sure, usually twist or compress it to her demands. Let Mary Austin loose upon marital relations and she will "understand" them all around the town. She likes her friends to call her "Chisera," which is to say "Witch Woman," or words to that effect. And this is not ridiculous. You may, if you resent ruthlessness and really bitter consistency, resent Mary Austin, but you do not laugh at her.

For she has that extraordinary completeness and self-sufficiency which makes a mess of many little matters and, on occasion, can cope fearlessly and triumphally with the authentic crisis. She is like an actress marked apart to play great rôles. Her writing and her thinking alike are set aside for noble subjects. When she comes down from her own standard and the desert's, her workmanship persists in all its beauty and sincerity; her inspiration abandons her. That is the decree laid upon her by her experience in the lonely west. And that is proper, too. The great mind is no less great for having only one idea so long as the idea remains a part of godhead.

There are two kinds of thinking: the purely emotional to which everything is important and inviolate, and the purely intellectual to which nothing matters very much. Mary Austin thinks principally through her emotions; her faults and weaknesses are all intellectual. She has great feeling and little skepticism.

One touch of humor would have made her less complete, would have marred the monumental integrity of her character. The desert has no need for landscape gardening; the mystic has no use for humor. When Margaret Fuller went to London to voice the transcendentalism of her generation she, too, accepted the universe. She did it, according to report, in public, arms flung wide and in so many words:

"I accept the universe!"

Said Carlyle, a little sourly: "Gad, she'd better!"

## XVII: *James Branch Cabell*

IT has happened a few times perhaps in the history of literature that a man has waked to find himself famous because of what he has written, but, so far as I know, it has remained for Cabell to open his eyes on a world wherein he was proclaimed as infamous because of what he did not write. It was "Jurgen" that "made" Cabell, but, in the eyes of the world, it made him something other than he was.

Cabell is a man of medium height, and of a somewhat stocky figure. His head is finely molded with the broad forehead of the æsthete and the thinker, not unlike that of the young Augustus; his eyes are heavy-lidded and sleepy, such eyes as one often sees in old portraits of the cavaliers and courtiers of the time of the Stuarts, rather insolent and a little bored; his mouth is delicately cut and sensitive, generous yet not too full, the mouth of a poet but not of a philosopher; and between those eyes and this mouth he has a quizzical little snout.

Cabell strikes me as a disappointed idealist who awoke from a fool's paradise to write "Jurgen" and "Figures of Earth." Within him Marlowe struggles with Congreve, and of the two is born frustration. His earlier books are realization through fantasy; his later work is fantasy baffled and broken by realization. Science, economics, sociology, he knows little of; his knowledge of history is erratic, of philosophy and religion, artistic; and his one political doctrine appears to be that hatred of Woodrow Wilson, the incongruous expression of which has, for me, marred two of his books. When Cabell tries to be topical he is usually lumbering. Like the courtier and the cavalier he places polish, urbanity, and elegance first on the list of virtues, and, like the cavalier and the courtier, he has no very keen sense of ethical values. He is amoral rather than immoral. His creed embraces that type of honor which combines romance with cynicism. Manner with Cabell is much more important than matter.

His philosophic credo, in so far as he appears to have one, seems to be the eternal repetition of life, the only object of which is procreation. Now this, after all, is essentially the philosophy of the cynic, for, while beauty is its idol, it invariably remembers, and takes care to point out, that the end of all beauty is decay. It is materialistic, because while it deals with abstract truths it admits them only as the impelling forces behind the physical world—which turns to mold. It is mechanistic, because it allows no space for a higher order of evolution which could only be expressed in metaphysical terms; it repeats itself endlessly, the old gestures, the old masks, and all to the sole end that men be born, beget others in their turn, and die. It sees no further, nor does it even admit the possibility of there being a "further."

The truth is that Cabell's work is almost entirely subjective. He is constantly in the throes of explaining and justifying himself to himself. He is able to face the general facts and conditions of life frankly and squarely —sometimes!—but this is only in moments of revolt, when his spirit is so sickened that it discharges perforce. Particular facts of life he is not able to face at all, but one may find them thrusting outward for expression in his symbols, between his lines, and in those fluent passages, the very intensity and facility of which have put him off his guard.

There are those, and Cabell is one of them, who simply

JAMES BRANCH CABELL

cannot face life as it is. Their means and methods of escape are many and varied and, sometimes, strange. Occasionally they have, like Cabell, creative ability. There is, for example, the actual instance of the man who felt compelled to do nothing but construct small models of cities. The models were of no practical value but, having made them, their creator was able to escape into them. The laying out of the streets, squares, parks, and public buildings satisfied in some measure their maker's sense of beauty and of pattern. In time these fancied cities grew so real to him that he lived only in them, and gradually lost touch altogether with the world about him. He succeeded in escaping. Cabell is not unlike him. One finds in his elaborate genealogy of the characters in his books as set forth in "The Lineage of Lichfield" several significant indications. There is of course the recurrent expression of his hopeless philosophy of repetition, and there is likewise manifest a sense of satisfaction in almost geometrical pattern, such as the other man found in the laying out of his streets, cross-streets, and squares. Beyond this there is still the attempt to clothe his mimic world in the garb of reality. And this desire for the semblance of reality is not primarily for his audience, but for himself. It makes escape more easy.

Cabell escapes into his imaginary world more and more as time goes on, as his powers strengthen, and as the actual drops from him. When one knows him one gradually comes to realize that the world of his creation, with its creatures sprung from Manuel as from Adam, constitutes the only real world to him. His eyes dull and his eyelids droop when he talks, as he seldom does, of the people and events of the life wherein he is embodied; but his interest quickens and brightens when he speaks of his mimic world, and of the persons and happenings there. He is Jurgen, and he is Charteris, and, in one form or another and under one name or another, the thread of self-identification can be followed through his work. He believes that he is writing an epos of humanity, a cycle of man, but in reality he is only writing the subjective autobiography of Cabell. It is not all life recurrent in different forms with which he deals, but simply the endless recurrence of himself within himself. The form may change, but the essence remains the same. He evidently feels that the means that lead to his ultimate destination are few, somewhat tediously few, though the combinations of which they are capable are considerably varied. For example, there are some 600,000,000,000 possible combinations of cards in bridge, but there are only fifty-two cards in the pack and the object of each hand is the same—to score. This is Cabell's tragedy, and it is from this that he endeavors endlessly to escape altogether.

Here is the man whom that strange uncertain quantity, the New York Society for the Suppression of Vice, lifted to attention and whose *apologia pro vita sua* they succeeded in suppressing for a long two years.

A disappointed idealist: why not? Life has held great tragedy for him, and he is endowed with qualities that in themselves court and provoke tragedy almost wantonly. Many lurid tales have been circulated about Cabell, but they are untrue. Most of them have originated with the gossips of Richmond who, after looking upon Cabell as an F. F. V. gone wrong, are now forced to regard him as a bona fide celebrity whether they like it or not. And they do not like it, for they do not at all understand Cabell, and hence are unable to patronize him as they would like to. Richmond will never forgive Cabell for the bitter truths he has told of it in "The Rivet in Grandfather's Neck," and in "Cords of Vanity."

Richmond realizes that while Cabell knows it inside and out, it can really never know Cabell. Such knowledge is unpalatable.

James Branch Cabell lives a little way outside of Richmond in a middle-aged house that has in it much of the Victorian, and nothing of the traditional Colonial of the south. The house is comfortable and uninteresting inside and out with little traces here and there of a certain modern efficiency—as in the folding typewriter desk in Cabell's study—that stand out baldly against a background of antimacassars and whatnot stands. The truth is that Cabell is blessed with a wife who is blessed with a sense of humor, and who sees to it that while the major portion of her husband has emigrated to Poictesme the part of him which remains at home is well cared for, let alone, and humored. It takes genius to write as Cabell does, but that genius is as nothing to the genius it must take to live happily with a genius. And Cabell stays at home. To get him as far as New York takes months of urging on the part of every one interested, and when he finally is ousted from his small workroom with its three windows and its rows of books, it is almost impossible to make him meet people or to say anything when he does meet them. They do not speak his language nor does he speak theirs.

His library is astonishingly meager both in the quantity and quality of the books that compose it, and this in spite of Cabell's just claim, made for, not by, him, to real erudition. He cares nothing for fine bindings or for old editions. The author most in evidence among his books is Hewlett, but one should not deduce from this that he owes much to Hewlett, any more than he does to Anatole France whom he read really carefully only after he had been compared to him. The materials that Hewlett has used in all seriousness Cabell has burlesqued, as in "Jurgen" and "Figures of Earth." Yet how he did lose his temper when Hewlett attacked him! The attack was bad, but Cabell's reply was worse, shriek upon shriek of wounded vanity. It was childish to give his spleen any permanence in "Taboo."

He is one of the founders of that exclusive little club apparently created for the purpose of mutual admiration by Mencken, Hergesheimer, and himself. Cabell cannot stand criticism, a weakness that serves his work poorly. The success that has come to him in such a strange and ironic way after years of neglect and even contempt has embittered rather than mellowed him. Most emphatically Cabell does not belong among those who, like St. Paul, "suffer fools gladly." He first entered the lists young, ardent, and unsuspicious; but, as the years went by bringing the sting of new wounds upon old ones, he incased himself more and more in the armor of unreality, and with the sword of satire fought on.

The key to Cabell's cynicism lies in the story of the fox and the grapes. He knows he cannot reach them, and so he proclaims them sour. But, unlike the fox, Cabell has compromised. He has deliberately given up the grapes, and hence his fury is double because it arises not only from his sense of failure but from the knowledge of his own responsibility for it. He chose the fleshpot with his eyes wide open, *vide* "Jurgen," and now all that is left to him is to hurl the pot with savage bitterness at the head of his readers.

The chief note in his later work is that of regret, regret for the youth and beauty which seem to him to pass together. Almost he feels with Dunsany that time is the most terrible enemy of man, for time, to him, is the destroyer. He is not unlike Dunsany in other ways, though I do not by any means intend to compare the two. They both, however, have a curious magic of phrases, and a cadenced prose that turns to pure verse: they both have invented a cosmogony of their own, and Cabell has in the bargain traced a very earthly dynasty which is descended from his gods. And yet . . . in all this by means of which he intends to embrace all life, he has only succeeded in embracing—Cabell. Like Narcissus he has been enchanted by an image in the pool of thought but, unlike Narcissus, he does not realize that the image is his own.

One finds always in Cabell the wail of the violins of Venusberg in combat with the long surge of the trombones of the Pilgrims' Chorus.

What is it in Cabell that we find admirable? It seems to me to be simply that he has done that which he has said again and again he wanted to do, to write beautifully of beautiful things. Not that he confines himself to that. He writes of ugly things too, but he writes of them grotesquely as is most fitting. He has the ability to an extraordinary degree of creating moods, of making a living atmosphere through which and into which the reader passes to walk with those that dwell therein, somewhat as Alice went through the Looking-Glass into the country beyond. Cabell is a rebel against the bonds of flesh that hold him, and he awakens in his readers a desire to rebel likewise. The most significant passage in all his work is, to me, that in which Jurgen stands by the bedside of the sleeping Queen Helen. Even there Cabell pauses to mock a little, but his mockery rings hollow, for he knows that rail as he may at his dream, the dream is stronger than he. Here, as elsewhere, his attitude is sheer bravado. But . . . it is very human. What makes all his bitterness and all his rebellion is his knowledge of the real beauty, the beauty he has somehow missed, that eternally tangles the heartstrings of man. He knows, and he knows well, how little the flesh matters, and he is infuriated at his realization that it matters even as much as it does. After a little time with Anaitis, goddess of love, Jurgen was so unutterably bored that he left her, and went to play with the children. There is no cynicism here, only a mild chuckle at the endless foolishness of man. For, whimsical as he often is, and cynical as he is upon occasion, Cabell is more quizzical than either.

What he will do next it is futile to conjecture. It may be another attempt to rationalize the literature of procreation—and whatever it is I very much fear that it will be an addition to the already too voluminous "Lineage of Lichfield"—but in any event Cabell may be trusted to do the two things he desires most to do, to conceive beautiful things and to write of them beautifully. It is for this that he is read, and it is for this that he will be remembered.

## XVIII: John Farrar

JOHN FARRAR has a quaint and rather creepy capacity for undergoing a gradual but complete metamorphosis before your very eyes. You look, and while you look the lines of his thin, hungry face assume new relations among themselves: what was before an obtuse angle slowly closes to the acute, and the straight lines forming it bend at the unjoined ends with the sinuous undulations of an angle-worm that has been partially crushed. This metamorphosis is not that swift facility for assuming protective coloration with which we associate the salamander; for Farrar, though outwardly the most socially amenable of party-hounds, has actually a most meager faculty for identifying himself with the moods and manners of a group: it is rather a matter of a painful sensitiveness to disturbing contacts. And most contacts to Farrar are disturbing. What we see, then, is the unconscious performance of a sort of quick-change artist, who foregoes the advantage of a momentary retirement behind a screen. One moment he is a pink-cheeked seraph with all three pairs of wings aflutter and at the end of the next moment he is a bent old man, disconsolate and agape at youth. One moment he appears a case of arrested development, with immaturity, even pubescence, soliciting your forbearance and kindly patronage; the next, he is an austere and censorious ascetic frowning his disapproval of gaucheries and frivolities. He is, in the course of a single evening, child and birch-

[1] Editor's Note.—This article was submitted anonymously for the Spotlight series. The editor feels it only fair to the others who have been attacked in these pages to open them to this sketch of himself.

man, pupil and lecturer, defender and carper, Pierrot and pedant, monk and playboy.

He has a way of clicking his teeth together, compressing his lips, lowering his chin to close proximity with his Adam's apple, and murmuring through his nose an ambiguous and non-committal "Ooom!" That is about the only time he ever has his mouth closed. Not that he is adenoidal; he isn't; but silent or loquacious, meditative or interested, his mouth is agape. That comes of an almost abnormal inquisitiveness combined with a New England conscience: he is very eager to know, but knowledge very often shocks, irritates, or troubles him; he would learn the bitter or ugly truth, but not until it has paid toll to his moral sentiments is that truth allowed to enter his head; he enjoys being aghast at scandalous gossip and is ever on the hunt for it. His mouth opens and stays open in a pained and hurt kind of expression.

I have never known any man, woman, or child who so thoroughly as Farrar constitutes himself his brother's keeper. Farrar assumes a paternal protectorate over every friend he has or makes, watching after his friend's health, counseling him in money matters, advising him against the pitfalls of a big city, choosing his acquaintances, censoring his pleasures, defending him against criticism, tooting his horn, giving him a leg-up with people of influence, and worrying himself ill lest through some failure in his plans his friend will go to the dogs. I spoke of a paternal protectorate; but Farrar's solicitude is maternal rather, even grandmotherly or, perhaps even more accurate still, grand-auntly. He is always arranging love matches, furthering courtships, trying to straighten out marital difficulties, reconciling estranged couples, making young poets sign the pledge, trying to distract the sentimental attentions of ingenuous novelists and playwrights away from dangerous women, advising

JOHN FARRAR

fresh air, wholesome amusements, and hard work against the claims of temptresses, the flesh and the devil.

Let some designing baggage cast a salacious or approving eye at one of Farrar's brood of talent—and they include men old enough to be Farrar's father—and his protective wings spread about his ward, his feathers go up in fear and fight, his countenance brews a thunderous and angry look, and that night he gets no sleep, wondering how he is going to circumvent the evil machinations of the harassing hussy. Let some one of his wayward wards be seen at lunch with a woman not his wife, and Farrar experiences a profound sense of discouragement at his life's work and muses with audible despair upon man's frailties, the decay of virtue, and the treacherous, insistent demands made upon character and moral stamina by the feverish, fretful life of a metropolis.

It is rather difficult to associate this pink-cheeked, reddish-haired, angular, and very young, young man with the moral preoccupations and proclivities of the elder Cato. But there they are, and there's no escaping them. It is, in a way, admirable; and I have no doubt but that, had Farrar not been so vigilant and censorious, any number of young and not so young people would have been sinful, though happy, and would have gone to pieces with a certain degree of uncountenanceable enjoyment. He has saved a lot of people from hell and illicit happiness; he has made them work with that feeling of thwartment which is the mother of all art; and he has laid up his treasures in heaven against the thieves and rust of a corrupting and demi-mondaine world.

This much must be said for Farrar, whether in consoling reflection that he is not an unmitigated busybody or in criticism of the fleet endurance of the white flame of his reclamatory and directive zeal: he will waste only just so much time on a fellow, and if he proves incorrigible, unamenable to reason, an implacable enemy of his own best interests, a resentful weakling, a consummate rake, and a vain believer in his own ability to regulate his life, Farrar will just simply not bother about him any more. After all, Farrar is the youngest editor of any conspicuous and influential magazine published in English; he is a novelist, a poet, an essayist, a critic, a playwright, a lecturer, a first-nighter, a university professor, a before-and-after-dinner speaker, a frequent best man at weddings, an impresario, a club director and organizer, an amateur actor with ability, a pianist, a music composer, a discoverer and encourager of talent, a philanthropist, and a circumspect man about town. He can give only so much energy and no more to the saving of souls. He is willing to spend at any time a decent, even more than a decent—a considerable—amount of time and energy in helping any deserving young man to make the most of himself and his abilities. He will go to any reasonable lengths for him: provide him, if necessary, with food and shelter, read his work with critical advice and encouragement, interview editors in his behalf, protect him from the invidious demands of the world, stave off the tempter and the temptress. But if the man shows no sense, no gratitude, no self-respect, no inclination to live a better and more fruitful life, at once an artist and a commendable member of the great social organization, Farrar will, with complete justice, lose interest in his case, give him his ticket to perdition, sigh, frown, run his hand dejectedly through his hair, and have no more worries about him.

I, for one, congratulate Farrar upon his attitude, believing that if once a man of mental maturity has been shown, and encouraged upon, the right path, and he still perversely chooses to follow the wrong and thorny one, it's his own business; life is too short to bother too much about him. Farrar has his own work to do, his own ambitions to realize, his own way to make in the world, his own designs which God has given him the talents to accomplish, and it would not only be a waste of time and energy to worry about such fellows, but would be depriving the world of such literary creation as he has been granted the ability to achieve.

But, you may possibly ask, how does Farrar get that way? how does he assume this prerogative of ethical and social direction? how does one so young acquire wisdom which is so old and experienced? Well, a certain amount of it was innate; Farrar was a prodigy at Yale; he lisped in numbers (and he lisps them still); he had a commanding personality even as a youth and his senior as well as his junior college mates early entertained respect for and deference to his wit, his talent, his energy, and his knowledge. He had, even as he has to-day, a way of impressing you with a definite belief that he could do things expertly well. He had no more than to indicate to an employer that he was, for the moment, at leisure and he was forthwith given any job he had set his mind on having. He who had been a poet, a collegiate actor, playwright, and cheer leader,[1] got first, I think, a responsible job as a special reporter. He convinced the editor—this pink-cheeked seraph who, in becoming serious, can look like Jonathan Edwards or St. John of Patmos—that there were strange and colorful stories to be had for the papers by one with his ability who possessed also the courage to mingle with the more cut-throat and unethical of the lower social strata.

"I ask no more," announced Farrar, "than an opportunity to become friendly with petermen and burglars, hired assassins and bums, sustainers and their déclassé

[1] The anonymous author here fails in his facts. Mr. Farrar was never a cheer leader.

women, yeggs, hopheads, swindlers, harness-bulls, crooked cops—the dregs and scum of humanity in the great Cloaca Maxima of a great city. I shall undertake to furnish you with stories to make your hair stand on end, and which will, incidentally, inculcate in the hearts and minds of the young a respect and liking for sane and wholesome, if less colorful, living. Let me choose as friends the lowly and outcast, the sullen and revengeful, the rotters and throat-rippers, the sodden, coke-stupefied, and degenerate, and I will bring you news and entertainment, cast in smooth and entrancing words which your respectable householder will read to his young daughter, even if he is a Supreme Court justice, with interest in the matter, disapproval of the acts, and sanction for the writer's sentiments. You will, sir, by hiring me, increase circulation and, what is more important, exercise a salutary effect upon the minds and inclinations of the young."

And so Farrar was hired, with complete later justification of his boast. He likes to tell now how he counts among his best friends men who have committed murders at ten dollars a head and have sandbagged salaried fathers for as little as the price of an evening's meal; he has listened as a pretended accomplice while sinister lychnobites laid plans over a low back bar-room table for outlaw depredations involving theft and manslaughter. He has seen, he informs you, iniquity in its most shameless, depraved, and incredible forms; he has gone, in his daring search for news and stories, hand in hand with death; and, as if to round out his adventures, he enlisted in the air service and saw war and life here and abroad with the peeled eyes of disillusion and the calm philosophy of a man who knows that of experience we may have a surfeit, and of waywardness too sickening a sight.

Farrar, who was at Yale when the war broke out,

won, within a short space, a first lieutenancy in the air service. His first work was under Colonel Hiram Bingham, the South American explorer, in the department which started the ground schools for active service. Later he toured the country investigating these schools and reporting on them. His first public address of any kind was delivered at Ohio State University before a crowd of rookies. His subject was military discipline. He had, at the time, not even been taught how to drill. His first training and experience as an executive editor came when he was sent overseas in the intelligence department of the air service. He assisted in the editing of confidential bulletins, issued by a huge organization, with a publishing plant and with representatives in various war zones. He helped also to gather material for the air service history. It was, however, his experience in the ground schools here and abroad that gave Farrar his initial interest in welfare work, that desire to help young men to acquire a knowledge of themselves and their relations to their fellows, and to develop their highest potentialities. It was an experience, he says, which grayed him spiritually and lent him a seriousness beyond his years.

It would be, then, presumptuous to question Farrar's qualifications as an advisory critic of literature and life. He has known, he tells us, the good and the bad, the saintly and the evil, the dangerous and the safe; and he counsels moderation in literature as he would counsel sanity and moderation in life. That is why he seems, at times, so elderly sagacious. Himself one of the very youngest members of the younger generation, he writes occasionally with the umbrageous impatience of a Dr. Henry van Dyke about the scatterbrain and obstreperous youths. He clings, as to the Rock of Ages, to the valetudinarians of literature, grieving that a devastating wave of heedless, reckless, youthful license and looseness is sweeping over the world and threatening home, happiness, and country.

But then, again, Farrar is capable of changing his mind. He is not one of these one-track fellows. He is not always a Cato. There is no one, at times, who has more belief in and sympathy with youth, even gay and obstreperous youth. He has, probably, encouraged as much new talent among young men and women as any editor in America. He has a vast, an amazing fund of energy; and no little of it, for all the kidding in the above paragraphs, is devoted without hope of reward or gratitude to the fostering and development of promising work among fledgling poets, novelists, short-story writers, essayists, and other artists. He has taken what was once a desuete and uninteresting house organ and made it a lively and interesting magazine, playing up to no clique or cult, fair, intelligent, well informed, steering a clear course between the radicals on the one side and the mossbacks on the other. He is at once a good editor and a good business man, having a regard both for the end and the means to that end of literary development. He has ideas; he is by nature something of an impresario. But, so great is his vital energy that his activities are incredibly numerous. It is difficult to imagine how Farrar finds time to do all the things he does, or, doing them, to carry them off so well.

## *XIX: William Rose Benét*

WHEN one flings one's soul to the air like a falcon flying it sometimes suggests more than venery. It also postulates a certain innate knack at juggling. Perhaps it would be going too far to assert that William Rose Benét is a juggler, for that intimates an obvious basis of deception. Mr. Benét may be "a devil an' a ostrich an' a orphan-child in one" besides an occasional impersonation of an "injia-rubber idiot on the spree" but he is never a base deceiver. He is as transparent as a pane of glass, and though he may skip blithely over the great wall of China and burglarize the Zodiac he does it with the frank ingenuousness of a child. He is our most naïve poet, his naïveté being the direct product of a wholehearted abandonment to his métier. He always jumps into Helicon with his galoshes on. He splashes about in his overcoat, an umbrella gripped in one hand, and he comes out dripping. And then he shakes the drops from him until they dance in the sun sparkling with all the colors in the rainbow. He adores the most variegated hues and those literary connotations that bring to mind the barbaric braveries of the past. Starting with "Merchants from Cathay" one may skim through his poetry to "Moons of Grandeur" and happen upon all sorts of heroes and fabled beasts from Sir John Mandeville to Luke O'Connor and from unicorns to the aforementioned falcon. His rhythms in the past have been emphatic, sonorous, rolling. Rhyme and inter-rhyme clash and kiss. He is a tonal artist, a felicitous verbalist, a juggler in a city square (preferably New York) flinging up gold and crimson and emerald globes.

All this should be set down first as a prelude to the affirmation that William Rose Benét (known to his more or less familiars as "Bill") is an incurable romanticist vaguely attempting to set his sail in a perplexing windstorm of cerebration. Indeed, for a time his acquaintances feared that the mellifluous regurgitations of Old Alf Noyes were about to sweep Benét into a treacly ocean from which there would be no escape. But they didn't. Bill put the snaffle on his unicorn and cantered decorously away from the syncopated remarks that the wild waves were saying. He is a much better poet than he is generally given credit for, but he has several disastrous handicaps in putting this fact over. He is not inclined to stop where he should stop. He is apt to overlard his matter a bit with color. And he *will* read his own work. For instance, when he starts his falcon off on its well-known "fling" one gathers from Bill's voice that it is taking the air much as an old-fashioned aeroplane or a glider does. It must have a long run first. When Bill reads a poem it sounds like a Druid incantation.

There was no particular reason for William Rose Benét, in the first place. His family was a military family and it will take more than Dr. Freud to figure out why an entire generation should suddenly turn poet. But they did; and the result is that Scarsdale, once the home nest, might have been likened to that famous pie wherein the four and twenty blackbirds caroled so sweetly. It is regrettable that Bill did not go into the regular army, even for a short while, because there is in existence a portrait of Our Hero in uniform that is joyous to behold. He looks like the Duke of Wellington the morning after Waterloo. Such pride and poise betokened anything but a poet. Instead of going into the regular army Bill went to Yale. Now the influence of Yale on poets—but then, this is a matter for the consideration of Harvard men.

WILLIAM ROSE BENÉT

At Yale Bill wrote poetry voluminously and he has kept at it ever since. His subsequent career has been a series of mild jumps from position to position. Sometimes they weren't positions; they were just jobs. He worked on the staff of "The Century Magazine." He worked for an advertising firm. He worked for "The Nation's Business." He once published a little magazine of his own, "The Chimæra," which beat most little magazines by one month. It ran two months. He helped win the war. He doesn't talk about it. He is now associate editor of "The Saturday Review." Also, he is the husband of Elinor Wylie.

Two of the gestes enumerated above deserve particular attention, for they throw light on Bill's personality. First there was the advertising agency. Its name shall be kept secret forevermore, but certain feats perpetrated by Bill while attached to that mercenary undertaking must be set down. It is quite possible that the majority of virile young men who read these lines will have had no occasion especially to note the advertisements of Mennen's Talcum Powder. But for those people who have, a gentle prodding of the mind may recall to them a catch-line reading, "The petal texture of baby's skin." *That* was created by William Rose Benét. *That* is one of his most famous lines. And then there was that charming assertion which accompanied the advertisements of Murphy's Varnish, "Your house under glass." For six months Bill labored with this advertising agency, striving mightily to inoculate its callous ad men with a more æsthetic feeling for their calling. Alas, it was no go. He cast his eyes elsewhere. Strangely enough they landed pop upon "The Nation's Business." Now "The Nation's Business" is conducted by the Chamber of Commerce of Washington, D. C., and its purpose is—well, the nation's business. It is possible that the editor mistook Bill for a merchant, and so he is; but not the kind of merchant that "The Nation's Business" would be especially interested in. Bill is a merchant from Cathay. He swaps unicorns and sells patches from the sunset to anybody that requires them. This being so (and the place being the United States of America), Bill went to work on "The Nation's Business" and wrote lengthily about the coal situation. It was from that dark and forbidding labor that Christopher Morley (looking for kinsprits, possibly) rescued Our Hero, brushed the coal dust out of his hair, took his mind off the nation's business, and incontinently ran him back into the literary game. To show how callous he was Bill immediately wrote a novel. People thereupon decided that he was a very good poet, indeed.

At this point (resting on one's oars while doping out the Reasons Mainly Spiritual why William Rose Benét should be permitted to Remain in America) it may be apropos to inject a few personalia. Bill is long and lean and lissom with spidery legs. He speaks slowly and smiles readily at bad and pointless jokes. This is courtesy, however, not stupidity. He never loses his temper except when a stranger puts his hat on. He likes spaghetti. He is anti-Prohibition. He is assiduous in doing things for people. His neckwear (nothing to speak of in the old days) has taken on a Renaissance flavor and hue of late. He is brown and smooth-faced and guileless. One has to look twice before discovering his eyebrows. His eyes are small. His nose looks as though it had been gently pushed by somebody and had not sprung back into shape. He takes his coat off when he works. He resembles Vachel Lindsay in that he loves to draw, and his artistic creations are sometimes marvelous to behold. He will draw a picture for anybody who asks him. He is good company because, unlike most modern poets, he is always ready to listen. He has his faults, too. He is aggravatingly patient. He is altogether too equanimous. In a brown suit he looks like a Venezuelan blood, a rakish South American who still goes to Sunday School.

And now for the Reasons Mainly Spiritual. Bill is one of the few American writers who have passed the dangerous age of thirty-five and still continue to respect the substance more than the form. He can find virtue in both Stuart P. Sherman and Ezra Pound. The excellencies of "Ulysses" are as apparent to him as the excellencies of "Pride and Prejudice." He does not necessarily detest Maxwell Bodenheim because he likes Matthew Arnold. His own poetry must be regarded as essentially conservative and yet he carries no brief for it as against the manifestations of the younger experimentalists. He loves poetry and that is all there is to it. Wherever it may be and in whatever guise, he will willingly recognize it if it be there. Naturally such an attitude is both admirable and annoying. He will never be a militant figure, never fight furiously for a movement, never go into the thick of the wordy battles and take blows as well as give them. In other words, Bill is not fashioned from fighting timber. He was wise in not joining the regular army. He is, at his best, an intelligent appreciator and he does not bow under the heavy misapprehension that the future of American letters rests upon his shoulders. We may guess that he likes to be comfortable, that he desires to be neither a Solomon nor an Ishmael.

The prophets have their place and so, too, do the valiant fighters for doubtful causes. As these more hardy ones, in a certain way, do represent the future so does Benét represent the present, the wise, tolerant, unaffected, not-too-radical day of established values. He possesses the open mind that will welcome and admit nascent achievements and really make much of them when he is satisfied that they contain the authentic ingredients of poetry. He is an intelligence and he is much further from the old, mossback traditionalists than he is from the younger men. It is true that his own poetry is conservative and that he appears to be well satisfied with the place where it is broadly established to-day. But it is to be suspected that in his reading he is quite willing to go further than he does in his actual composition. His methods of self-expression have matured; as a writer he will go no further; he is content with that. He has shaken the thin ghost of Noyes from his work altogether and has definitely established himself as a born balladist. He is not a great poet and he will never be a great poet. Certain things are lacking, profundity of thought, for instance, and the high peak of inspiration. But he grows with his work; he combs it better. The difference in values between "Merchants from Cathay" and "Moons of Grandeur," for instance, should be perceptible to all. A reckless flamboyancy has been shaken off and in its place is a rich, colorful, melodic strain that is arresting with distinguished imageries and an extraordinarily fine technical precision. He is an intelligent, albeit rather easy, critic of letters and his prose is invigorated by a certain deftness and whimsical lightness. "The First Person Singular," his solitary novel, might have been much better if he had taken it more seriously and wrought it more carefully. He needs time and leisure, perhaps, to do his best work.

He is essentially the child of erudition, and all that is bizarre and colorful and marvelous and strange in letters makes an extremely forceful appeal to him. Because of this it is frequently true that the smell of the study lamp may be sensed in his poetry. It is often there quite frankly, and the deliberateness with which it is set forth should silence most fault-finders. True enough, this leaning toward books for inspiration is a danger, for it is likely to squeeze a deal of life out of the composition. But there is another side to it. One must admit that there is an equal chance of breathing life into these figures and situations which, for the most part, are as motionless and faded as figures of an old tapestry.

This Benét does when he is at his best. Then, too, he turns with frequency to life itself, to his own reactions toward that restless tiger, and when these moods result in such things as "Fire and Glass," for instance, there is no reason to be worried about the poet's future. He is here to stay and for some time.

## *XX: Heywood Broun*

THIS assignment to lift the veil and let the readers of THE BOOKMAN see something of "The True Heywood Broun" is, if I may filch a phrase from the *opera* of Dorothy Parker, like being asked to carry gilded lilies to Newcastle. There is no one—not Calvin Coolidge or Peggy Joyce nor any other celebrity—who dwells more continuously or more openly in the public eye. Any reader of the New York "World" knows something of Broun's age, weight, income, and dimensions, knows whether he has bought a new suit and what fortune his amorous adventures have had and in what condition are such inner possessions as his pride, his faith, his parental emotions, his courage, and his hope of immortality. Such a reader must be an exceedingly hasty one who cannot tell offhand how Broun is feeling this week about Mayor Hylan, God, Jack Dempsey, and Ruth Hale.

Philip Moeller tells the tale of some tourists arriving so late at Oberammergau during the season of the Passion Play that they were in desperate straits for sleeping quarters but finally persuaded one pious shopkeeper of that hamlet to put them up for the night. It was not until next morning, when they awoke to find a group of interested villagers and pilgrims gazing at them from the sunlit sidewalk, that they realized he had turned an honest mark by renting his shop window as a bedroom. Their predicament would strike most of us as a chapter out of some familiar but dreadful nightmare. I do not see how it could have ruffled the calm of that singularly expansive New Yorker, Heywood Campbell Broun.

HEYWOOD BROUN

Not long ago one of the more handsome and more roguish matrons in the rapidly aging younger set asked Alexander Woollcott if he thought she would derive a compensatory enjoyment from an affair with Broun.

"My dear," replied that sagacious critic, "I know no other way in which a struggling young girl can get so much free publicity."

Among Broun's friends—and while he is close to none of them, his acquaintances, with a few negligible exceptions, all like him enormously—this candor of his is not only a byword but an endless source of surprise and entertainment. Not one of them would think of telling him anything that was not to be repeated. Not one of them but has heard him open a conversation somewhat in this wise:

"Hullo, I've just heard something I've promised never to tell. I'll tell you, however, if you'll tell me a secret in return."

"But," you may answer, cannily, "I don't happen to know any secrets to-day."

"Well, then," Broun will resume with a thwarted look, "I'll tell you anyhow."

And the tale begins. Now all such talk comes from him not in malice or in vanity or from any of the motives which set most tongues a-wagging. It comes, some say, from a sheer inability to retain information. Or rather it comes from a natural response to his own favorite motto, "Sieve and let sieve" (not, as one might legitimately imagine, by any means the worst of his puns). More exactly, I believe, it comes from his lack of respect for the conventional standard of privacy—one of many standards such as those of dignity, modesty, self-sacrifice, reverence for gray hairs and the like, of which his exploring mind long since challenged the validity. To a person thus released, conversation is an emptying of the mind. In speech and in writing, Broun turns *his* inside out, as a woman dumps her purse, himself genuinely curious as to its contents. Certainly Broun will tell things to his own discredit and embarrassment quite as freely as he will tell those which discomfort others. Conceivably he might steal a thousand dollars from you if you left it lying around, but the next time he saw you, he wouldn't be able to resist saying, "I took that thousand dollars from you."

He was engaged some time ago to speak in Rochester. Absurdly enough the local agent had booked him incongruously at a basket party, to follow after a long minstrel show full of local talent. No one could have been good in such an emergency, not even Broun, who is a capital speaker. He was a flop. He had made notes on the train which he planned to consult from time to time in the opportunities created by the laughter at his sallies.

There was no laughter and he soon vanished ingloriously from the platform. Now most of us, thus trapped to our discomfiture, would have buried the episode deep in memory and said nothing about it on returning home. But Broun, on arriving next noon at the Round Table at the Algonquin in New York, began by saying that he had been lecturing in Rochester the night before. The question as to how it had gone came automatically from several directions.

"It went very well," said Broun in an offhand manner and then, after the briefest of pauses, he added, "That was a lie. It didn't go well at all. I was rotten." And out poured the whole story.

And if it had not been for him, no one would have heard the diverting tale of his venture into high society last spring. It was before his recent conversion in the matter of style and tidiness. Now, on an impulse imparted by I know not what force, he has suddenly emerged as a well-dressed man. He is well groomed, well tailored, slim. His ancient resemblance to the Barrymores has come back in full force and girls who had laughed at him tolerantly in other years have been caught recently in the act of trembling at his approach.

But last spring a thousand anecdotes about his hopeless externals enlivened the town. They were all justified. He weighed two hundred and forty pounds, wore slovenly and spotted clothes, let his hair grow like the lawn of a deserted house, and scuffled along the street without a vestige of polish on his No. 13 shoes. "He always looks," said the most acid of actors, "as if he had taken the coal out of the bathtub and then decided at the last moment *not* to take a bath after all."

It was such an object that rolled up to the front door of one of the finest houses on Fifth Avenue last spring in response to an invitation to play bridge. The page looked at him in cold surprise and suggested that he go to the rear door. He mumbled something about being expected. The door was closed as a precaution but in a moment the head footman opened it a crack and inspected the visitor. "Go away," he said, "and come some other time. Madam has company this afternoon." "But," said the visitor, "I'm part of the company. You go tell her Heywood Broun is out here on the door-step." This sounded so authoritative that, after a wavering instant of indecision, the footman again closed the door and disappeared into what probably, for the purposes of this story, ought to be called "the mansion." When he came back it was to open the door wide, stare incredulously at Broun for a moment and then say grudgingly: "You are to come in."

Every one told this story, but no one told it so well as Broun told it. And the point of its relation here is that no one would have told it at all if he had not told it first. What we have as the protagonist of this anecdote is the only primitive wandering free among the sophisticates. He is the only simple person in the lot but I believe we could prove, if we put all the stories together, that it is a recaptured simplicity—the simplicity of a man who, after a shy and intimidated and conventional youth, has grown freer year by year as, year by year, he realized how meaningless were the taboos which held most folk in thrall. Yet, in trying to prove this, I should be wrecked by a thousand contradictions.

He is simple about money, yearning for the possession of it in actual shining currency. If, in payment for a piece of work, he were to be offered his choice between a heavily guaranteed six months' note for ten thousand dollars and a neat pile of five thousand-dollar bills, he would, I am seriously certain, choose the latter. In poker he is merciless, caring only to win and seeing no sense at all in the conventional rule among sportsmen that a loser should smile. This loser never does anything so artificial. On the contrary, when thus bereft, Broun's face darkens and he slouches off into the dawning day, refusing even to walk up the street with a lot of yapping winners. Yet I have known him to go to New Haven to lecture for fifteen dollars, have known him to make secret gifts of prodigal dimensions. And he is more totally oblivious to what becomes of the money he does gather in than any one I know.

He is kind, with unfailingly gentle manners, but I cannot imagine his planning a good time for some one else.

He is almost universally liked and so enormously gregarious that he cannot endure solitude. Yet there is just a faint film covering him like a capsule, so shutting him off that he has reached his thirty-sixth year without winning a nickname, except for a brief time in France when his calamitous efforts to order eggs won for him among the other correspondents the *nom de guerre* of "Oofs" Broun.

He is timorous and will cower at the very thought of an embarrassing interview and yet, when he was passing a street-corner meeting and heard a silly and cowardly thing said about Michael Collins, he walked up to the speaker and threw two pennies in his face, a reckless thing to do, as was afterward intimated by the five Irishmen who followed him up the street and blacked his eye for him. He is honest, and in all matters of any importance will say what he believes in his column though the world scoff and the "World" wince. Yet having agreed solemnly to speak at a certain dinner on Wednesday night, he will, when the hour comes, heave himself up from the poker table and leave it only long enough to telephone to the committee and in an astoundingly croupy voice explain that he has been struck down with laryngitis and cannot get out of bed.

As you see, there are entirely too many contradictions here to permit this large person to be squeezed into the strait-jacket of a formula. If ordered to find such a formula or be shot at sunrise, I should probably try to write of Broun as one who, like primitive man or any Newfoundland dog, lives only in the current moment and, in matters of courage, honesty, kindness, and possession, forgets yesterday and has never heard of to-morrow. Yet I should know that that formula left a lot of pieces of him strewn about. After all, it is as silly to try to sum up so abundant, miscellaneous, and accidental a being as Heywood Broun in a few words as it would be to reduce Charles Dickens or the Mississippi River to an epigram.

I hereby abandon the attempt and will wind up by telling the most characteristic anecdote of them all. George Kaufman tells the tale of how Broun was idling in Woollcott's office at the "Times" one midweek afternoon when in bustled Annie Nathan Meyer, bent on getting publicity for a benefit in which she was represented by a one-act play. She ingenuously brought along some photographs of the cast for publication on Sunday. Woollcott, whom the superficial always regard as rude, explained to her bluntly that with limited space there never was room to celebrate a negligible and fleeting performance and that therefore it would be a waste for her to leave the photographs. They wouldn't be printed.

A fortnight later, Broun was relating the incident to some friends.

"Woollcott was terribly gruff and rude to poor Mrs. Meyer," he said. "I had to come to her rescue."

"And what did you do?"

"Why, I told her I should be glad to take the photographs and have them printed in the 'Tribune' the next Sunday. She went away happy."

"And where are the pictures now?"

"Oh, I forget. No, wait a minute. Here they are in my pocket. I forgot to throw them away."

## *XXI: Robert Frost*

ROBERT FROST is what the bucolic Virgil might have been, had Virgil, shorn of his Latinity and born of Scotch-New England parentage, spent most of his life where thermometers remain near and often below zero for three months of each year. If Mr. Frost had lived in classical Italy or Greece, he would probably have tended sheep. And only his flocks would have heard many of his poems, so seldom does he write and so much of his poetry is little more than contemplative conversation. He is a poet of mountain land and of pasture; but how foreign to him would be the mellow temperament of a Virgil! His farms are on rugged hillsides, his meadows too filled with stones. He knows the orchard wall and the mountain, the barn and the birch tree, the Vermont farmer in the fields at haying time or on log roads in winter. All these are not only the properties for his stage set. They are the tools with which he has worked. He *is* a farmer—Massachusetts, Vermont, New Hampshire, what state you will—but a farmer! A poet of the *minutiæ* of a locality, a singer of Yankee moods, he yet succeeds in being both national and universal because of his intuitive understanding of the stark motivation of simple minds. His "North of Boston" is a series of dramatic portraits of New England farm folk; but it is more than that, it is an epic of the lives of isolated and lonely people, wherever in the world they may be.

Frost, the man, gives an impression of great force, combined with a sort of tentativeness. Perhaps this is because thoughts are so vital to him. He thinks slowly.

He acts slowly. Sensitive, upright, dignified, Mr. Frost is a *good man* moving in a world of wickedness. His New England consciousness of the wicked, he has tried to lay over with a gloss of tolerance. His extreme gentleness of spirit has resulted. He has determined to preserve this gentleness, this freshness of viewpoint in the face of all disillusionment. Consequently he has few prejudices. A tolerant, wise man, with less pity for mankind than willingness to observe people and accept them without superimposing an emotion. His close friends, though not many, are diverse. Among them can be found such contrasting personalities as the brittle-minded Louis Untermeyer and the blunt-souled Wilfrid Wilson Gibson. Mr. Frost's life has been filled neither with the physical indecision nor the moral ramblings of undisciplined genius. His ethical firmness partakes of the nature of the hills. His adventures are those of a soul carefully tempered by corporeal decision. Many of the things that are most important to most men are not important at all to him. Of pride of possession he has none. His ambition is the development of his art, not the successful understanding of writing as a possible business. His home is important to him. So is his family. So is his poetry which, in its essence, is a simple facing of the facts of life. Beyond this, he does not go. He fights no glorious combats with existence. He is not a propagandist for God or Puritanism—no, not even for the back-to-the-farm movement.

Frost's body, which is sturdy and square, makes little impression on one who meets him for the first time. It is the eyes: bright blue, steady, gentle yet canny, two vivid lights in a face that is otherwise gray. There is the loose, coarse, now almost white hair, the full but finely cut lips, the nose that is a trifle too broad to allow the characterization "Greek" for the whole head, which is indeed a noble one. Physical movements are casual. In old age, they

ROBERT FROST

may become soft and shambling. Loose clothes become the poet. If he were to wear a Snappy Cut suit, it would take on the appearance of homespun. He is a dignified figure as he sits on the back porch of his stone farmhouse on a rise of the road near South Shaftsbury, Vermont. One or two of his four children are usually there with him, and Mrs. Frost, a quiet, beautiful woman of steadfast purpose. A mood of calm industry prevails in her household. The family have made a fountain in the back yard, which slopes by bushy meadowland away to the Green Mountains. Frost works late into the night and sleeps far into the morning. He likes to walk. He likes to sit watching that fountain and letting his mind play along its rising and falling waters. Occasional visitors there are, hospitably received.

For a part of the year now, Frost travels. Recently he returned to his post as professor of English at Amherst College. He speaks occasionally in public, does it well, but does not enjoy it. If he had his own way, he would spend his time alone with his family, thinking and, from time to time, writing. He has never taught himself to write when occasion demands. Apparently he indulges his moods and waits upon them. He has taught his soul to listen too long, to express itself too seldom. In this, he is more poet than journalist. The charge of laziness which has been brought against him seems false. He prefers to write only well, and consequently makes firm demands of his inspiration and his intellect. His control is sometimes a little too studied, his intent too often philosophical rather than lyrical. The body of his work is dryer than need be. You feel that he has often intended a lyric which turned out an eclogue.

The only note of bitterness in his make-up is his attitude toward the writer who despoils his art, and the public which does not countenance comparative indigence in the artist. He feels, perhaps, that the leisure of poets is misunderstood, that periods of contemplation seem times of drought to the average intelligence. The sound of literary claques is annoying to him. If he is intolerant of anything, it is of a certain type of literary personage chiefly to be found in New York clubs.

At various times in his life he has been a teacher; once at Derry, New Hampshire, where his grandfather, despairing of his grandson's business acumen, had bought him a farm. Later he was at the Normal School in Plymouth, New Hampshire, and at the University of Michigan, where he was appointed "poet in residence." His connections with colleges, however, seem irksome. He practically ran away from Dartmouth where he attempted an undergraduate career, and subsequent studies in Latin at Harvard pleased him little. Teaching, in so far as it does not interfere with his real work, is apparently palatable; but the restrictions of academic life beat sadly upon him and he stands puzzled and amazed in the presence of professorial bickering and arraignments. On the campus of the great western university he was ill at ease, though grateful. Not worldly enough to cultivate the manners of a lion, he yet understands those who would lionize him. Though he could actually despise no one, he is at a loss before the self-conscious hero worshiper. Contact with real talent he doubtless enjoys, and as poetry reader for a publishing house he has shown wisdom as a critic; but the merely determined aspirant to literary honors must necessarily fill a true poet with despair.

His ten years in San Francisco, where he was born, seem to have made as little impression on the body of his work as those spent in Beaconsfield, Buckinghamshire, England. He commenced writing poetry at fifteen, and American magazines published his work, but it was during his English stay that his first volume, "A Boy's Will," appeared. "North of Boston," too, was published in England before American publishers awoke to the worth of Mr. Frost. This fact, however, seems to worry him not at all. He has no quarrel either with publishers or public.

There is seldom easy and facile grace in the poetry of Robert Frost. The loveliest of his lyrics are in his latest Pulitzer prize-winning volume, "New Hampshire." An almost rigid adherence to the colloquial prevails; where Lowell and Whittier observed and reported the New England peasant, Frost has become one. He writes stories of their most vivid moments with unswerving power of dramatic presentation. Some of his best pictures are of grim and terrible events, and the whole body of his writing indubitably shows a decaying and degenerating New England. That he fails to see the other side of life is untrue. Passages of great beauty shine from drabness. His events and his characters have moments of warmth and of happiness. Always, however, is manifest the sense of fairness to events as he sees them. He is seldom, if ever, the protagonist. His characters speak for themselves. If he prefers one to another, he conceals his preference with care, as in "Snow," where the reader must be judge between Meserve's impetuosity and the narrowness of the Cole family.

He is a natural dramatist: he sees things as pictures rather than hears them as music. He has written short plays and intends to write longer ones which are still slowly germinating. Soon these projected dramas will become actual plays in Frost's mind. Whether they emerge upon paper or not really matters little to him.

Frost's humor, often of satirical intent, is clumsy. It is intended to catch the dryness and drollery of the Yankee, but it succeeds often in being only very dry. His truest moments of humor are probably accidental and spring simply from his deep understanding of humanity. Like most realists, he is occasionally unconsciously funny. He can write a quatrain that matches Wordsworth's most grotesque ruralism—

> She wheeled the dung in the wheelbarrow
>   Along a stretch of road;
> But she always ran away and left
>   Her not-nice load.

And this is the same hand that pens the following superb lines:

> I'd like to go by climbing a birch tree,
> And climb black branches up a snow-white trunk
> *Toward* heaven, till the tree could bear no more,
> But dipped its top and set me down again.

From "The Black Cottage" there is a passage whicn typifies Frost. Here is the realist groping for truth, letting the world as it is play upon the character of his work; yet after all fundamentally aware that even the realism of the present may come to be the romance of the future, the truth of the past fade out in the light of new discovery. This would be profound pessimism were it not for the fact that Mr. Frost apparently believes that he has discovered the secret of rotating events. He has found stability in this unstable course.

> It will turn true again, for so it goes.
> Most of the change we think we see in life
> Is due to truths being in and out of favour.
> As I sit here, and oftentimes, I wish
> I could be monarch of a desert land
> I could devote and dedicate forever
> To the truths we keep coming back and back to.
> So desert it would have to be, so walled
> By mountain ranges half in summer snow,
> No one would covet it or think it worth
> The pains of conquering to force change on.

Scattered oases where men dwelt, but mostly
Sand dunes held loosely in tamarisk
Blown over and over themselves in idleness.
Sand grains should sugar in the natal dew
The babe born to the desert, the sand storm
Retard mid-waste my cowering caravans—

While Frost permits the world to mold his work, the world can never leave its imprint upon his personality. Let it call him what it will, shiftless, irresponsible, lazy; his primary purpose is as firm as the rocks in his own back-door yard. If Mr. Frost starts out to think a deep thought, the house may burn about his ears, but he will think his thought to the conclusion that satisfies Mr. Frost.

## *XXII: Edgar Lee Masters*

EVERY now and then a tremor of apprehension invades literary Chicago. Edgar Lee Masters has been reported off the reservation. He is on the warpath, somewhere in the east, denying the existence of the Chicago literary school. Presently it is whispered that Masters is back within the corporate limits of Chicago or in Michigan where he does most of his writing; and the flutter subsides. Only the fact remains that Masters has had his fling, and has again asserted himself as the spirit that evermore denieth. For Masters that loose federation, the so-called Chicago literary school, does not exist. Only Masters exists, a magnificent solitary, marooned in a desert of the arts. If Masters is aware of the feasts and gambols of the Society of Midland Authors, he watches them, like Crusoe, from concealment, shocked to the soul at the barbaric pastimes of these literary savages. He has never been enrolled in the centuries of the Bookfellows. He never sits in at journalistic lunches. In the encomiastic literature of the various groups the name of Masters gets no mention, nor does it appear in those eulogia which anoint the Chicago group as a whole. One of the most impressive things about Edgar Lee Masters is the fact that he has constituted himself the exception, the distinguished and outstanding exception, which proves the Chicago literary school.

Though Chicago finds it politic to be officially unaware of Masters, it will never go so far as to deny his existence. In fact few persons in that city are better known where reputation counts. Long before he made himself

EDGAR LEE MASTERS

really felt as an author, Masters was recognized as an able and aggressive lawyer, with a flair for economic and humanitarian questions. His defense of the striking waitresses attracted considerable attention. His shrewd and pitiless cross-examinations in conducting libel cases for a Chicago newspaper are still remembered. He dabbled to some extent in democratic politics. Such practical successes, however, were small satisfaction to a man who at an early age had been bitten by the writing bug. When Masters was at his busiest as a lawyer, he had already established quantity production as his literary sideline. He turned his hand to essays, plays, and poetry, but principally this last. A procession of little books of well-wrought innocuous verse came from his pen without making any particular stir. Most of this early work was in the grand manner from which Masters's muse has made but one fortunate escape—an escapade as he at that time considered it. There can be little doubt that "Maximilian," a drama in blank verse, was much nearer to the author's heart than the "Spoon River Anthology." But by a curious irony "Spoon River," the nadir as it seemed of Masters's poetic flight, brought the zenith of his fame—and rightly. The genesis of "Spoon River," a literary freak of the first order, caused amazement at the time, which the author's subsequent work has not abated.

There are those who think that Masters would have gone on mixing law and letters indefinitely without making more than a local reputation, had it not been for his close friend, the late William Marion Reedy. "Bill" Reedy, as he was always affectionately known in Chicago and St. Louis, helped many a young author, doing thereby as much for letters in the middle west as any man to date; but his greatest *coup,* all things considered, was in bringing out Masters. The two were fast friends, and when Reedy was reported in Chicago his many admirers would look him up at "Lee" Masters's office. It was a great place to smoke and listen to real talk, racy often and with more from life than from books. "Bill" Reedy, aside from his brilliant literary attainments, was a singularly vigorous full-blooded midwesterner with a fund of experience which few could match. Masters, though he lacks the human quality which clinched friends and even the merest acquaintances to Reedy, has in other ways much the same equipment. The peculiar service of Reedy to Masters seems to have been in showing him that the common life and knowledge of raw human nature which he had in abundance was the best sort of literary material.

Much of Masters's early work appeared in "Reedy's Mirror." This should not be regarded as a service of friendship, for the worst of Masters's loftiest verse, undistinguished and reminiscent as it seems, is quite up to the run of common or garden verse, and "Reedy's Mirror," though it had a keen eye for the best, was sometimes obliged to print the best it could get—unless of course editor Reedy chose to write the whole magazine, as he now and then did, with very satisfactory results. Besides his literary fertility, another peculiar virtue of "Bill" Reedy as editor was his habit of studying and advising his contributors, as much for their sake as for his own. He seldom returned a manuscript without detailed comment of the sort that is most valuable to a writer.

Reedy had been advising Masters for some time before results became evident. He had impressed on him the value of realism. He induced Masters to read "The Greek Anthology," whose poignant brevities, as Masters has himself said, were most influential in determining the form of "Spoon River." Some time before the impulse came to publish, Masters had begun casting his Illinois material into epitaphs, encouraged to this flier in poetic realism, as Harriet Monroe asserts, by the appearance of Sandburg's first poems in the new "Poetry" magazine. The impetus to print these experiments, according to a close friend of Reedy and Masters, was supplied as follows. After some hesitation Reedy arrived at the conclusion that although Masters's regular verse had been good enough to print, it was not good enough to print indefinitely. He returned a batch of manuscript to Masters with the blunt comment that this was leading nowhere. The reaction, as the story goes, was the first numbers of "Spoon River," which Masters petulantly signed with a pseudonym, and fired into the "Mirror" office more or less as a joke. The joke proved intensely practical. The editor read "Hod Putt" and "Amanda Barker" and pronounced them real stuff; to confirm his own judgment Mr. Reedy sent the manuscript, along with a fourteen-page letter of comment, to a well-known Chicago journalist, who was equally impressed. Accordingly the assay office reported to the prospector in the field that this was pay dirt, a bonanza strike, and urged him to file on this claim and work it for all it was worth. Masters filed and dug. In a short time he had raced through the God's acre of Spoon River in which every headstone, as it developed, was to prove a milestone to the hall of fame. This, or something very like it, was the genesis of the most successful—and deservedly successful—book of poetry in the past three decades.

Even while "Spoon River" was appearing in the "Mirror" over the pen name of Lester Ford it attracted general attention, and the success of the book was instant and amazing. For once a book of verse went with all the *éclat* of a popular novel, and most valuable of all, it was in part a success of reprobation. This was the first blast of the new realism to a large part of the general public, and there are many good people in Chicago and elsewhere who still hold their noses at the mention of "Spoon River." Critical opinion was nearly unanimous that this was an original and permanent contribution, a verdict which time has not altered. The countless parodies and obvious imitations are the most conspicuous tribute to "Spoon River," but not nearly so important as the profound influence it has undoubtedly exerted on the younger novelists.

In this way Masters had the conventional though not too common experience of waking up to find himself famous. It is likely, however, that he was less surprised than most people to whom such happy dawns have come. He had never lacked confidence in himself. His subsequent work displays in part a stubborn confidence that his earlier vein had not received due consideration. To Masters's credit be it said that he has not, like so many sudden successes, resorted to imitation of his lucky strike. The books of poetry published since "Spoon River" have been medleys, in part revivals of his early grandeurs, in part experiments of many sorts. There are poems, romantic and biblical, tirades, catalogues, and psychopathic sketches. Masters has made a number of attempts to use scientific material in poetry, with results that give the impression of an undigested technical vocabulary. Then there is the amorphous "Domesday Book," a kind of modern "Ring and the Book." As poetry this, to put it mildly, is a work of more magnitude than magnetism but it made an excellent bridge to the pure prose that Masters is now writing. His novels "Mitch Miller" and "Children of the Market Place" reflect Masters's intense interest in Illinois history, a field in which he is well fitted to do valuable work.

Curiously enough, the one spontaneous literary sensation Masters has scored since "Spoon River" was again in the "Mirror" and again by pseudonym. Shortly before the death of William Marion Reedy there began to appear in the "Mirror" a series of remarkable sonnets, signed by the arresting name of Elmer Chubb. Suggesting, as it did, an elderly cherub, the name suited the sentiments to perfection. The language of the sonnets was Miltonic, the content the essence of Puritanism. Fulsome praise of William Jennings Bryan, adoration of the Anti-Saloon League magi, and anathema on a lewd generation were the prevailing themes. One of the most overpowering dwelt in mild Maryolatry upon the perfections of Mary Garden, concluding with a pious wish that she might be shielded from the temptations of her artistic career. The manner was perfect, and it was not overdone. The "Mirror" public, a comparatively small but discriminating one, was completely imposed on and the editor was deluged with letters and telegrams for information on that egregious ass, Elmer Chubb. Masters kept up the joke for some time, even going so far as to have Chubb letterheads printed for replies to indignant correspondents, but of course the truth leaked out.

The Chubb sonnets have a peculiar interest as showing the humorous side of Masters better than anything in his acknowledged work. The humor, to be sure, is elephantine but it is there, the savage twinkle of a rogue elephant. The simile of a rogue elephant seems to suit Masters, not only in these ponderous gambols, but throughout his career. He has that aversion to other successful authors which Joe Hergesheimer pronounced distinctive of a first-class man. He has run amuck among his fellow poets, lampooning some of them, yea! even Amy Lowell, publicly, and planting drastic opinions on others where they would do the most harm. Certainly it is no vulgar inflation over sudden success that tends to make Masters more and more a solitary. It is rather what one who knows him well has pronounced an "ingrowing lugubriousness," again a quality of the rogue elephant. This is the black pessimism which has marked most of his work since "Spoon River." Masters despairs of the race and of the Volsteaded nation. In revolt against the herd, he despises even his prospective audience, and is continually in contempt of the court of critical opinion. Probably this explains a peculiar platform experience related of Masters. According to the story, he was sent by a lecture bureau in Chicago down to Kansas City to address the woman's club there. His speech seems to have been ponderous, dogmatic, pontifical. All the ladies understood about what they were getting, was that they didn't like it; and for once the worm turned. The club notified the bureau that they must refuse payment.

Chicago has not known Masters well of late, but it grudges no artist his privacy. It admires his great and permanent achievement. It feels him as an imminent presence out of whose pregnant frown some new portent may flash at any moment. As for his occasional aspersions on the city, some verses borrowed from Keith Preston, the pert poetaster of the "Daily News" book page, may express the general attitude:

GAUDEAMUS IGITUR

Edgar Lee Masters doesn't like Chi;
Furthermore he tells us the why!
Firstly he finds we are drying as drinkers:
Second he thinks we are trying as thinkers.
Edgar Lee Masters doesn't like Chi.
What'll we do? Lie down and die?

Never, no, never! Edgar would laugh,
Write us a helluvan epitaph.
Read the Anthology, brothers, and shiver!
Shall we be dumb as the dead of Spoon River?
Lo, those poor hicks that lay under the asters!
Living at least we annoy Mr. Masters.

Live and let live is the motto of the so-called Chicago literary school.

## *XXIII: Sherwood Anderson*

I HAVE never known a man who was worth his salt who was not in some way vain, proud, puffed up, or conceited. There are vanities and vanities and the sagacious mind will not resent the one and be taken in by the other.

Sherwood Anderson has the most gorgeous vanity of any writer I have ever seen. It is gorgeous because on the surface he is the least vain of men. On the surface he displays a charming modesty and a sweet humility, a companionable deference and a willingness to listen.

Many are taken in by this. They speak of him as a delightful and lovable fellow, which he is, indeed, but for reasons beyond this gracious exterior. These same people upon encountering Ben Hecht, say, or Joseph Hergesheimer, are often repelled and disconcerted by the elaborate surface vanity of these men and are soothed and comforted by the much more extensive vanity of Sherwood Anderson.

Hecht and Hergesheimer wear their vanity like a chip on the shoulder, but it is not so deep and significant as Sherwood's vanity which he conceals from all but the most penetrant eye. Hecht cocks his hat on the side of his head, cultivates a repertoire of gestures and facial expressions, and speaks with a swagger that has overtones of insolence. This is because he has not at bottom a self-assurance half so sure as Sherwood's. Hergesheimer dresses for morning, for afternoon, and for evening even when he is alone and he talks at you rather than with you, except when he remembers that Meredith or some one once said that conversation must not be a monologue

SHERWOOD ANDERSON

but a spontaneous exchange of ideas, at which time he tells you that he dislikes people who orate but do not converse, and gives you all of two minutes to get a word in.

These two men pass for vain and conceited while Sherwood escapes. In sheer truth they are amusing and entertaining, and their vanity is a matter of ingenuous surfaces while Sherwood's is a question of his whole being, his very existence. Both Hecht and Hergesheimer are capable of viewing their work in a critical and disinterested light; they are capable of maintaining a certain skepticism as to its ultimate worth. Sherwood is not. He would, however, valiantly deny this contention of mine. When he is brought to speak of his work he does it in a modestly evasive manner, very pleasing for the gullible to see. Hecht would have no hesitancy in *telling* you that he is the greatest writer living; but Sherwood *believes* that *he* is.

I doubt whether Sherwood, when the time comes for him to be embalmed in a uniform collected edition, will alter a line that he has written. He's that much stuck on himself as a writer. Mind you, I think that is an excellent and by no means a reprehensible thing. It accounts for the phenomenon that is Sherwood Anderson, a great and original figure in American literature. It is a beautiful vanity, but it is a vanity no less. I would not, for one, have him be otherwise.

To illustrate: Sherwood's "New Testament" which ran in "The Little Review" and some of his poems in "Mid-American Chants" are often unintelligible, incoherent, and disconcerting. He wrote these things down without effort of will, without a plan, simply as they came to him while he sat alone in his room. They are uncorrelated, crotchety mental associations, unraveling under a personal stimulus. The usual artist's point of view would be to regard this material as the makings of poems which should be rounded, traditional, and comprehensible. Not Sherwood. They are, as he regards them, the unhampered, free progeny of a rich, untutored, creative urge. They are Sherwood Anderson and you can take them or leave them, call them art or nonsense; but he will not change them to suit your preconceptions of what art should be and he will not cease to regard them as important and significant. And I think perhaps he is right.

Again, take his paintings. Until that summer he stayed down in Alabama near Mobile Bay he had never painted anything except wagon spokes and barns. And he can't draw a better likeness than I can. But he had the urge to paint—to express himself in form and color, so he sent north for paint and canvas and started feverishly to work. He did not paint what he saw before him: that is, he did not attempt to reproduce what he saw as photographic reality. He painted what was in his mind's eye. He put reds on and smeared greens and dabbed yellows where something inside him told him to place these colors. It was a sort of automatic painting, undirected, unguided by will, except the will to create.

He had the effrontery to exhibit these paintings. Again his superb vanity. The vanity of a man who believes that nothing that he does is shallow, weak, useless, or unimportant because he is absolutely honest and sincere in expressing himself. His paintings met with ridicule, incomprehension, derision; but this did not phase him. He sent them on from Chicago to New York to be exhibited. In New York two of them were sold, fetching a hundred dollars apiece. Sherwood was grateful that there were two who appreciated his work. Maybe they didn't. Maybe they bought them out of curiosity or out of sentimental regard for the handiwork of a man they considered a fine writer of stories. But, whether any one thought well of the paintings or not, you may be sure Sherwood does not underestimate their value. He rates this value pretty high. So do I. It may be that I am under the spell of him as a writer and as a personality; but I think that these paintings are not only interesting, but strangely, curiously beautiful. And I know there is no insincerity, hokum, or trickery in them.

No, Sherwood is not modest. His vanity peeps out, like those atrocious socks he wears with red and black checks in them, each block of color two inches square. Most people are not likely to notice these socks, because his suit is usually a quiet and comfortable tweed. They are not likely to pay close attention to the violent multicolored muffler he wears, because his overcoat is a decorous raglan. They are not likely to notice the guinea feather in his hat band, because his hat is cleverly chosen to show off his head most effectively and unostentatiously. They are not likely to notice that his hair is trimmed more often than a movie star's, because it looks so unkempt, unwieldy, and romantic. They are not likely to observe that he is fastidious, because he so adroitly conveys the opposite impression.

You see, Sherwood is a Scotchman with the uncanny canniness that is traditional with the race. He is shrewd as well as talented; he has social sense as well as genius. People are charmed by his conversation, because he sets them up a bit. Any one who gives assurance to another always wins his admiration, sympathy, and championship, especially if the latter is suffering from a sense of inferiority. Sherwood always gives that assurance to every one. Not, however, because he is particularly interested in everybody, but because he is particularly interested in himself and that presupposes a definite, disinterested, but assumed interest in the petty opinions, worries, and convictions of others.

Sherwood will spend hours listening to doddering and garrulous old men who lie about their early escapades, adventurous enterprises, and deeds of strength, amour, and bravery. I have seen him listen in apparent fascination to a windy old fraud backed up to a building on the busiest street in Chicago. In the Kentucky mountains where he has gone for several years on business connected with the advertising company he occasionally works for, he is the most popular "furriner" who ever went into those parts. This is because he interrogates every one in a pleasing fashion, draws them all out, displays an interest and a sympathy with them. He listens to isolated men and women, who for years have been shut up in the silence of routine monosyllables, without the stimulus to talk of a sympathetic ear.

He is a sort of lay confessor to all and sundry. A wise and tolerant priest, he violates the confessional only in an unmalicious and disguised way. There is something about him that makes people want to recount their life histories to him. He is the confidant of enterprising business men who tell him their dissatisfaction with life, their secret aspirations, the difficulties they get into over their sweethearts. Hard-ups and frustrated geniuses, neurotics and racehorse touts tell him all about themselves. Give Sherwood twenty minutes in the corner with a married woman and he knows every blessed grievance she has against her husband, from his habit of wearing nightgowns to his silly preferences in women, from his humming idiotic snatches of song in his bath to his shallow lies, petty trickeries, and empty vanities.

What is more, he has a sinister talent for telling you just what is wrong with you, for diagnosing your case with amazing accuracy. He is like a clever mind reader or an Indian fakir. His intuitions are so sure that they act as prompters to your own easy disclosures. He has acquired this talent by a persistent and patient interest in people, by an insatiable curiosity, by an early Christian belief in the profound significance of all human life.

To get back to his vanity. His vanity is such that it presupposes that his own life and work is important, significant, and invaluable. Such is his profound belief in himself that this belief precludes his active sympathy with the work of any other writer, especially of any one working in a different field from his own. Thus he may profess in an amiable fashion that he likes the work of Hecht, of Hergesheimer, of Waldo Frank, of this or that one he meets; but actually he not only dislikes it and can't read it, but is very suspicious of it. He has hurt the feelings of many a fellow writer by telling him, in effect, that in his opinion the inquiring and hopeful writer wasn't honest or sincere. A novelist should know better than to ask another novelist what he thinks of his work: in reply, if the questioned is truthful, he must either admit that he considers the other fellow's work bad or have doubts about the value of his own work. And Sherwood has absolutely no doubts whatever.

He is, indeed, one of the few consistent artists in America, one of the very few men who have had the courage to deny the American god of monetary success and devote themselves to their highest self-realization as artists. Even at the height of his run of acclamation, he has refused to be lionized. While lesser men would have accepted every tea and dinner, every opportunity to appear before women's clubs and school societies, every chance to give readings in arty eating places, Sherwood stuck to his shack in Palos Park, Illinois, and worked. Once a week he went into Chicago and had lunch at Schlogl's with Harry Hansen, Carl Sandburg, Ben Hecht, Keith Preston, T. K. Hedrick, Llewellyn Jones, Richard Atwater, Gene Markey, and J. P. McEvoy (the true and only claim Chicago has to be the literary center of America, the only group of people who are vitally interested in literature in the whole sprawly town). That is about the extent of his social activities.

He has refused to tie himself for any protracted length of time to any industrial endeavor, because money means nothing to him beyond its power to purchase the few necessities of life and give him the leisure in which to write. It is for this reason that the "Dial" award meant much more to him than it would to most writers, accustomed to expensive scales of living, self-indulgence, and extravagance. Sherwood knows how to use the money so that it will, in very truth, give him the opportunity to write.

But had he not got the award, had his books never sold beyond a number affording him a pitiable royalty, he would yet have done perhaps precisely what he is doing now. He would continue to create, for he has the soul of an artist, a soul uncorrupted by the exigencies of a material civilization. He began to write late in life, to keep himself, so he says, from "going crazy." Writing was a relief from the strain of years of bitter experience and trying hours in the cut-throat, nerve-racking game of commercial competition. He wrote, and he writes now, from an inner necessity, and even did he never get his work between covers he would still continue to write, and still continue to keep his faith in its very high personal (and that is, ultimate) value. Such is the triumph and the apology for Sherwood's inordinate, magnificent vanity.

## *XXIV: Louis Untermeyer*

HE was born in New York City, October 1, 1885, and is probably the least educated poet in America. His Alma Mater is the De Witt Clinton High School, from which, having flunked twice in geometry, he failed to graduate. He has been successful in concealing (1) his mathematical shortcomings from his business associates, (2) his middle name from the public. It was first intended to give him his mother's family name (Michael) but, yielding to a repressed romanticism, only the initial was kept. It was finally used for his middle name, which is Milton. He has never allowed it to appear in print.

He is five feet seven inches in height, stocky, inclined to take on weight because of an uncontrollable lust for sweets; is equally worried about the state of the world and the thinning of his hair; puns as often (and as atrociously) as Christopher Morley, and is as fussy about his neckties as a Wall Street stockbroker. The absurd smallness of his ears is overcompensated by the prominence of his nose. He has a long slanting forehead, wears eye-glasses, and affects racy colloquialisms that are not suited to his temperament. The shape of his head is dolichocephalic.

Although he prefers Virginia mixtures, he smokes any and every brand of cigarette. However he cannot stand tobacco in any other form. Once a year B. W. Huebsch persuades him to finish a cigar, which he does with unhappy consequences. He has a collection of fourteen pipes which he has tried to "break in" without success.

He originally expected to be a professional musician;

he wrote a few sentimental songs in the styles of MacDowell and Schumann at eighteen, and at nineteen his first printed poem (a fulsome sonnet to Nazimova) appeared in "The Theatre Magazine." Since then he has not composed a note. But he continually deplores the fact (to any one who will listen) that his creative gift is not musical, and he still plays the piano creditably. His favorite method of entertaining guests is to play the accompaniments while his wife sings the less well-known songs of Brahms and Hugo Wolf, and he never tires of saying that he would rather have written the "little" Eighth Symphony of Beethoven than all the tragedies of Shakespeare.

He married a girl from the incredible town of Zanesville in 1907. His wife is Jean Starr Untermeyer, also a poet. They have one child, a boy, Richard, sixteen years old, who worships only two gods: Babe Ruth and the late Nikolai Lenin.

His work is full of absurd self-contradictions. He bangs the drum for all the modern tendencies, scorning anything that is even faintly "academic"; yet his own poetry is as orthodox in form as the most conventional of his *bête noires*. Similarly, as a critic, he occupies almost opposite positions. He exposed the "Others" group to derisive laughter both in his parodies and his articles in "The New Republic." Yet he wrote a more than friendly introduction to Maxwell Bodenheim's first book of fantasies. His chapter in "The New Era in American Poetry" on the intraverted music and morbidity of Aiken's verse was vitriolic and almost libelous; yet on this vehement critique was founded a close friendship, and he will rush to Aiken's defense if any one on the "other" side attacks the blond hermit of South Yarmouth.

This grotesque inconsistency needs no psychoanalyzer. His exaggerated pugnacity is a shield; his belligerent at-

LOUIS UNTERMEYER

titude is what the Freudians would call a defense mechanism, a protection against an inherent sentimentality to which he is always in danger of yielding. He is, like many of his race, highly sensitized, extremely adaptable, and hence open to any strong influence, subject to a succession of sudden attachments. Thus one finds him absolutely uncritical, even as a critic, of the work of intimate friends like Robert Frost and Carl Sandburg. Thus, also, one finds him, in spite of the abandon and more-than-suggested infidelities in "The New Adam," a fiercely monogamous husband, a possessive householder, a traditionally Hebraic parent.

His critical attitude leans heavily on the following terms: *banal, glib, technique, derivative, racy, indubitably, authentic, illuminating, acerbid, exaltation* (usually as opposed to *exultation*), *physical* (often accompanied by *as well as metaphysical*), *fulgent, inhibited,* and *neurotic.* His poetry, when it is most his own, seems to be ringing the changes on such favorite words as: *urge, flesh, red, triumph, fuse, wave, surge, fires, stark, rushing, energy,* and *abandon.*

As a critic, he has had the dubious advantage of occupying a strategic position close to the center, thus receiving the direct fire from both the opposing camps. The members of the extreme left regard him as a damnable reactionary, while such defenders of the conservative tradition as Cale Young Rice and Stuart P. Sherman consider him a red-eyed Bolshevik.

As a poet, he is similarly contradictory. His themes, figures and points of view are radical, but his form is, if not always orthodox, at least fairly regular in shape. He would rather, he has said, write one intense, concentrated quatrain than all the carloads of free verse shipped annually to the offices of "Poetry."

He would, incidentally, be a better poet if he were not

so fond of intensifying his phrases. He continually attempts to make his verbs too active; his adjectives stagger under a burden of vehemence. The rhyme "urge-surge" should be forcibly extracted from his system!

He suffered from catarrh for several years, but after an incision of the nasal septum, now breathes without difficulty. He has never had a day's illness since he contracted chicken-pox at the age of five, hence his "Challenge" poetry, obviously influenced by Henley, is insufferably bouncing and muscular. However, he complains occasionally of seborrhea.

In the business world, which he entered at seventeen, he is known both as a designer and a manufacturing jeweler with radical tendencies. This is because he has espoused the cause of labor, is one of the contributing editors of "The Liberator," was connected with the trial of "The Masses" in 1918, and was one of the first manufacturers to come out for the forty-four hour week, closing his factory (in Newark, New Jersey) all day on Saturdays. What puzzles his fellow manufacturers is the fact that his "socialistic ideas" seem to have been not only pleasurable to him but profitable to his partners.

He takes a perverse pleasure in posing, especially when he is among literary persons, as a satisfied merchant, a member of the Board of Trade, a capitalist, a lowbrow. Yet he regards the manufacturing of jewelry as a parasitic and essentially immoral trade, and has recently handed in his resignation. He hopes, he says, after a year or two abroad to retire to some farm in Connecticut, study for several years, and then settle down as—God save the mark!—a lecturer in some lesser university.

He has a sprawling, hodgepodge library of thirty-five hundred books containing most of the dramas and practically all the representative poetry since 1890. It also contains two shelves which he calls his Chamber of

Horrors. Some day he intends to use this material in an anthology to be entitled "The World's Worst Poetry." He expects to insert, among verbal atrocities by James Byron Elmore ("the Bard of the Alamo"), Julia Moore (Mark Twain's "Sweet Singer of Michigan"), J. Gordon Coogler, and other queer fowl, some of the gaudiest banalties of Cale Young Rice, Robert W. Service, and George Edward Woodberry.

He is fond of books as books, but he is no bibliophile. The only first editions he ever collected were those of H. G. Wells, D. H. Lawrence, and (at twenty-one) Richard Le Gallienne. He will sell the last at less than cost. His only prized possessions are a first edition of "The Tinker's Wedding" sent to him and autographed by J. M. Synge (he claims to have written the first American review of Synge's work), a manuscript notebook of unpublished poems by Siegfried Sassoon, and a Bible sent to him by H. L. Mencken which bears the legend "Property of the Hotel Astor" on the cover and is inscribed on the title-page: "To Louis Untermeyer, with the compliments of The Author."

He always eats too much and never has indigestion.

He is continually harping on "individuality," he derides "influences"; yet he is vastly tickled when any one compares him to Heine.

He is a Jew by birth and by preference, yet some of his best friends are Jews.

He has published a dozen assorted volumes of prose and verse. Yet one of them has never been offered for sale in any book store. It appeared in 1917, a pamphlet of forty pages with illustrations, and was distributed anonymously. It was called "The Wedding Ring." It does not appear in any list of his works.

He likes to think of himself as a sardonic and even silent person; and yet he is effervescent to the point of continually bubbling over nothing. Once started on an enthusiasm, he will talk at any opportunity to any audience for any length of time.

A most aggravating and unreasonable combination. A poet, yet a practical business man; a passionate propagandist, yet a critic without any axes to grind; a reviewer who has made dozens of enemies, yet an anthologist with little prejudice or partisanship. . . . A creature mythical, fantastic, incredible—but nevertheless very much alive.

## *XXV: Burton Rascoe*

THIS has happened so many times, it must be significant. Some sweet creature, sufficiently lacking in sophistication to extract a thrill from meeting celebrities—by which one means nowadays any one whose name appears in print occasionally—is confronted by a smooth-faced, elegantly leggy lad, to whom at sight one would hardly credit more than twenty-four summers. His hazel eyes have the wandering alertness of a fox terrier's; his remarkably long nose emphasizes this impression of pouncing inquisitiveness, for it terminates in a hexagonal knob, and the planes reflect light, so that in motion it positively twinkles. And its owner is never still. But a touch of hobbledehoy uncertainty checks his patent eagerness; an evident desire to please and to be liked obviously interferes with a natural impulse toward eloquence. His conversation resembles the outpouring from a full decanter abruptly inverted, a decanter containing a pousse-café, whence the components emerge in unblended gurglings. He stammers, never quite finishes a sentence, trails off into vague non-sequiturs. Poising on tiptoe like dawn new lighted on some heaven-kissing hill, he bows from the waist, gestures with his hands, straightens his tie; he beams and blushes engagingly. In short, he betrays all the symptoms of being painfully young. And he answers to the name of Burton Rascoe.

Whereupon the lady never fails to exclaim, in accents of astonishment: "But I thought you must be a dignified old gentleman with long white whiskers!"

This a priori concept, though absurd, is not difficult

to account for. It is derived from Mr. Rascoe's correctly journalistic habit of chatting in print about Aristotle and Sophocles with the easy familiarity of a contemporary. Realizing instinctively that a dead man cannot furnish news, he proceeds on the assumption that any one he writes about is still alive; and he gets away with it. The naïve lady has merely reasoned from the wrong end of the syllogism.

The deceptive appearance of juvenescence which Mr. Rascoe presents in his proper person is rather more puzzling. Chronologically, he is thirty-one; by the time this achieves publication, maybe he will be thirty-two. That isn't so terribly young, and neither is Burton Rascoe, altogether. But then again, he is. His is a case of belated maturity, resulting from extreme precocity. Psychologically he is a sixteenth cousin of Ninetta Crummles, the celebrated Infant Phenomenon, who discovered the fount of eternal youth in a bottle of Hollands, flavored with midnight oil. Mr. Rascoe also sat up of nights in his boyhood, and drank too deeply of the Pierian spring. He has not yet had time to catch up mentally with himself. Very likely he never will; and when he leaps nimbly into his grave at the age of seventy or eighty, folks will shake their heads and remark upon the pity of such a promising youngster's being cut off in the flower of his years that way.

They will feel so because whatever the intellectual mode of the moment may be, Burton Rascoe will be at least a day in advance of it. His chosen place in the procession is that of running footman, clearing the street for the bandwagon. When at the age of twelve he lent his concentrated and unavailing attention to Kant and Socrates, it was not from any innate desire to imbue himself with the wisdom of the ancients. No, he wanted to be neck and neck with his high-school teachers, to

BURTON RASCOE

gain a few laps on his elders. Chill apprehension seized upon him at the thought that some one might spring the categorical imperative at a dinner party before he knew the correct comeback. Subconsciously he is still embarrassed by that infantile dread.

This is his solitary inhibition. Otherwise, he simply does not know the meaning of timidity or repression. Reverence, respect, and restraint are alien to his nature. As a human being he possesses not even rudimentary principles; and as a critic, he hasn't any æsthetic standards. He has preferences, but they are either purely personal or utilitarian. These are sweeping statements, and require to be elucidated carefully to avoid misunderstanding; but it doesn't matter, they will be misunderstood anyhow. Yet let it be appended hastily that he has something just as good, for all practical purposes, being firmly seized of the Pauline doctrine that while all things are lawful to him, all things are not always expedient. The only drawback to this rule of conduct is that a slight flaw in his taste occasionally leads to errors of judgment in the matter of what is or is not permissible.

For he makes quite terrible gaffs occasionally by overshooting the mark, failing to distinguish between the thing that may be cried in the market-place and that which must be murmured in confidence, among friends. Upon this colorable evidence, there are those who charge him with malice. They are totally mistaken. He has no enduring grudges, and never bothers to pay off scores in cold blood. When he indulges in controversy, it is for an ulterior motive; and if he is accused of not fighting fair, so was Napoleon, for the same reason, because they aimed at victory and hit at the weakest point. Moreover, Burton Rascoe really does not perceive why any persons should mind what he does to them, since he would not be put out if they did the same to him, and is not when they repay him sevenfold. To say the least, this sounds improbable, but it has been proved. Some years since, a man who stood on the footing of a friend endeavored to inflict upon him a grave injury, with no possible justification. Mr. Rascoe must have been annoyed, but contented himself with avoiding that person thereafter; and lately, when the false friend published a novel, Burton hailed it as a masterpiece. "How could you?" asked a third person who was acquainted with the circumstances. Burton looked surprised, and replied simply that the novel was good.

Thus his lack of a code of ethics is of no material import, being counterbalanced by an equal absence of envy, greed, or rancor. He is amiable to a fault, full of generous enthusiasms, excessively sociable. He gets on with the tetchiest of our younger literati in spite of themselves; and there are a lot of violently inflammable egotists among them. One in particular has wasted as much nervous energy trying to pick a quarrel with him as would have sufficed to make an epic. This morbid poetaster writes Burton an insulting letter at least once a month, announcing a complete severance of diplomatic relations—and comes around a few days later to find Burton unruffled and unchanged. The letter likewise remains unanswered. But it is filed away somewhere; it might be valuable years hence.

As a critic, he is a wonderful newspaper man. If he goes down to history at all, it will be as the encourager of new talents. He smells them out not by their artistic fragrance, but by virtue of as keen a nose for news as ever any one was gifted with. His flair for the author who is going to write something startling is downright uncanny. No one else in the world could have anticipated "Jurgen" by reading "The Cream of the Jest." One is already a classic; the other is just a *jeu d'esprit.*

The men who have arrived don't interest Rascoe very much. You can learn all about them in the morgue. What he is looking for is some one who will make fresh copy for to-morrow's paper. If he can get a novel angle on an established author, that is worthwhile; but otherwise, what's the use? Always there must be the perpetual slight novelty, with a timely application. The search for the absolute is no quest for him. If Plato had just given us "The Republic," and Burton Rascoe got a review copy, he would play it up as a proposal for the nationalization of women. For the past year, his favorite word had been "pornography," on account of the censorship fight. But if he had lived during the twilight of the post-Elizabethans, he might have been a Puritan and the discoverer of John Milton. Green apples suit his literary digestion. He can make a full meal of caviar. A hint of the scandalous never comes amiss to him, because newspapers build their circulation largely upon scandal decorously presented. It is the fact or theory which a book embodies rather than its artistic value which engages Mr. Rascoe's attention. He is preoccupied with what he can make of it instead of with what the author has already made of it.

Indeed, his ear for verbal music is slightly defective; and he searches for the unusual word rather than the *mot juste*. Neither euphony nor precision appeals to him so much as oddity. It hardly matters if he doesn't know just what the word means, so long as it is not hackneyed he will employ it. His sense of humor is unripe, tending toward crudity. But he is brilliant, intuitive, quick to perceive an author's intention, and hence prone to give as much credit to a promise as to a definite performance. The future owes him a considerable debt —which he is entirely competent to collect.

For this blushing youth knows where he wants to go

and how to get there. When he came to New York he left an established reputation in Chicago. (The phrasing is exact.) Most Chicagoans believe that New York is supercilious, whereas it is simply provincial. Burton's disregard of tradition kept him from this error. He had absorbed the lesson of the frontier: that it does not matter where you came from, nor what you have done; present performance is the important thing. Oklahoma is his native state, which originated the "sooner," the fellow who hopped in ahead of time and settled down without waiting on formality. That was his procedure in New York. He perceived that the quickest way to get in was to take introductory conventionalities for granted. Placidly appropriating an unoccupied chair among the self-elect, he began talking to them with affable arrogance. The arrogance was calculated, for the purpose of provoking rejoinder. He "drew" the inner circle; to one a compliment, to another a thrust, whichever would best serve the turn; and they bit. By talking back to him, they tacitly admitted him.

Calmly looking over their various means of keeping in the public eye, he adapted anything he could use. His Bookman's Daybook has been called the most striking journalistic innovation of the past decade. So it is, but as Shakespeare helped himself to Holinshed and Plutarch, Burton Rascoe took and transmogrified "Kenelm Digby's" Literary Lobby and F. P. A.'s Pepysian parody to make his bookman's holiday, just as a point of departure. He had both the nerve and the ability to go beyond his preceptors. The Daybook required a lot of courage to begin, and even more talent to continue, to walk the invisible chalk line between dulness and vulgarity. Personal revelations are of absorbing interest, when not insufferably boresome. Betwixt Scylla and Charybdis Burton has steered his frail bark deftly, only occasionally grazing the proprieties, for he has a constitutional list to the Left.

The original quality in the Daybook is that it reports the intellectual news of the day; here is the newspaper man to the fore, though he happens to be "covering" literature. The superficial gossip is mere window dressing. Mr. Rascoe is intent primarily upon giving a reflection of contemporary thought. And he goes after it like a reporter; gets it from the source. Probably a good deal of it is inaccurate in detail, colored by his own theories and predispositions; but essentially it is truthful. His victims sometimes object that they never said what he imputes to them. Maybe not, but the substance of the conversation is generally characteristic; he conveys the speaker's personality, though it be by means of an imaginary dialogue. It is what they were leading up to, or might have said; it sounds like them. And one must bear in mind that few of us can recall exactly what we did say on a given occasion.

Mr. Rascoe himself does not talk so well as he listens —when compelled to. But he is not hard to compel. He never seems to get an idea fully formulated, *viva voce,* because another steps on its heels. At whiles he acts in the same erratic and disconnected manner. At a party, along toward the middle of the evening, he springs from girl to girl as a chamois from crag to crag. Seizing one by the hand with glad enthusiasm, he trails her limply protesting form in pursuit of another. He emulates the military hero in "Penguin Island" who strode unhampered on his triumphant career, with a countess floating scarfwise from his neck and a duchess clinging fondly to his knees. Accused of Don Juanistic proclivities, Mr. Rascoe asseverated fervently: "You wrong me, you wrong me; I just like to be with nice women"— and therewith bounded away in full cry after a newly discerned bevy of girls, leaving his character to speak for itself. Women appreciate his appreciation; they pour their sorrows into his confiding ear, while his wife looks on with a mingling of amusement, exasperation, and resignation.

A sketch which included no glimpse of him in his parental and domestic rôle would be sadly incomplete. Seeing him *en famille,* one realizes that he is fortune's pet. His wife, Hazel, so frequently mentioned in the Daybook, is a compendium of the graces, grave and sprightly, with a wistful childlike face and a remarkable fund of plain common sense. She looks like a butterfly and serves as his ballast. He would have run himself to death in pursuit of excitement long ago if she hadn't seen to it that he got all he needed at home. Almost one suspects that she selected their children with sagacious prevision of his moral requirements. Children are inevitably a responsibility; but his are a burden that any man would be glad to shoulder. There are two, a boy and a girl, as good as gold and eminently soothing to the proprietary paternal eye. When they grow up they are going to find father a good deal of a problem, on account of his insouciant habits and incorrigible youthfulness; but they have the stamina to grapple with it. After all, they will decide, he is their father, though he does not seem to realize it; and they will do their duty in respect of holding him to the straight and narrow path. They are bound to disapprove of him, but they will not be able to help loving him. His wife, on being diplomatically invited to enumerate his faults, replied after long cogitation: "Well, he snores, grinds his teeth, and moans in his sleep; but otherwise he is perfect!"

His family counts enormously in his life. If he writes for posterity, it is in the most direct sense; he does it for his wife and children. The artistic impulse comes in a very bad second. The most likely sign of genius about him is that he works solely for the reward. Nothing but an imminent deadline and bread and butter considerations can spur him to write. He would rather just live. But with those incentives, he is highly industrious and prolific. He will accept any commission that offers, and fill it too; but his copy is not turned in until the eleventh hour and fifty-ninth minute. For years he has been preparing a collection of essays for the press, and it is not yet finished, because the returns on such a volume are problematical. If a check were assuredly forthcoming on delivery of the manuscript, it would have been ready long ago. In the only leisure period he has enjoyed since the age of eight or thereabouts, he wrote the rough draft of a novel, but it may never be brought to completion, because fiction is seldom remunerative and he was obliged to get back on a salaried job.

His obvious mannerisms are mostly misleading. The exigencies of the daily grind make him appear brusque at times; but he is never really out of temper. As intimated above, his bad breaks are intentional, not slips of the pen but mistakes. A streak of harmless vanity keeps him tolerably modest; he worries over the fact that his eyebrows do not extend the full width of his lofty brow, that his nose is not of a classical straightness, that he is not five feet ten in height instead of an inch and a half below that standard. His self-confidence is the outcome of a tolerably accurate estimate of his genuine capacities, and a rooted determination to make the most of them. His biggest achievement to date is the immortalizing of a member of the American Academy. But unless his sudden and violent demise follows some similar exploit, he will be heard from further.

## *XXVI: Padraic Colum*

OCCASIONALLY one runs across a miracle of manhood, a personality which possesses no animosities and would not know what to do with them if he had them, a naïve recipient of life whose essential gentleness is so singular as to set him in the midst of all groups and apart from the internecine warfare that is the ordinary occupation of groups. Padraic Colum is such a personality. He has been likened to a leprachaun, one of the Siddhas, an inspired child, and an adorable phenomenon in a nation that would rather fight than eat. The truth is that such comparisons weaken him and lessen his stature, for he is all of these things and much more besides. He does not stop short at the leprachaun stage, and it is to be suspected that this comparison is more the result of his size than of his brain and personality. In other words, he is more skilled in threading the labyrinth of life than his gentleness suggests. He has discovered (or, perhaps, it is a congenital gift of clairvoyance) the precise media to ensure success in a literary existence. But before going into this his outward aspects should be noted.

His clearly cut features, wide-set eyes, large head of hair (now, alas, thinning), suggest an intelligence that gathers added strength from a blithe simplicity in mannerisms. An unfailing cheerfulness of demeanor in all meetings and argumentations posits an impartiality of judgment that is suspect. He is not really impartial. Rather is he perpetually generous in his approach to all things, the possessor of a mind that is insistently cau-

PADRAIC COLUM

tioned by tolerance. Behind this aspect of tolerance loom certain adamantine convictions which are yet so broad in their manifestations as to include many seemingly contradictory things. He believes, for instance, that the literary creator should love all his characters, and this belief induces a broadness of sympathy which partially impairs his position as a potential writer. One understands therefore that he moves within certain limitations, that he can never actually get out of himself, that no book that he may write can ever be really bigger than he is. There will be no accidents in his career but rather a continual self-expression consistently bounded by his personality. Yet these statements must not be taken as belittlement, for as much as any writer living to-day he possesses that mystic substance that we call genius. This deliberate circumscribing of himself is merely an intimation of the direction which his demon will pursue. His sympathy closes certain gates of departure into darkness for him but it flings wide other egresses to fair prospects.

This tolerance, now so emphatic a portion of his being, is not an acquired characteristic, nor the result of speculations which have shown him the relativity of all things and therefore induced the conviction that the phenomena of life and æsthetics are all limitations of organic existence. In other words, he is not a cerebral philosopher. It is rather the continuation of a childlike acceptance which admits magic and fairies and divinity and goodness as a supernal pulse animating the universe. It is a sensitivity that is quite unclassified and which defeats analysis. It was present in him from the first. His novitiate was served in that Dublin wherein James Joyce existed, but it is safe to assert that he did not live in the same Dublin that Joyce saw. It was in another city altogether that he began life as a clerk in a railway office and used the ledgers for poetry scribbling. It was a city of admirable impulses, of nationalistic fervor, of untrammeled enthusiasms. He sprang fully endowed from the forehead of Dana.

Legends have crystallized his gentleness and simplicity but they do not do him justice. We hear of him timidly calling on the directress of a small amateur company with a play about Brian Boru under his arm. We hear that among the very first poems he ever wrote was the marvelous "A Poor Scholar of the Forties," certainly a definitive proof of genius. We hear of him playing in one of A. E.'s plays and constantly being twitted for years after by a line addressed to him in that play, "Be still, hasty boy!" We hear of him marrying his charming and brilliant wife with but a few pounds in his pocket and setting off for London with no more than sanguine hopes of success. We hear of the respect he commanded by his first plays, "The Fiddler's House," "The Land," and that dark triumph, "Thomas Muskerry." We hear of the hegira to America and years of struggle. We—but what is the use of going on? All of it combines into a portrait of a man whose gentleness is an indubitable source of strength, whose simplicity is merely the consistent development of self-expression, of a high degree of actual achievement.

There is a unity in Padraic Colum, a deep-seated belief in destiny that has given him courage and strength to pursue his career. He has remarked that he writes nothing of his own volition, that he must be told what to do and then he will do it. He has also remarked that he can do anything that he is told to do; and this is, by far, the more important statement. Of course, he can. It really doesn't matter what he does. Poems, plays, novels, essays, criticism, description, fairy stories, studies in folk lore—all of these things are merely outlets to that rich substance which is his mind and which is quite unalloyed by any ulterior impulses. For this reason he is not always a good critic; he is too much himself; his personality strikes fire from the tiniest flint.

There is a lesson to be read in the story of the bee. It happened at Peterboro, New Hampshire, where, seated on a screen-enclosed porch, Padraic Colum noticed a bee trying to buzz its way out. He took the bee in his hand and, opening the screen door, flung the bee to freedom. The ungracious insect stung the poet on the hand during the gesture. "The poor little bee didn't know I was trying to help it," remarked Colum, without any rancor whatsoever. The same thing would have happened to any critic who tried to sting Colum. It would have happened to any person foolish enough to display enmity of any sort. His tolerance is the result of his own convictions as to the fairness of his attitude toward life. When the gods fashioned him they left out jealousy.

Now and then he becomes aware of his own extreme tolerance and it troubles him. It may be possible that deep in his heart there are instants when he would like to be Napoleon or Casanova. Who knows? But his equanimity is too deep-seated for any painful self-proddings. His cult of cheerfulness negates any morbid inward analyses. Besides that, he is really religious. His religion is a natural inward growth, partially a result of national characteristics and the actual dependence of his scheme of things on the principle of divine guidance. If he were not religious he would not be Padraic Colum. Religion reacts to something that was deep-seated in him from the very first, from the days before he realized what religion meant. It is that something that accepts fairies as actualities and manifests itself in numberless evidences of superstitions.

We may believe that he is naturally sure of himself. It could only be a man sure of himself who, when welcomed in Hawaii by government representatives, calmly pledged the friendship of Ireland to the Pacific island. Hawaii might have been a turning point in his career if he were not already so firmly grounded in himself. But even in that faraway land thoughts of the birds on Irish beaches touched his soul. And it is here that another point may be brought out which throws light on his personality. He is of unchangeable quality. The Padraic Colum of the Dublin of 1903 is the same Padraic Colum of the New York of 1924. Like all real ideals, he does not shift. There are times when he neglects his proper expression, when he wastes himself on unending series of children's books that retell classics, when he attempts to broaden a poetical vein which really should not be broadened; but even this neglect cannot be called a dissipation of genius. There is really no lessening in the man. He merely fails to speak with the proper accent. It is Longford.

An amazing amount of knowledge is concealed in his mind, and here again is a reason for not taking his simplicity too much at its face value. No man can know as much as he does and be simple. Rather is his simplicity a directness, a refusal to play with masks of any sort and an understanding that literature need not be a ceremonious affair. He is animated by a deep enthusiasm that is concerned less with the mode of expression than the actual expression itself. Consequently he will not be found indulging in experimentations for the sake of technical development. His output is the natural deliverance of himself to his readers, and it may come through any channel that is suggested.

Having said so much, it becomes imperative to insist again that Padraic Colum be not misinterpreted as one of those simple geniuses who are stung by bees, fall into ditches, get lost in the woods, mislay their hats, and exhibit all the other so-called "cute" mannerisms that are supposed to be associated with the unspoiled personage. He is of vaster stature. All of these things may happen to him, of course, but they are of secondary import so far as his actual self is concerned. The man who may be perverted into a gentle sort of clown is not so infinitely capable as Padraic Colum assuredly is. The gentleness of strength, the simplicity of assurance and accurate assumption, the unconsciousness of natural confidence, these are the things that move behind his unassuming exterior. He is a scholar in the best sense of the word, as any one talking to him for half an hour will know. His approach to a subject is always broad and reasonable.

One may not always agree with him but no one can doubt his intelligence. It is quite possible that he is altogether too much concerned with loving his characters. This tendency rather tempts him to love other people, to love people in general, in fact. And so broad an inclusiveness is not good for great literature. It destroys values. But, curiously enough, Padraic Colum will rarely be found loving the things that do not distinctly aid his self-expression in some measure. If he must love all the characters in a book, he will be sure to write a book in which all the characters should be loved. There are two things that he is on record as *not* loving: they are the Algonquin and "Vanity Fair." Also there are two traits that will never be found in his books; and they are brittle wit and superficial sophistication.

## XXVII: Fannie Hurst

I REMEMBER very well an April day some six years ago, when I was coming slowly home from the village post office with the morning's mail in my pocket and an open magazine in my hand. The world was ringing with shouts for battle, on every corner men were gesticulating and arguing. The United States had at last been stung to action—we were going to war.

But I was utterly indifferent. The interest aroused in me by the black, four-inch type headline in the morning paper had evaporated; for the moment it mattered not to me whether the French capitulated, the Germans triumphed, or the United States entered the fray. I was reading "Sob Sister," by Fannie Hurst. I was absorbed, thrilled, fascinated by this living, breathing, throbbing glimpse of an older war—the war that is as old as Eve's oldest daughter.

The position of Fannie Hurst in the world of letters cannot be properly estimated without taking into account this truly remarkable short story. It is as daring a literary achievement as we have in the language; perfect portraiture, a superb example of the art of writing and the conquest of a field almost untouched by English and American authors. That it came from the hand of a woman, and an extremely young woman, makes it all the more astonishing; but "Sob Sister" is an astonishing story on all counts.

I am often reminded, in beginning one of Fannie Hurst's short stories, of the pitcher in a baseball game, who winds himself up into various contortions and bow-

FANNIE HURST

knots before he lets fly the ball. Miss Hurst does something of the sort, almost invariably prefacing her tales with an involved sentence or two full of mouth-filling and eye-filling words, as if winding up for the start.

Unlike the pitcher, whose delivery is uncertain, this particular writer almost inevitably delivers a strike. Out of the sixty or seventy short stories which constitute the most important part of her work to date, it would be hard to select five that are not notable, unusual, and stamped with the peculiarity and passion of her genius.

Fannie Hurst has many idiosyncrasies as a writer; I cannot call to mind any great writer who has more. Besides this somewhat stilted and artificial commencement, she likes to use outlandish words throughout all her stories, words harsh and guttural, filled with consonants. She is not an easy, a lucid and graceful writer. Quite the opposite, her style is involved, ponderous, awkward. But back of it is a marvelous knowledge of human nature, a marvelous feeling for the exact and subtle values of words—perhaps no other writer to-day can use a single word, or a brief phrase, with the stunning force and power she displays. It is exactly here that her genius lies.

For there can be no question that Fannie Hurst is a genius. Whatever her method of approach, whatever her medium, her attack is sure. The tears blur one's eyes, a salty thickness catches one's throat, and one looks about furtively, laughing shamefacedly—it is only a story, after all! There isn't really a Ghetto mother trying, so clumsily, so pathetically, to keep her boy safely home on Sunday night; there isn't really a man's outworn mistress struggling to hold him with freshly broiled steaks and baby talk—there is only Fannie Hurst!

Fannie Hurst, who wrote "Humoresque," and "Ice Water, Pl——!" "A Petal on the Current," "Just

Around the Corner," and "Back Pay." Fannie Hurst, who goes her serene, her independent way—analyzing, diagnosing, vivisecting, doing exactly as she pleases, never varying her course to a favoring wind, never stooping to sex stuff, or pollyannism, or any of the other fancies of the hour, never holding out her hat for pennies.

They tell me that she never permits cutting in any editorial office, be it the greatest or the smallest. And one may readily believe that cutting would be death to the very essence, the bouquet, the effervescence of her work. It is easy to imagine the brisk young thirty-dollar-a-week clerk dealing with one of her heart-stopping and soul-wringing passages that consist simply of broken monosyllables: "Mama—" "What, Baby?" "Mama—" "Mama's here, Baby!" "Mama—"

"Why, this is just space-filling," the young clerk, told to cut a thousand words, might blithely decide. And *viva* the blue pencil.

But the young clerk would be wrong. Not easily, not carelessly, has the least of those phrases been set there. Fannie Hurst works literally by the sweat of her brow, hammering her stuff out word by word, changing, altering, rewriting, deleting. You examine one of her scratched and erased and altered manuscripts wonderingly: why was this word substituted, this phrase changed?

There is no doubt, however, in the writer's mind. Every word is weighed, every phrase studied, everything shifted, wearisomely pondered, despairingly readjusted until it is, somehow, mysteriously and finally *right.* And her reward is that men and women from the Seal Rocks to Good Ground echo the word in deep content of soul: "That's like Ma. Isn't that Pa all over? That's *right.*"

It amuses me now to recall my mental picture of Fannie Hurst, before we met. She seemed to me likely to be a sour-faced person, angular, moustached, crabbed and profound, instructress in English in a genteel academy for young misses—that type. Yet the woman herself is anything but this.

She is opulent, oriental, beautiful, with very black hair and very red lips, a creamy skin and magnificent dark eyes. She dresses characteristically, in daring tam-o'-shanters, in gorgeous brocades and heavy embroideries. But despite the splendor and the beauty, she is feminine in manner, gentle, a little shy, almost girlish. Modest and tongue tied about her own work, she is full of enthusiasm about that of others. Her friends are almost all women—one feels that she has but small interest in men.

This extraordinarily, joyously successful person, to whom life has been so generous, began her days in a quite commonplace fashion in St. Louis. Success in a high-school play aroused in her the usual histrionic longings, and she came to New York not very many years ago, backed by a devoted father, and anxious for theatrical training. By a curious fillip of fortune she obtained a small part with Leo Ditrichstein in "The Concert." Miss Hurst was merely in the first act, one of the languishing ladies who study voice culture with the impressionable musician. She held this part for several weeks, until she came out of the theater after a certain matinée to find her father waiting for her by the stage entrance. Her parent appears to have disapproved of this venture, and Fannie went back with him to St. Louis. She never returned to the theater, and the evening's performance was presented without her.

But she came back to New York, and this time turned to writing as a natural outlet for what is really unusual vitality. Bob Davis of "Munsey's"—that friend of young writers, whose kindly word and constructive criticism have helped so many of our fictionists to fame and fortune—was the first to give her encouragement. He accepted many of the early stories, and finally urged her to submit one he felt to be especially good to "The Saturday Evening Post." Her first manuscript sent to Mr. Lorimer's weekly she herself priced at $125; but the check that was immediately sent her was for three times that sum.

Long before this exciting bit of encouragement, however, Miss Hurst had determined that writing was her ordained profession. She had taken a college course, obtained a degree of Ph.D. from Columbia, and plunged into various experiences with the sole idea of enlarging her sympathies, and her knowledge of life. She boarded with a Jewish family in the Ghetto for two years, which perhaps explains her answer, a few years ago, to a young girl who asked her how she could ever imagine the things she did.

"Some of it is just remembering," said Fannie, with her eyes thoughtful and the corners of her mouth twitching.

With tremendous difficulty she obtained a position as waitress in a Childs restaurant. This job she held for two weeks, and for a similar period she worked as a salesgirl in Macy's basement. Some years after this, she returned from Europe by steerage. She wanted a first-hand knowledge and she got it, and later found good use for it.

From the Macy job she admits she was humiliatingly fired, because she was unable to keep her sales-book correctly. Successful on half a dozen counts, among them that of obtaining a doctor's degree, this genius of the pen confesses that she could not rise to the simple mathematical requirements of Macy's basement.

No one in the profession to-day is more ambitious or

more hard-working than she. To what new triumphs she will progress is a question that is giving her admirers much concern. Some years ago she tried play-writing, and collaborated with Harriet Ford in "The Land of the Free," in which one of the Nashes, Mary I think, most beautifully starred. The first act of this play, in which a Russian mother back in the old country parts with the little daughter who is going to America—this act had not a word of English in it, by the way—was entirely the work of Miss Hurst, and was one of the most striking, the most touching and exquisite presentations ever made on Broadway. But the play failed.

During wartime Fannie Hurst dramatized "Humoresque"; the production, however, was made only last winter. Despite Laurette Taylor's great art, and another unique and memorable first act, it scored only another failure. It was produced at the end of a bad season, and the wartime flavor told against it from the start. A third trial, this time with the dramatized short story "Back Pay," was also unsuccessful, and "Fannie re-Hurst," as one of her friends affectionately calls her, is somewhat discouraged on this score. She has turned her full force upon novel-writing, and that "Lummox" is a big story is the conviction of a majority of the critics. "Lummox" is her second novel.

"Star-Dust," its predecessor, had some of the faults of a first novel and was surprisingly amateurish in places. But in many passages there was the sure flashing of genius, the golden streaks that marked it apart from the other thousands of novels of the year. Had it been the work of a beginner it would undoubtedly have been acclaimed with tremendous applause.

But Fannie Hurst is no beginner. She is supreme in her own sphere—the sphere of Kipling and O. Henry, neither of whom ever wrote anything worth considering in more than ten thousand words. She has the field to herself; Kipling's great voice is almost silent now, and O. Henry is dead. Who else?

Yes, there are promising beginners, and there are old favorites. One sees the name of Edna Ferber, Booth Tarkington, Wilbur Daniel Steele—"I like everything she—or he—writes!" one says. But "Alice Adams" and "The Girls" were big novels, and from the pens that wrote them other big novels will come. From no other pen will ever come the big short stories Fannie Hurst can write. They are all-American, but they are as big as the heart of the world. They are all simple, but they are as subtle as the delicate chambers of the brain. We form ourselves into an Oliver Twist club, we follow her dazzling tams and her sweeping embroideries appealingly, and we cry out, "Short Stories, Pl——!"

## *XXVIII: Don Marquis*

SIGNS and portents heralded his appearance upon this whirling globe. He was born about four o'clock in the afternoon, with a white head and probably its concomitant; in the mid-most of an eclipse of the sun—a total eclipse, mark you, no mere tentative or partial obscurity. The date may be ascertained by consulting an astronomical calendar, guided by the additional information that he is now just past his ninth lustrum, or if you prefer a more homely term, his fourth decade—the prime and fruitful period of life.

The spot, which future generations will doubtless recognize by some suitably simple token, something in the line of marble or gilded monuments, was evidently a forester's hut, being in the town of Walnut, Bureau County, Illinois. The period was that of fretsaw work and antimacassars, which may or may not have made a permanent impression upon his subconscious but which left no evidence in his personal architecture; it has the charm of simplicity. Holbein would have been the man to limn those ruggedly honest features. Not to bandy words, he is handsome in a virile way, with a strong square jaw, a straight nose, good gray-blue eyes, a ruddy color, and a fine head well thatched with silvery hair. These, added to a robust frame, ought to content the most fastidious. Needless to say, they don't. What he would have preferred, had his wishes been consulted, is a willowy elegance, aquiline features of the type known as patrician, and perhaps a touch of æsthetic languor. Fothergil Finch—certainly! He has been heard to claim that his soul is all of these things, and furthermore, that it is adorned with a silky mustache. He does not altogether like the dimple in his chin. It is inconsistent, but natural, that the portrait of himself which he most heartily approves is an etching by Muirhead Bone, which makes him look stern and masterful to the verge of grimness. Above everything, he hates the habit of caricaturists in giving him a curvilinear aspect indicating jollity and careless ease. He desires to be either swankish or dominant: Châteaubriand or Napoleon. (By what irony did Châteaubriand give his name to a beefsteak and Napoleon his to a cream puff?) It is a fact that the only consideration which stays Don Marquis from raising whiskers—whiskers are for dignity, Ophelia—is that they persist in emerging in three different colors, red, white, and black, not harmoniously blended, but in exclusive streaks. The prospect of unfurling to the breeze a hirsute appendage which would resemble the flag of some infant nation of Central Europe is enough to daunt the stoutest heart—and he is not really stout. Neither literally nor figuratively, or more so than a man needs to be to contain multitudes, in the apt phrase of Whitman.

Of these, his outward similitude is but a mask, a jaunty gesture intended to deceive the world. Here we approach his dark, long-guarded secret.

One hesitates—seeks for circumlocution and honeyed phrases to soften the blow. You have, of course, imagined Don Marquis as a roistering blade who would have been completely at home in the Mermaid Tavern, among the swashbucklers and hearty tosspots of that spacious age. He has voluntarily elected the part of Advocatus Diaboli, of an iconoclast battering down the fortress of tradition, convention, and all the vested interests of respectability. You suppose him another Aucassin who, given the choice between heaven and hell, would unhesi-

DON MARQUIS

tatingly take the left hand turning, because "thither go all the great lords and lovely ladies, the jongleurs and scholars and knights," the merry company who keep the primrose way beaten smooth and broad. That is the import of his writings; that is what he would have you think. The bitter truth is far otherwise.

Don Marquis is incorrigibly moral, hopelessly inhibited, a prisoner of virtue. His literary works are but a vain appeal to a non-existent baser nature which he hopes may some day materialize and liberate him from his own Puritan spirit. His life has been ruled and ordered by a conscience which would have carped at the Roundheads as spiritual slackers and reproached the Theban hermits for sybarites.

Captain Fitzurse and the Old Soak have neither part nor lot in him. They are wish projections, gay mirages with no basis of reality. Mehitabel, the amoral cat, is a bright and glittering ideal. But Aunt Prudence Hecklebury is a cold fact; that is why his jesting is tinged with the bitterness of defeat when he mocks at that militant prude. She has him licked. She is his oversoul; and when he reflects that he has only one life to live, and that she has had the directing of it, what wonder he expends such store of wistful tenderness upon Mehitabel, glorious waster of nine several existences simultaneously?

If Aunt Prudence were all of Don Marquis, the matter would be simple; though of course he would then be some one else. But she is only one phase of his personality, though she has proved the dominant one. And he might be a little sorry for her. She has her troubles. A Covenanting Scotch conscience set on guard over the heart of a troubadour and the soul of a Utopian reformer is not in an enviable position; which three elements make up the man, with one important addition. Very important, since lacking it he would long ago have exploded like the chameleon who tried to repose upon a plaid. His sense of humor has been the cohesive force, holding the balance among his warring qualities. While they, fighting against one another, have estopped him from working out a notable career as poet or crusader, his sense of humor has gently nudged him into fame. He might have been Shelley; he might have been William Jennings Bryan; he might almost have been Nietzsche or Carrie Nation. His sense of humor resolved him into Don Marquis.

It is the polestar of the personal philosophy by which he contrives to exist. For each of his entities—excepting the humorous imp who is rather an accompanying Socratic demon than a fiber of his being—each phase of his multiple personality is simple and single. There is something childlike about his attitude toward life. He has always wanted a positive answer to everything, and cannot be fobbed off with a complicated series of probabilities dignified by the name of a creed. His intelligence works with the lucidity of a Euclidean formula, operating in the realm of the abstract; and failing of a definite, demonstrable solution, his sense of humor always murmurs, "Which is absurd." His laughter is his sole shield against the appalling incomprehensibility of the universe. But for it he would not know how to stand up to life. Life is ruthless, and he does not understand ruthlessness. Life is hard, and at the core Don Marquis is shrinkingly sensitive. Life is limited, and he is a dreamer who could never set bounds to his aspirations. And life is strangely abrupt, which is most disconcerting to a shy and modest nature.

For he is excessively shy, because his intelligence warned him, sooner than any one else, that he is singularly candid and guileless. Though he is as good company as any man in the world, he is not, in the broad sense of the term, a "good mixer," welcoming casual contacts. He has no other defense than a certain reserve, which cannot be maintained except by some literal distance from his fellows. The truth wells from him naturally; yet he is not unaware that to be transparently truthful is to be at a perpetual disadvantage. It would be quite impossible for him to practice deception. That is where the poet in him undoes him, for a poet's business is to wear his heart upon his sleeve.

Of all living creatures he is most afraid of women, not through any misogynistic tendency, nor because he holds them in low esteem, but to the contrary. His romantic imagination invests them with strange powers and mysteriously dangerous enchantments; while observation has shown him that women much more than men really listen to what is said to them, ponder over and disentangle the meaning of chance revelations. Women have been trained to the task; that is what is called intuition. The amiable and careless egotism of man enables him to forget that he is always in the exposed condition of a glass eel in an aquarium. But women—they look at you, and seem to hear what you say! They are on. And he is not blessed with that jaunty confidence in his own superlative merit which enables other men to bask complacently in feminine glances. He avoids women through an excess of respectful admiration. If he had lived during the Middle Ages, he would have dashed off to the Crusades and stayed there, out of sheer gallantry toward the ladies of his home town.

Failing this resource, he has manufactured the inadequate mask above referred to. It was a desperate expedient. It is purely external, and barely serves to shield him from the hurrying public. In private, he frankly abandons it; he is serious and straightforward. But his need of some protection came near expressing itself in an extreme manner when he was quite young. He yearned to be an actor, tempted by the vast array of ready-made characters which the stage affords for the shelter of the uncertain ego.

Actually, he went on tour with "East Lynne" and "The Hidden Hand," but the company blew up and threw him back into the blazing anonymity of a newspaper office. At the same time, he was toying with the graphic arts, as a student in the Corcoran Galleries at Washington. There were the velveteen jackets and flowing tie to inveigle him. In all these projected activities may be discerned also a hankering for reassurance as well as concealment. Each of them, with luck, brings some reward not only in coin of the realm but in audible applause and praise. The only reason he did not pursue three different careers at once was because of the relativity of space and time. And the reason newspaper work has held him is that of all employments it most gives the sense of being temporary, a mere period of incubation and preparation for some larger effort. On a newspaper, to-morrow is always fraught with magnificent possibilities.

That is where his sense of humor has had a sly chuckle at Don Marquis. It kept him writing until his career could catch up with him, instead of allowing him to use up his energy running after glory.

For he has not consciously striven for the bitter bay leaf, nor its golden equivalent. No man who is in haste to "arrive" will spend a precious day polishing ten lines of verse for an ephemeral newspaper column. Though he has always been a hard worker, it was in the interests of perfection, not for the pay envelope. A profound and genuine idealism made him hold everything easy as suspect. His extensive and obscure apprenticeship to his craft irked him very little. Taking any job that came along, as printer's devil, reporter, section hand, special writer, he cherished no rankling consciousness of injustice. The time would come! Once he was let out of a position as copy reader, and on inquiring, with an honest desire for information, wherein he fell short, was told that he had no sense of humor and no command over the English language. He accepted the verdict without protest, and is not sure yet if he has been able to change that editor's opinion.

On the other hand, he was "discovered" more than once by editors and critics; but it didn't matter. He had not engineered the discovery, nor did he ever utilize any extraneous means of advancing himself. Accepting the ups and downs of existence with puzzled equanimity, he was reasonably content so long as he had an opportunity to do his own work in his own way. The fair rewards were not of the tangible variety. It is himself he is mocking, not unkindly, in the person of Hermione, with her anxious query: "Have I, or have I not, developed myself to-day?"

He would like to do some good in the world; but then he takes a long look at the said world, and another at himself—and bursts into laughter. The Almost Perfect State is a bit of gentle satire directed toward his own tendency to dream of impossibilities. He commutes, not only between Garden City and New York, but between our poor old earth and Cuckoo-Cloudland; he gladly wears the livery of the sober bourgeois so that no one may suspect whither he is bound; and he tells his adventures freely, day by day in his column, so that no one shall guess. They think he is talking about them, not about himself! He is always running into his other selves in unexpected places, tripping himself up. With the manuscript of a religious drama secreted in his pocket, he is capable of denouncing Browning as no better than a Dissenting hot gospeler. His brain teems with the germs of gigantic and weighty *opera,* plays, novels, epic poems; while his hand is turning out the history of Archy the Cockroach. Fundamentally he is so darned serious that he can't keep a straight face over it.

## *XXIX: Joseph Hergesheimer*

JOSEPH HERGESHEIMER is an exquisite, thwarted by adiposity and a malicious Circean fate. He is at heart an eighteenth century dandy in plush pants and ruffled lace; but he looks like a bread-and-pastry dealer with eyebrows arched in perpetual inquiry as to what the customer will have to-day. His soul is the soul of William Hickey, groomed by a Wetzel of a former day, his satin boots spattered by spurting blood in a duet of rapiers, as an entr'acte between epigrams and cocktails. And he lives in West Chester, Pennsylvania, a settlement of Quakers and Scots Presbyterians.

He has his compensations for this disparity between essence and exterior, spirit and flesh, desire and circumstance. He dresses three times a day. He reads "Vogue," the "Gazette du Bon Genre," and the memoirs of the court of Louis XIV. He writes beautiful books, luscious with pretty words, about marionettes whose charm is a matter of fragility, cosmetics, and linen carefully draped. He winks at women with an air of self-confidence and smiles at them as if there were something between him and them. He has assignations with adjectives, love affairs with nouns, and capricious liaisons with adverbs and prepositions. He believes he is an authority on women.

He never wearies of repeating that art comes from the heart and not from the mind. What he means by the heart one is hard put to conjecture. Certainly it is not tenderness and compassion and pity, for his work has the cold shimmer of the glazed surface of a porcelain trinket.

He is a momentarian in his philosophy, with a polite and airy skepticism about the worth and value of character and steadfastness, denial and sacrifice. Like that fanciful philosophic nihilist, Santayana, he is an advocate of "fluttering tip-toe loves," and when he depicts passion it is always with a left impression that it is wasting and a little messy.

He has an oriental's attraction to fabrics, spices, essences, and tinsel items of indulgence. Silks and stained glass, wrought silver and carved panelings catch his eye not only in ensemble but in minutiæ. This suggests an artistic strain at war with a chill impulse to respond reverently to the plastic loveliness of the Winged Victory and the Cytherean goddess. There results at once a balance and an anomaly: his work is neither austere nor hedonistic; it is decorative and Schnitzleresque, with the sub-acid pathos of a Punch and Judy show. It has the ironic sentiment of banjo chords on a moonlit lake while a child of eighteen out of finishing school is drowning herself for love of a gardener.

Hergesheimer's sensory impressions are predominately tactile and visual. There are no odors in his books: he describes even perfumes in terms of sight, as liquids of certain hues and exotic names in beribboned bottles pleasingly shaped. His sense of taste is rudimentary; food interests him only as an arrangement of words in the depiction of a dinner party, and drink is to him a fluid in graceful glasses and with a connotation of luxury. In "Cytherea" he describes a champagne bottle in detail and expatiates upon the process involved in releasing the cork; but he is not concerned with taste and savor. His ear is as deficient as Meredith's, which explains their affinity in style—thought as a sequence of two-dimensional pictures, set off as conversation that is elliptical and funambulesque and is meant to be precise. He thinks in terms

JOSEPH HERGESHEIMER

of sight and touch; and should one seek to reduce his search and interest in life to two words, they would be "elegance" and "charm."

He is extremely sensitive to criticism and this sketch will make him hopping mad. It shouldn't, because it is written by one of his most loyal admirers, by one who thinks that, without question, Hergesheimer is one of the finest novelists now writing in English. But it will.

Four years ago he talked entirely about himself, and the subject became a little shopworn after two hours and a half. But of late he has got about and has achieved a more general fund of ideas. His conversation is brilliant and witty, keen, amusing, and to the point. He talks less about himself, and even when he is his theme, he endows it with a glamour and an interest that is stimulating and entertaining. He is an impatient auditor, but a perfect companion. Believing nothing, he first senses and then feeds one's tastes and biases. He is a facile sophist and the soul of reassurance. He delights to say the thing that will please or irritate; and half the time he doesn't believe what he is saying. He is merely talking from a point of view. And he changes his point of view almost as often as he changes his underwear. His dress is chosen for smartness and for comfort. In the mornings he wears flannel shirts and tweed knickers, in the afternoon a lounge suit, not too snugly tailored, and in the evening dinner dress with a shirt and soft collar of thick silk.

One of his favorite expressions in speech is "utterly charming," and utterly charming describes perfectly his home in West Chester. It is an ancient house built of boulder stones, with huge fireplaces and heavy, seasoned timbers. It sits away from the road on a rounded knoll, a little somber and commanding. Airedales disport themselves on the lawn. Two cars, one Joe's and the other his wife's, are in the ample barn, now equipped as a garage. Servants perfectly trained; furnishings a continual surprise and delight, inevitably placed; and plenty of hot water, a rarity in country homes. Over this demesne rules Mrs. Hergesheimer, frank, cordial, unaffected, wholesome, pretty, and lovable. An agile and alert little bundle of energy, her most constant thought is to make her scribbling husband comfortable and happy.

With such a home one would think that Hergesheimer would do all his writing there, isolated and quiet, among familiar surroundings. Instead he rents a small office opposite the court house in West Chester and arrives there at nine o'clock in the morning, like a business man. He has steel filing cabinets in which he keeps his notes, his correspondence, and the manuscripts of everything he writes. He uses a stub pen and writes the first draft carefully in a grade school composition book. Then his secretary makes a triple-spaced copy on the typewriter. He goes through it carefully, making innumerable changes and corrections. She copies it again, and again he makes corrections. The third draft and even the printer's proof are not free from his rearrangement of words.

He is naïve about these manuscripts. He refuses to part with them, because he believes, rightly, that they will some day be of high monetary value. He is a shrewd business man; knows how to think in terms of money. One of his recent hobbies is the collection of rare books and first editions. He plays this game, I believe, because it is less expensive and pleasanter than playing the stock market. But at bottom it is the same sort of gambling with him. He gets catalogues from the rare-book dealers in every mail, and he reads these through for the rise or fall in the quotations on certain books, just as a gambler in stocks watches the market quotations. He spends at least an hour every morning studying these catalogues, making out his orders to dealers, and figuring out what some of his books are worth. Most of them he has never read.

Hergesheimer inherited a bit of money and a weak constitution. As a boy he was a bookworm, shy and reserved. When money fell into his hands he forthwith got married and lived in Florence. There he suffered a nervous breakdown and was nursed back to health by his wife after months of care and anxiety. He wrote for fourteen years, urged on by a dogged belief in himself, without having a single manuscript accepted. He and Mrs. Hergesheimer bore the pinch of adversity and the rebuffs of editors with fortitude, and the final triumph was therefore all the sweeter. In these years of apprentice work, his masters were Conrad, Henry James Meredith, and Flaubert. His style, even yet, is not fixed and inflexible. It varies between a highly tenuous and involuted prose and a smoothly cadenced manner which is simple and clear. To my mind the very finest writing he has yet published is to be found in two pieces which are widely dissimilar in manner: one of them, "A Scots Grandfather" in "The Reviewer"; the other, "Eight Novels" in "Vanity Fair."

One of Hergesheimer's weaknesses is that of speaking before women's clubs. He is in great demand for that sort of thing. But usually he does not get a second invitation to speak before the same club. He has a faculty for getting himself in bad; he is a consummate egotist and he takes a sadistic delight in saying things which make his audience uncomfortable. Probably nine-tenths of his readers are women, but when he has an audience of women, he usually asperses their intelligence categorically and in detail.

That is a cultivated attitude which feeds his own vanity. When he was in Chicago, he felt called upon to upbraid the citizens for the physical unloveliness of the city. He lamented that the architecture there was not the same as that of Florence. He was invited to speak before a certain club and in sheer perversity failed to show up. When no one later showed concern for his negligence, he called up his hostess five times, trying to get her to arrange another lecture date for him.

Hergesheimer's talents, I believe, are just maturing. He is just now arriving at a mastery of his media of expression. He has only recently attained an æsthetic attitude. He has produced, to date, only two novels with themes which were not factitious: "The Three Black Pennys" and "Cytherea." The others are full of sensuous beauty, colorful, more carefully and more exquisitely written than these two. But it is safe to predict that his forthcoming novels will be novels wherein a finished and polished style will be wedded to a content which itself shall command an interest.

## XXX: *Henry Seidel Canby*

HENRY SEIDEL CANBY—a slice from his life: We rise at 7.30. While we shave we get an idea for an article. At breakfast we recall three engagements which we should have kept, and did not keep, yesterday. Never mind; don't worry! We'll fix them somehow. At nine o'clock we are at the office and we set about editing the review of the moment. This consists of carrying on for several hours the following activities simultaneously. (1) Reading our letters. (2) Dictating replies. (3) Answering telephone calls from (a) the representatives of those three engagements, (b) a man who wants to insure our car, (c) our wife in New Haven to tell us that our eldest child has the mumps, (d) other persons too numerous to mention. (4) Trying to repel, but finally having to interview, the following persons: (a) eleven enthusiasts who, although they are wobbly on spelling and punctuation, want to try their hand at reviewing; (b) an indignant author to protest against the review of his book; (c) a lady who wishes us to endorse her campaign for Pure Literature; (d) some old friends from Wilmington who remember when we were a child and what our curls looked like.

A strenuous and exasperating morning! But we, being Henry Canby, are not ruffled; only a little heated. We lunch with a publisher, an English novelist, and a newspaper man from Washington with a lot of inside information. During luncheon the novelist talks intimately about his work and the newspaper man turns his information inside out. We have a highly interesting time, consent to write an introduction for the American edition of the novelist's work which the publisher has just agreed to bring out, and arrange to dine with the novelist to-morrow—no, let's see, to-morrow we have to represent the older generation at a banquet of the Younger Lions, so we will say the day after to-morrow.

We return to the editorial sanctum—say rather the editorial forum—exhilarated by fresh ideas, new information, and a sense of accomplishment. We try to settle down to do a review, but we are interrupted by a call from an advertising gentleman with ideas of his own about the function of a literary review. It takes us nearly two hours to convince him that while his plan for printing his advertisements upside down would certainly call attention to his books, it would distract attention from the more serious literature which, strangely enough, an editor has sometimes to admit.

After this, dinner at the Players', where we meet more interesting people, is soothing, and we are about to retire to our room to write that review when we are offered a seat for a play we have long wished to see. We accept.

The next day's editorial experiences are like the first, with some conferences and some intricate problems about "overhead" and things like that thrown in. In the evening we dine and speak at the banquet of the Younger Lions. The next evening we dine with the English novelist. He talks until 2 A.M. On the following day we leave for New Haven. We look forward to a quiet week-end there where we can read some contributions and get some writing done. Arrived in New Haven we dash to the University and conduct a class in English. As we reach our home we remember that our eldest child has the mumps. We grow doubtful about that quiet week-end. Our fears become certainties when we find a heap of fifty shrubs by our front door. For, in the intervals of a busy

HENRY SEIDEL CANBY

life, we have found time to build a new house and the shrubs are part of the exterior decoration. They have been deposited here three days too soon by the nurseryman. They must be planted at once. We can get no one to plant them. We plant them ourself. That night we immerse ourself in a bath of Omega Oil and go to sleep murmuring, "Shrubs—mumps, mumps—shrubs, mubs—shrumps."

The next morning our neighbor, Lee Dodd, strolls over. He finds us contemplating thirty unplanted shrubs.

"Better get these shrubs in to-day, Henry," says he.

Any other man would agree and would ruin his muscles, his temper, and his Sunday getting them in. Not so we. Cheerful, confident, playing our luck to the limit, we reply:

"Oh, they will be all right for several days."

We are justified. They get planted eventually. They grow. For any one else they would die.

Monday we take the eight o'clock to New York. We edit until noon, when we entrain for a lecturing tour. We address university audiences, library associations, Rotarians. We compose our speeches en route. After our New York office a Pullman is peace.

We return after a week. Tired? Not a bit of it! We have enjoyed ourself vastly. Our lectures went off well, we made new friends, added to our stock of information, lost our suitcase once, missed trains at least twice, wrote two editorials in the Pullman coming back, and are now all ready for another week of editing.

I hereby declare this to be a truly representative section of the daily life of Henry Canby.

It has been said that the Christian idea of heaven as eternal life is precisely what the Buddhist means by hell. To most men—and by that, of course, I mean to myself—such a daily round as Canby's would be hell, but *he* really enjoys it, thrives on it. I assert this although I am aware that there is a legend in the Canby family that Henry is "not strong." But these things are, after all, relative. I can imagine Delilah remarking to Samson after he had been working in the forest for some hours, "If I were you, dear, I wouldn't pull up any more trees this morning; you know you're not really strong."

But it is not, after all, strength that explains Henry Canby. It is *gusto*. He has an enormous capacity for enjoying experience. Life for him is a series of adventures, exciting, inspiring, or informative. Other men do not happen upon such adventures, or, if they see them coming, they try to dodge them. He either creates them, because man's character is his fate and what one is, that one finds, or, if they come his way, he goes to meet them. Engagements and responsibilities which to others would be a torment in apprehension and in actuality a nightmare mean to him, variously, a railroad he has not traveled on or a range of mountains he has not seen before, new acquaintances, the intimate and amazing confessions of three total strangers, a chance to make the Review better known, another glimpse of the human comedy. He lives in the present because it is absorbing; if it is absorbing that is because he makes it so.

That is the positive side of his temperament. The negative side is this. First, he never worries. He does not borrow trouble. He trusts that the future will take care of itself. If it shouldn't, he is confident in his own ability to take care of it by the time it shall have become present. His bland indifference to the calamitous possibilities of existence is often alarming. I have seen him setting out on a long motor trip in a car which is little more than a fortuitous conglomeration of parts, with four tires which I can best describe as ribbon tires. I have met him an hour before a speech and he has confessed that he did not know even then what he was going to say. On both occasions he arrives. No one else would. Henry Canby's successes are a standing refutation of all the maxims of prudence.

In the second place, he is devoid of self-consciousness. He is always natural, always himself. I will not say that you always know where to find him; on the contrary, he is generally somewhere else; but when you do find him, no matter what his environment, he is always the same man. This goes with living in the present. His eye is on the task in hand. He has no margin of attention to be concerned with a vision of himself in relation to the task.

Such a description, as a man absorbed in the present, is open to misunderstanding, for it implies that critical detachment is absent, and H. S. C. is far from being the victim of his love of life. He is an alert observer and reflects upon what he has observed. How he finds time to think I do not understand. He must do it, as swallows drink—on the wing.

What then is his philosophy, or, if he would disclaim the term as too pompous, what is the general policy of his thinking?

I answer at once: liberalism. And by that I mean two things: first, tolerance; second, sanity. The second is the fruit of the first. For if tolerance increases your sense of the complexity of a problem it also shows you the inadequacy of any one formula or doctrine, with whatever power of passion or of logic it be urged. These virtues are the natural expression of Canby's catholicity of sympathy and they are evident in nearly everything he has written. Read that early volume of his on "College Sons and College Fathers" and see how just he is to the maligned undergraduate, to the harassed instructor, to the well-meaning but ignorant parent. Or turn to his essay on "The Irish Mind." Henry Canby went to Ireland when the clamor of parties and doctrines was loudest and most confusing. He had made no special preliminary study of Irish affairs. He stayed there only a few weeks. Yet his analysis of this most difficult problem was measured, sympathetic, and acute: altogether a notable piece of interpretation. It is this spirit of open-mindedness which recognizes divergent claims, combined with the will to achieve a harmony between them, that really brings about advance in human affairs, and in the world of literary criticism "The Literary Review" was the expression of it. That was its policy, that has been its contribution. Two quotations will give an idea of the way in which Canby, as editor, defined his task.

*The New Republic,* the present *Nation, The Freeman, The Weekly Review,* and, in a little different sense, *The Dial,* were founded by groups held together, with the exception of *The Dial* coterie, not by any common attitude towards literature, or by any specific interest in literature itself, but rather by a common social philosophy. These journals, again with the one exception, were devoted primarily to the application of their respective social philosophies. Even when in reviews or articles there was no direct social application, there was a clear irradiation from within. When *The New Republic* is humorous, it is social-liberal humor. When *The Freeman* is ironic there is usually an indirect reference to the Single Tax. And *The Dial* will be modern or perish. . . . Something more was needed; and specifically literary mediums that should be catholic in criticism, comprehensive in scope, sound, stimulating and accurate.

The reviewer as a liaison officer is a homelier description than soul affinity or intellectual mate, but it is quite as honorable. Books (to the editor) represent, each one of them, so much experience, so much thought, so much imagination, differently compounded into a story, poem, tractate on science, history, or play. Each is a man's most luminous self in words, ready for others. Who wants it? Who can make use of it? Who will be dulled by it? Who exalted? It is the reviewer's task to say. He grasps the book, estimates it, calculates its audience. Then he makes the liaison. . . . The house of the interpreter has become the literary journal.

I think it is fortunate that Henry Canby emerged from academic life into his present sphere of wider activity and wider influence. Not alone because he has found work more congenial to his temperament and greater scope for his talents, but because the public judgment needs to be inspired with his kind of tolerance and sanity. The misfortune of criticism in this country is that it is controlled largely by extremists on one side or the other. Those who achieve reputation and leadership do so not because they are good interpreters, but because they are good fighters. We get much cleverness, much wit, and a skilful scoring of points, but we do not get sweetness or light or understanding or wisdom. Meanwhile, the unhappy individual who looks to the critics for guidance discovers that he is being asked only to exchange his own prejudices and antipathies for those of the critics. The function of the liberal in this predicament is to act as mediator, to put an end to a situation where able minds waste their energies in mutual antagonism. He will teach them to understand one another; he will gently suggest that, whether it be a question of a new idea, or a new book, or a new movement, the critic's business is to make not an issue but a study of it.

Now it is this genuine meeting of minds that is, in Canby's judgment, the proper object of education. This, I think, is the major theme in much that he has written. It informs his discussion of the problems of college education, it appears more than once in "Education by Violence," while his volume of critical essays called "Definitions"—a volume which contains his most mature, vigorous, and incisive work—is prefaced with these words:

Literature in a civilization like ours, which is trying to be both sophisticated and democratic at the same moment of time, is so much involved with our social background, and is so much a question of life as well as of art, that many doors have to be opened before one begins to approach an understanding. The method of informal definition which I have followed in all these essays is an attempt to open doors through which both writer and reader may enter into a better comprehension of what novelists, poets, and critics have done or are trying to accomplish.

Thus the partial transition from the professor's chair to the editor's office has not meant the abandoning of the work of education but an extension of it. For Henry Canby has not only imported fresh meaning into that vague term "a liberal education"; he is helping measurably to establish the thing itself.

# PART TWO

## BOOKS FOR GENERAL REFERENCE

## REFERENCES, BIOGRAPHIES AND BIBLIOGRAPHIES

## BOOKS FOR GENERAL REFERENCE

*Contemporary American Novelists,* 1900-1920, CARL VAN DOREN, The Macmillan Company.

*The Women Who Make Our Novels,* GRANT OVERTON, Dodd, Mead & Company.

*The New Era in American Poetry,* LOUIS UNTERMEYER, Henry Holt & Company.

*New Voices,* MARGUERITE WILKINSON, The Macmillan Company.

*An Anatomy of Poetry,* A. WILLIAMS-ELLIS, The Macmillan Company.

*A Critical Fable,* ANONYMOUS (AMY LOWELL), Houghton Mifflin Company.

*Taking the Literary Pulse,* JOSEPH COLLINS, George H. Doran Company.

*Many Minds,* CARL VAN DOREN, The Macmillan Company.

*The Men Who Make Our Novels,* GEORGE GORDON, Dodd, Mead & Company.

*The American Novel,* CARL VAN DOREN, The Macmillan Company.

*Tendencies in Modern American Poetry,* AMY LOWELL, Houghton Mifflin Company.

*An Introduction to Poetry,* HUBBELL and BEATY, The Macmillan Company.

*The Bookman Anthology of Essays* (1923), JOHN FARRAR (editor), George H. Doran Company.

*Some Contemporary Americans,* PERCY H. BOYNTON, University of Chicago Press.

*Authors of the Day,* GRANT OVERTON, George H. Doran Company.

## SHERWOOD ANDERSON

Sherwood Anderson was born at Camden, Ohio, September 13, 1876. He was educated in the public schools. In addition to his career as a novelist and short-story writer, he has been a writer of advertising copy. Though he has long been identified with Chicago, he is at present living in New Orleans.

---

REFERENCES:

*Contemporary American Novelists,* CARL VAN DOREN, Macmillan.

*A Story Teller's Story,* SHERWOOD ANDERSON, Huebsch.

*Midwest Portraits,* HARRY HANSEN, Harcourt, Brace.

*The Promise of Sherwood Anderson,* ROBERT MORSS LOVETT, *Dial,* January, 1922.

*Sherwood Anderson,* PAUL ROSENFELD, *Dial,* January, 1922.

BIBLIOGRAPHY:

*Windy McPherson's Son,* New York, 1916.
*Marching Men,* New York, 1917.
*Mid-American Chants,* New York, 1918.
*Winesburg, Ohio,* New York, 1919.
*Poor White,* New York, 1920.
*The Triumph of the Egg,* New York, 1921.
*Many Marriages,* New York, 1923.
*Horses and Men,* New York, 1923.
*A Story Teller's Story,* New York, 1924.

## MARY AUSTIN

Mary Hunter Austin was born at Carlinville, Illinois, September 9, 1868. She was graduated from Blackburn University in 1888, and was married to Stafford W. Austin, of Bakersfield, California, in 1891. She is a constant contributor to the magazines, lecturer, novelist, poet, playwright. She has made a deep study of the American Indian. She divides her time between New York City and California and New Mexico.

---

REFERENCES:

*The Women Who Make Our Novels,* GRANT OVERTON, Dodd, Mead.

*Contemporary American Novelists,* CARL VAN DOREN, Macmillan.

*Many Minds,* CARL VAN DOREN, Macmillan.

BIBLIOGRAPHY:

*The Land of Little Rain,* Boston, 1903.
*The Basket Woman,* Boston, 1904.
*Isidre,* Boston, 1905.
*The Flock,* Boston, 1906.
*Santa Lucia,* New York, 1908.
*Lost Borders,* New York, 1909.
*Christ in Italy,* New York, 1911.
*A Woman of Genius,* Boston, 1912.
*The Lovely Lady,* Garden City, 1913.
*Love and the Soul-Maker,* New York, 1914.
*The Man Jesus,* New York, 1915.
*The Ford,* Boston, 1917.
*The Young Woman Citizen,* New York, 1918.
*Outland,* New York, 1919.

*Twenty-six Jayne Street,* Boston, 1920.
*The American Rhythm,* New York, 1923.

PLAYS

*The Arrow Maker,* Boston, 1911.
*Fire,* 1914.
*The Man Who Didn't Believe in Christmas,* 1916.

## WILLIAM ROSE BENÉT

William Rose Benét was born at Fort Hamilton, New York Harbor, February 2, 1886. He was educated at Albany Academy and was graduated from the Sheffield Scientific School, Yale University, in 1907. He has been twice married, the second time to Elinor Wylie, the poet. He has been free lance writer, editor and journalist. His home is in New York City, where he was associate editor of the *Literary Review* of the New York *Evening Post.* He now occupies this post on the new *Saturday Review of Literature.*

---

REFERENCES:

*The New Era in American Poetry,* LOUIS UNTERMEYER, Holt.
*New Voices,* MARGUERITE WILKINSON, Macmillan.
*The Poetry of Benét, Dial,* January 16, 1914.

BIBLIOGRAPHY:

*Merchants from Cathay,* New Haven, 1913.
*The Falconer of God,* New Haven, 1914.
Collaborated with wife in translation of *The East I Know* (by PAUL CLAUDEL), New Haven, 1914.
*The Great White Wall,* New Haven, 1916.
*The Burglar of the Zodiac,* New Haven, 1918.
*Perpetual Light,* New Haven, 1919.
*Moons of Grandeur,* New York, 1920.
*The First Person Singular,* New York, 1922.

## HEYWOOD BROUN

Heywood Broun was born at Brooklyn, New York, December 7, 1888. He was a student at Harvard University for some years. He was married to Ruth Hale, a writer, in 1917. He has been a reporter, feature writer and columnist with various New York newspapers. He is still active in his journalistic career, being connected with the New York *World*. He lives in New York City and is known as essayist and novelist as well as dramatic critic and sport writer.

---

REFERENCES:

*Many Minds,* CARL VAN DOREN, Macmillan.

*Heywood Broun,* by Himself, *Nation,* October 10, 1923.

BIBLIOGRAPHY:

*The A. E. F.,* New York, 1918.

*Seeing Things at Night,* New York, 1921.

*Pieces of Hate,* New York, 1922.

*The Boy Grew Older,* New York, 1922.

*The Sun Field,* New York, 1923.

## JAMES BRANCH CABELL

James Branch Cabell was born at Richmond, Virginia, April 14, 1879. He was graduated from William and Mary College in 1898. He has taught French and Greek, and has made various studies in genealogy. His present home is at Dumbarton Grange, Dumbarton, Virginia.

---

REFERENCES:

*The Art of James Branch Cabell,* HUGH WALPOLE, McBride.

*The American Novel,* CARL VAN DOREN, Macmillan.

*Contemporary American Novelists,* CARL VAN DOREN, Macmillan.

*The Men Who Make Our Novels,* GEORGE GORDON, Dodd, Mead.

*James Branch Cabell;* an introduction, JOHN GUNTHER, *Bookman,* November, 1920.

BIBLIOGRAPHY:

*The Eagle's Shadow,* New York, 1904.
*The Line of Love,* New York, 1905.
*Gallantry,* New York, 1907.
*The Cords of Vanity,* New York, 1905.
*Branchiana,* Richmond, 1907.
*Chivalry,* New York, 1909.
*Branch of Abingdon,* Richmond, 1911.
*The Soul of Melicent,* New York, 1913.
*The Majors and Their Marriages,* Richmond, 1915.
*From the Hidden Way,* New York, 1916.
*The Certain Hour,* New York, 1916.
*The Cream of the Jest,* New York, 1917.

*Beyond Life,* New York, 1919.
*Jurgen,* New York, 1919.
*Jurgen and the Censor,* New York, 1920.
*Figures of Earth,* New York, 1921.
*Taboo,* New York, 1921.
*The Lineage of Lichfield,* New York, 1922.
*Joseph Hergesheimer,* Chicago, 1922.
*The High Place,* New York, 1924.

## HENRY SEIDEL CANBY

Henry Canby was born at Wilmington, Delaware, in 1878. He was graduated from and took postgraduate work at Yale University, where he shortly afterward became a teacher. He has never completely given over his professorial connection at Yale and still lives in New Haven, commuting to New York City where he has undertaken the profession of literary journalism. He edited for a time *The Literary Review* of the New York *Evening Post.* From this he turned to his own magazine, published in association with *Time,* and called *The Saturday Review.*

---

REFERENCE:

*Modern Essays,* Second Series, CHRISTOPHER MORLEY, Harcourt, Brace.

BIBLIOGRAPHY:

*The Short Story,* New Haven, 1902.
*The Short Story in English,* New York, 1909.
*A Study of the Short Story,* New York, 1913.
*College Sons and College Fathers,* New York, 1915.
*Education by Violence,* New York, 1919.
*Our House,* New York, 1919.
*Everyday Americans,* New York, 1920.
*Definitions,* New York, 1922.
*Definitions,* Second Series, New York, 1924.

EDITOR

*Antony and Cleopatra,* New Haven, 1921.

Co-author or Co-editor

*The Book of the Short Story,* New York, 1903.
*English Composition in Theory and Practice,* New York, 1909.
*Selections from Robert Louis Stevenson,* New York, 1911.
*Elements of Composition,* New York, 1913.
*Selections from Masefield,* New York, 1917.
*Facts, Thought and Imagination,* New York, 1917.
*Good English,* New York, 1918.
*War Aims and Peace Ideals,* New Haven, 1919.
*Saturday Papers,* New York, 1921.

## PADRAIC COLUM

Padraic Colum was born in the town of Longford, in the Irish Midlands. At eighteen he entered a railway office in Dublin as a clerk. He learned about verse from W. B. Yeats and A. E. and about plays from the men and women who were building up the Irish Theatre. His wife, Mary Colum, is a critic of ability. He has become strongly identified with America, and makes his home in New York City.

---

REFERENCES:

*Irish Plays and Playwrights*, CORNELIUS WEYGANDT, Houghton Mifflin.

*An Irish Folk-Dramatist, Padraic Colum,* ERNEST BOYD, *Irish Monthly*, Dublin, 1917. V. 45, P. 718-725.

*Poetry of Padraic Colum,* LEWELYN POWYS, *Freeman,* June, 1923.

---

BIBLIOGRAPHY:

* *The Land,* Dublin, 1905.

* *The Fiddler's House,* Dublin, 1907.

* *Thomas Muskerry,* Dublin, 1910.

*Wild Earth,* Dublin, 1907. New York, 1922.

*My Irish Year,* London, 1912.

*Mogu the Wanderer,* Boston, 1916. New York, 1923.

*The King of Ireland's Son,* New York, 1916.

*The Adventures of Odysseus and the Tale of Troy,* New York, 1918.

* Included in *Three Plays,* Boston, 1916, New York, 1924.

*The Boy Who Knew What the Birds Said,* New York, 1918.
*The Girl Who Sat by the Ashes,* New York, 1919.
*The Children of Odin,* New York, 1920.
*The Boy Apprenticed to an Enchanter,* New York, 1920.
*The Golden Fleece,* New York, 1921.
*The Children Who Followed the Piper,* New York, 1922.
*Anthology of Irish Verse,* New York, 1922.
*Castle Conquer,* New York, 1923.

## FLOYD DELL

Floyd Dell was born at Barry, Illinois, June 28, 1887. He has been married twice. He has served in various journalistic capacities, as reporter, editor, literary critic, on various newspapers and magazines. Of late years he has devoted himself largely to novel writing. His home is at Croton-on-Hudson, New York.

---

REFERENCE:

*Contemporary American Novelists,* CARL VAN DOREN, Macmillan.

BIBLIOGRAPHY:

*Women as World Builders: Studies in Modern Feminism,* Chicago, 1913.
*The Angel Intrudes, a Comedy,* New York, 1918.
*Were You Ever a Child?* New York, 1919.
*Moon-Calf: a Novel,* New York, 1920.
*The Briary-Bush,* New York, 1921.
*Janet March,* New York, 1923.
*Looking at Life,* New York, 1924.

### PLAYS

*Sweet-and-Twenty, a Comedy,* Cincinnati, 1921.
*King Arthur's Socks and Other Village Plays,* New York, 1922.

## JOHN FARRAR

John (Chipman) Farrar was born at Burlington, Vermont, February 25, 1896. He was entered in the class of 1918 at Yale University, spent a year in military service, and was graduated in 1919. He is unmarried. He has been a reporter and is at present editor of *The Bookman.* His home is in New York City.

---

BIBLIOGRAPHY:

*Forgotten Shrines,* New Haven, 1919.
*Songs for Parents,* New Haven, 1921.
*The Middle Twenties,* New York, 1924.

EDITOR

*The Bookman Anthology of Verse (1922)*, New York, 1922.
*The Bookman Anthology of Essays,* New York, 1923.
*The Bookman Anthology of Verse, Second Series,* New York, 1924.
*The Literary Spotlight,* New York, 1924.

PLAYS

*A Pageant,* Burlington, Vermont, 1910.
*Firewater,* Burlington, Vermont, 1912.
*Dreams of Boyhood,* Burlington, Vermont, 1924.
*The Magic Sea Shell and Other Plays for Children,* New York, 1923.
*The Awful Mrs. Eaton* (with Stephen Vincent Benét), 1924.
*Nerves* (one act), Included in *The Atlantic Book of Junior Plays,* Boston, 1924.
*Nerves* (three acts) (with Stephen Vincent Benét), 1924.

## EDNA FERBER

Edna Ferber was born at Kalamazoo, Michigan, August 15, 1887. She was educated in the public and high schools of Appleton, Wisconsin. She is unmarried. She was a reporter on various newspapers until she took up short story writing for the magazines. Her time is divided between New York City and Chicago.

---

REFERENCES:

*The Women Who Make Our Novels,* GRANT OVERTON, Dodd, Mead.

*Odd Women and The Girls,* W. P. ALLEN, *North American Review,* November, 1922.

BIBLIOGRAPHY:

*Dawn O'Hara,* New York, 1911.
*Buttered Side Down,* New York, 1912.
*Roast Beef Medium,* New York, 1913.
*Personality Plus,* New York, 1914.
*Emma McChesney & Co.,* New York, 1915.
*Fanny Herself,* New York, 1917.
*Cheerful—By Request,* New York, 1918.
*Half Portions,* New York, 1920.
*The Girls,* Garden City, 1921.
*Gigolo,* Garden City, 1922.
*So Big,* Garden City, 1924.

PLAYS

*Our Mrs. McChesney* (with George V. Hobart), 1915.
*$1200 a Year* (with Newman Levy), New York, 1920.

## F. SCOTT FITZGERALD

(Francis Scott Key) Fitzgerald was born at St. Paul, Minnesota, September 24, 1896. He entered Princeton University in 1913 but left in 1917 to join the army. He was married in 1920 and has one child. His home is at Great Neck, Long Island.

---

REFERENCES:

*Contemporary American Novelists,* CARL VAN DOREN, Macmillan.

*What I Think and Feel at 25,* F. SCOTT FITZGERALD, *American Magazine,* September, 1922.

BIBLIOGRAPHY:

*This Side of Paradise,* New York, 1920.
*Flappers and Philosophers,* New York, 1920.
*The Beautiful and Damned,* New York, 1922.
*Tales of the Jazz Age,* New York, 1922.

PLAY

*The Vegetable,* New York, 1923.

## ROBERT FROST

Robert Frost was born at San Francisco, California, March 26, 1875. He was a student both at Dartmouth and at Harvard Universities. He was married in 1895. He has been farmer, teacher and poet. His home is at South Shaftsbury, Vermont; but he is at present teaching English at Amherst College.

---

REFERENCES:

*Friday Nights,* EDWARD GARNETT, Knopf.
*The New Era in American Poetry,* LOUIS UNTERMEYER, Holt.
*Tendencies in Modern American Poetry,* AMY LOWELL, Houghton Mifflin.
*New Voices,* MARGUERITE WILKINSON, Macmillan.
*A Critical Fable,* ANONYMOUS, Houghton Mifflin.
*Our America,* WALDO FRANK, Boni, Liveright.
*Many Minds,* CARL VAN DOREN, Macmillan.

BIBLIOGRAPHY:

*A Boy's Will,* London, 1913.
*North of Boston,* London, 1914.
*Mountain Interval,* New York, 1916.
*New Hampshire,* New York, 1923.

PLAY

*A Way Out* (one act), *Seven Arts,* February, 1917.

## HENRY BLAKE FULLER

Henry Blake Fuller was born at Chicago in 1857. He has lived there practically ever since. Intending to be a musician, he found himself a bookkeeper, saved enough money for a trip to Italy, and there gained the idea for his first novel. He has always lived a quiet, retiring life, although he retains an active interest in the affairs of writing and has been of much service as consultant to Harriet Monroe in the administration of *Poetry*.

---

REFERENCES:

*Contemporary American Novelists,* CARL VAN DOREN, Macmillan.

*The Men Who Make Our Novels,* GEORGE GORDON, Dodd, Mead.

*Heroines of Fiction,* W. D. HOWELLS, Harper.

BIBLIOGRAPHY:

*The Chevalier of Pensieri-Vani,* Boston, 1890.
*The Chatelaine of La Trinité,* New York, 1892.
*With the Procession,* New York, 1895.
*From the Other Side,* Boston, 1898.
*The New Flag,* Chicago, 1899.
*Lines Long and Short,* Boston, 1917.
*Bertram Cope's Year,* Chicago, 1919.

PLAY

*The Puppet-Booth,* New York, 1896.

## JOSEPH HERGESHEIMER

Joseph Hergesheimer was born at Philadelphia, Pennsylvania, February 15, 1880. He was educated at a Quaker School in Philadelphia and at the Pennsylvania Academy of Fine Arts. His career has been as a man of letters. He is married and lives in West Chester, Pa.

---

REFERENCES:

*The Men Who Make Our Novels,* GEORGE GORDON, Dodd, Mead.

*Contemporary American Novelists,* CARL VAN DOREN, Macmillan.

*Our Short Story Writers,* BLANCHE COLTON WILLIAMS, Dodd, Mead.

*Joseph Hergesheimer: the Man and His Books,* LLEWELLYN JONES, Knopf.

*Joseph Hergesheimer, an Essay in Interpretation,* JAMES BRANCH CABELL, The Bookfellows, 1911.

*Joseph Hergesheimer,* WILSON FOLLETT (pamphlet), Knopf, 1920.

*Friday Nights,* EDWARD GARNETT, Knopf.

BIBLIOGRAPHY:

*The Lay Anthony,* New York, 1914.

*Mountain Blood,* New York, 1915.

*The Three Black Pennys,* New York, 1917.

*Gold and Iron,* New York, 1918.

*Java Head,* New York, 1919.

*The Happy End,* New York, 1919.

*Linda Condon,* New York, 1919.

*Hugh Walpole, an Appreciation,* New York, 1919

*San Cristobal de la Habana,* New York, 1920.
*Cytherea,* New York, 1922.
*The Bright Shawl,* New York, 1922.
*Tubal Cain,** New York, 1922.
*The Dark Fleece,** New York, 1922.
*Wild Oranges,** New York, 1922.
*The Presbyterian Child,* New York, 1923.
*Balisand,* New York, 1924.

* Included in *Gold and Iron.*

## FANNIE HURST

Fannie Hurst was born at St. Louis, October 19, 1889. She was educated at Washington University and at Columbia. She has served in various capacities as salesgirl, etc., to gather material for her short stories and novels. She is married and lives in New York City.

---

REFERENCES:

*The Women Who Make Our Novels,* GRANT OVERTON, Dodd, Mead.
*Taking the Literary Pulse,* JOSEPH COLLINS, Doran.
*How I Got Where I Am,* J. ALDEN BRETT, *Success,* June, 1924.

BIBLIOGRAPHY:

*Just Around the Corner,* New York, 1914.
*Every Soul Hath Its Song,* New York, 1916.
*Gaslight Sonatas,* New York, 1918.
*Humoresque,* New York, 1919.
*Star Dust,* New York, 1921.
*The Vertical City,* New York, 1922.
*Lummox,* New York, 1923.

PLAYS

*Land of the Free,* 1917.
*Back Pay,* 1921.
*Humoresque,* 1923.

## OWEN JOHNSON

Owen (McMahon) Johnson was born at New York City, August 27, 1878. His father is Robert Underwood Johnson, the author and editor. He was educated at Lawrenceville and at Yale University, from which institution he was graduated in 1900. He is married and lives in New York City. He is a member of the National Institute of Arts and Letters and a Chevalier, Legion d'Honneur, France.

---

REFERENCE:

*The Men Who Make Our Novels,* GEORGE GORDON, Dodd, Mead.

BIBLIOGRAPHY:

*Arrows of the Almighty,* New York, 1901.
*In the Name of Liberty,* New York, 1905.
*Max Fargus,* New York, 1906.
*The Eternal Boy,* New York, 1909.
*The Humming Bird,* New York, 1910.
*The Varmint,* New York, 1910.
*The Tennessee Shad,* New York, 1911.
*Stover at Yale,* New York, 1911.
*The Sixty-First Second,* New York, 1912.
*Murder in Any Degree,* New York, 1913.
*The Salamander,* Indianapolis, 1913.
*Making Money,* New York, 1914.
*The Woman Gives,* Boston, 1915.
*The Spirit of France,* Boston, 1915.
*Virtuous Wives,* Boston, 1917.

*The Wasted Generation,* Boston, 1921.
*Skippy Bedelle,* Boston, 1922.
*Blue Blood,* Boston, 1924.

PLAYS

*The Comet,* 1908.
*A Comedy for Wives,* 1911.

## MARY JOHNSTON

Mary Johnston was born at Buchanan, Botetourt County, Virginia, November 21, 1870. She was educated at home and she is unmarried. For many years, she has been a novelist of popularity. Her present home is "Three Hills," Warm Springs, Virginia.

---

REFERENCES:

*The Women Who Make Our Novels,* GRANT OVERTON, Dodd, Mead.

*Contemporary American Novelists,* CARL VAN DOREN, Macmillan

BIBLIOGRAPHY:

*Prisoners of Hope,* Boston, 1898.

*To Have and to Hold,* Boston, 1900.

*Audrey,* Boston, 1902.

*Sir Mortimer,* New York, 1904.

*Lewis Rand,* Boston, 1908.

*The Long Roll,* Boston, 1911.

*Cease Firing,* Boston, 1912.

*Hagar,* Boston, 1913.

*The Witch,* Boston, 1914.

*The Fortunes of Garin,* Boston, 1915.

*The Wanderers,* Boston, 1917.

*Pioneers of the Old South,* (In "Chronicles of America Series"), New Haven, 1917.

*Foes,* New York, 1918.

*Michael Forth,* New York, 1919.

*Sweet Rocket,* New York, 1920.

*Silver Cross,* Boston, 1921.
*1492,* Boston, 1922.
*Croatan,* Boston, 1923.

PLAY

*The Goddess of Reason,* Boston, 1907.

## SINCLAIR LEWIS

Sinclair Lewis was born at Sauk Centre, Minnesota, February 7, 1885. He was graduated from Yale University in 1907. He has served in various capacities as a journalist and as editor to a publishing house. He was married in 1914. His first success as an author was with his short stories. He had written, however, several novels before the sensational "Main Street."

"Now 'Main Street,' a criticism of contemporary life with special reference to its interest and beauty, is important to us socially because, more thoroughly than any novel since 'Uncle Tom's Cabin,' it has shaken our complacency with regard to the average quality of our civilization"—Stuart Pratt Sherman.

---

REFERENCES:

*The Significance of Sinclair Lewis,* STUART PRATT SHERMAN, Harcourt, Brace.

*Contemporary American Novelists,* CARL VAN DOREN, Macmillan.

*How I Wrote a Novelette, American Magazine,* April, 1921.

BIBLIOGRAPHY:

*Our Mr. Wrenn,* New York, 1914.

*The Trail of the Hawk,* New York, 1915.

*The Job,* New York, 1917.

*The Innocents,* New York, 1917.

*Free Air,* New York, 1919.

*Main Street*, New York, 1920.
*Babbitt*, New York, 1922.

PLAY

*Hobohemia*, New York, 1919.

## AMY LOWELL

Amy Lowell was born at Brookline, Massachusetts, February 9, 1874. She was educated in private schools. She has received various degrees and honors from various universities. Her works of criticism and her poetry as well as her lectures at universities and elsewhere have made her well known as a literary figure in America. Her home is at Brookline, Massachusetts.

---

REFERENCES:

*The New Era in American Poetry,* LOUIS UNTERMEYER, Holt.

*New Voices,* MARGUERITE WILKINSON, Macmillan.

*An Anatomy of Poetry,* A. WILLIAMS-ELLIS, Macmillan.

*Amy Lowell, Sketches Biographical and Critical,* RICHARD HUNT and ROYALL H. SNOW, Houghton Mifflin.

*A Critical Fable,* ANONYMOUS, Houghton Mifflin.

*Our America,* WALDO FRANK, Boni, Liveright.

*Our Poets of To-day,* HOWARD WILLARD COOK, Dodd, Mead.

*Amy Lowell: a Personality,* HELEN BULLIS KIZER, *North American Review,* May, 1918.

*New Verse and New Prose,* W. M. PATTERSON, *North American Review,* February, 1918.

*The Poetry of Amy Lowell,* JAMES W. TUPPER, *Sewanee Review,* January-March, 1920.

*Amy Lowell and the Pretorian Cohorts,* JOSEPHINE HAMMOND, *Personalist,* October, 1920.

*Amy Lowell, Poet-Critic of Massachusetts Bay,* NORREYS JEPHSON O'CONOR, *Landmark,* January, 1922.

BIBLIOGRAPHY:

*A Dome of Many Coloured Glass,* Boston, 1912.

*Sword Blades and Poppy Seed,* New York, 1914.

*Six French Poets,* New York, 1915.

*Men, Women and Ghosts,* New York, 1916.

*Tendencies in Modern American Poetry,* New York, 1917.

*Can Grande's Castle,* New York, 1918.

*Pictures of the Floating World,* New York, 1919.

*Legends,* Boston, 1921.

*Fir Flower Tablets,* Boston, 1921.
(Poems translated from the Chinese.) With Florence Ayscough. English versions by Amy Lowell.

*A Critical Fable,* Boston, 1923.

*Pierrot Qui Pleure et Pierrot Qui Rit,* Boston, 1914.
By Edmond Rostand, translated by Amy Lowell.

## DON MARQUIS

Donald Robert Perry Marquis was born at Walnut, Illinois, July 19, 1878. He is a newspaper man, short-story writer, poet and columnist, a member of the American Institute of Arts and Letters. He lives on Long Island near New York and is at present a member of the staff of the New York *Herald-Tribune.*

---

REFERENCES:

*Day In and Day Out, Adams, Morley, Marquis and Broun, Manhattan Wits,* CARL VAN DOREN, *Century,* December, 1923.

*Don Marquis, American Minstrel, Current Opinion,* November, 1922.

*Don Marquis of the Evening Sun, Everybody's,* June, 1916.

BIBLIOGRAPHY:

*Dreams and Dust,* New York, 1915.

*Hermione,* New York, 1916.

*The Cruise of the Jasper B.,* New York, 1916.

*Prefaces,* New York, 1919.

*Carter and Other People,* New York, 1921.

*Noah an' Jonah an' Cap'n John Smith,* New York, 1921.

*The Old Soak and Hail and Farewell,* Garden City, 1921.

*Poems and Portraits,* Garden City, 1922.

*The Revolt of the Oyster,* Garden City, 1922.

*The Old Soak's History of the World,* Garden City, 1924.

*Pandora Lifts the Lid* (with Christopher Morley), New York, 1924.

## EDGAR LEE MASTERS

Edgar Lee Masters was born at Garnett, Kansas, August 23, 1869. He was educated at high school and at Knox College, Illinois, studied law in his father's office and was admitted to the bar in 1891. He was married in 1898. He is a member of the National Institute of Arts and Letters. His present home is in Chicago, Illinois.

---

REFERENCES:

*Tendencies in Modern American Poetry,* AMY LOWELL, Houghton Mifflin.

*The New Era in American Poetry,* LOUIS UNTERMEYER, Holt.

*Midwest Portraits,* HARRY HANSEN, *Harcourt, Brace.*

*New Voices,* MARGUERITE WILKINSON, Macmillan.

*A Critical Fable,* ANONYMOUS, Houghton Mifflin.

*Poets of the People,* MARGUERITE WILKINSON, *Touchstone,* May, 1916.

*Frost and Masters, Poetry,* January, 1917.

*Contemporary Poetry—News and Reviews,* JESSIE B. RITTENHOUSE, *Bookman,* May, 1918.

*Poets as People,* JOYCE KILMER, *Bookman,* November, 1916.

BIBLIOGRAPHY:

*Great Valley,* New York, 1916.

*Songs and Satires,* New York, 1916.

*Spoon River Anthology,* New York, 1916.

*Tendencies in Modern American Poetry* (in conjunction with A. Lowell), New York, 1917.

*Toward the Gulf,* New York, 1918.

*Starved Rock,* New York, 1918.
*Mitch Miller,* New York, 1920.
*Domesday Book,* New York, 1920.
*The Open Sea,* New York, 1921.
*Children of the Market Place,* New York, 1922.
*Skeeters Kirby,* New York, 1923.
*Mirage,* New York, 1924.

PLAYS

*The Locket* (Three act play), Chicago, 1910.
*Maximilian,* Boston, 1910.

## BRANDER MATTHEWS

(James) Brander Matthews was born at New Orleans, Louisiana, February 21, 1852. He was graduated from Columbia University in 1871 and has received post graduate and honorary degrees from various other universities. He was married in 1873. He studied law and was admitted to the bar in 1873; but turned to literature and is well known as teacher, critic, novelist, playwright, essayist, editor, and student of the drama. He lives in New York City and he is emeritus professor of dramatic literature at Columbia University.

---

REFERENCES:

*American Authors and Their Homes,* F. W. HALSEY, Pott.

*Cosmopolitan Critic,* W. L. PHELPS, *Forum,* January, 1908.

BIBLIOGRAPHY:

*The Theatres of Paris,* New York, 1880.

*French Dramatists of the Nineteenth Century,* New York, 1881.

*The Home Library,* New York, 1883, (Arthur Penn, pseud.).

*In Partnership* (in collaboration with H. C. Bunner), New York, 1884.

*The Last Meeting,* New York, 1885.

*A Secret of the Sea,* New York, 1886.

*Pen and Ink,* New York, 1888.

*Cheap Books and Good Books,* New York, 1888.

*A Family Tree,* New York, 1889.

*American Authors and British Pirates,* New York, 1889.

*With My Friends; Tales Told in Partnership,* New York, 1891.

*Americanisms and Briticisms,* New York, 1892.

*In the Vestibule Limited,* New York, 1892.

*A Tale of Twenty-five Hours* (in collaboration with George H. Jessop), New York, 1892.

*Tom Paulding,* New York, 1892.

*The Story of a Story,* New York, 1893.

*Vignettes of Manhattan,* New York, 1894.

*The Royal Marine; an Idyl of Narragansett Pier,* New York, 1894.

*Studies of the Stage,* New York, 1894.

*Bookbindings, Old and New,* New York, 1895.

*Books and Play-Books,* London, 1895.

*His Father's Son,* New York, 1896.

*Tales of Fantasy and Fact,* New York, 1896.

*An Introduction to the Study of American Literature,* New York, 1896.

*Aspects of Fiction,* New York, 1896.

*A Confident To-morrow,* New York, 1899.

*The Action and the Word,* New York, 1900.

*The Historical Novel,* New York, 1901.

*Parts of Speech; Essays on English,* New York, 1901.

*The Philosophy of the Short-Story,* New York, 1901.

*Notes on Speech-Making,* New York, 1901.

*The Development of the Drama,* New York, 1903.

*Recreations of an Anthologist,* New York, 1904.

*American Character,* New York, 1906.

*The Spelling of Yesterday and the Spelling of To-morrow,* New York, 1906.

*Inquiries and Opinions,* New York, 1907.

*Life and Art of Edwin Booth* (with Laurence Hutton), Boston, 1907.

*The Spelling of the Poets,* New York, 1908.
*The American of the Future; and Other Essays,* New York, 1909.
*Molière; His Life and His Works,* New York, 1910.
*The Study of the Drama,* Boston, 1910.
*A Study in Versification,* Boston, 1911.
*Fugitives from Justice,* New York, 1912.
*Vistas of New York,* New York, 1912.
*Gateways to Literature; and Other Essays,* New York, 1912.
*Shakspere as a Playwright,* New York, 1913.
*On Acting,* New York, 1914.
*Do We Want Half the Hemisphere* (with N. M. Butler), New York, 1916.
*A Book About the Theatre,* New York, 1916.
*These Many Years; Recollections of a New Yorker,* New York, 1917.
*The Principles of Playmaking, and Other Discussions of the Drama,* New York, 1919.
*Englishing of French Words,* Oxford, 1921.
*Essays on English,* New York, 1921.
*Vignettes of Manhattan; Outlines in Local Color,* New York, 1921.
*The Tocsin of Revolt, and Other Essays,* New York, 1922.
*Playwrights and Playmaking, and Other Studies of the Stage,* New York, 1923.

PLAYS

*Edged Tools,* New York, 1873.
*Margery's Lovers,* London, 1884; New York, 1895.
*A Gold Mine* (in collaboration with George H. Jessop), 1887, published, 1908.

*This Picture and That* (one-act comedy), 1887, published, 1894.

*On Probation* (in collaboration with George H. Jessop), 1889.

*The Decision of the Court* (one-act comedy), published, 1893.

*Peter Stuyvesant, Governor of New Amsterdam* (in collaboration with Bronson Howard), 1889.

EDITOR

*Comedies for Amateur Acting,* New York, 1880.

*Poems of American Patriotism,* New York, 1882.

*The Rhymester; or The Rules of Rhyme,* by THOMAS HOOD, (Arthur Penn, pseud.), New York, 1882.

*Sheridan's Comedies,* with a Life, Boston, 1885.

*Actors and Actresses of Great Britain and the United States* (in collaboration with Laurence Hutton), New York, 1886.

*Ballads of Books,* New York, 1887.

*Retrospections of America,* by JOHN BERNARD (in collaboration with Laurence Hutton), New York, 1887.

*Andre, by* WILLIAM DUNLAP, New York, 1887.

*Dramatic Essays,* by CHARLES LAMB, New York, 1891.

*David Garrick and His Contemporaries* (in collaboration with Laurence Hutton), Boston, 1900.

*American Familiar Verse; Vers de Société,* New York, 1904.

*Songs from the Dramatists,* by BELL, New York, 1905.

*The Short-Story; Specimens Illustrating its Development,* New York, 1908.

*The Oxford Book of American Essays,* New York, 1914.

*New Art of Making Plays in These Times,* by LOPE DE VEGA, New York, 1914.

*Mrs. Siddons as Lady Macbeth,* by FLEMING JENKINS, New York, 1915.

*Chief European Dramatists,* Boston, 1916.

*Shaksperian Studies* (in collaboration with Ashley H. Thorndike), New York, 1916.

*Theory of the Theatre,* by SARCEY, New York, 1916.

HUXLEY'S *Autobiography and Essays,* New York, 1919.

*Letters of an Old Playgoer,* by MATTHEW ARNOLD, New York, 1919.

*Chief British Dramatists* (in collaboration with Paul R. Lieder), 1924.

## H. L. MENCKEN

Henry Louis Mencken was born at Baltimore, Maryland, September 12, 1880. He was graduated from Baltimore Polytechnic in 1896. He is unmarried, and he has always engaged in the profession of journalism, being reporter, city editor of the Baltimore *Sun,* then magazine editor. For many years, with George Jean Nathan, he edited *The Smart Set.* These co-editors have now embarked on a new enterprise, the establishing and editing of a new monthly journal of literary and critical opinion, *The American Mercury.* Mr. Mencken lives in Baltimore; but spends a part of every week in New York City.

---

REFERENCES:

*Side Lights on American Literature,* FRED LEWIS PATTEE, Century.

*H. L. Mencken,* BURTON RASCOE AND VINCENT O'SULLIVAN, Knopf.

*H. L. Mencken,* ISAAC GOLDBERG, Haldeman-Julius.

*Smartness and Light: H. L. Mencken, A Gadfly for Democracy,* CARL VAN DOREN, *Century,* March, 1923.

*Near Machiavelli,* WALTER LIPPMANN, *New Republic,* May 31, 1922.

*Appreciation,* EDMUND WILSON, JR., *New Republic,* June 1, 1921.

*H. L. Mencken,* By Himself, *Nation,* December 5, 1923.

BIBLIOGRAPHY:

*Ventures Into Verse,* Baltimore, 1903.
*George Bernard Shaw,* Boston, 1905
*Philosophy of Friedrich Nietzsche,* Boston, 1908.
*The Artist,* Boston, 1912.
*A Little Book in C Major,* New York, 1916.
*A Book of Burlesques,* New York, 1916.
*A Book of Prefaces,* New York, 1917.
*Damn! A Book of Calumny,* New York, 1918.
*In Defense of Women,* New York, 1918.
*The American Language,* New York, 1919.
*Prejudices,* First Series, New York, 1919.
*Prejudices,* Second Series, New York, 1920.
*Literary Capital of the United States,* Pamphlet, Chicago, 1920.
*Prejudices,* Third Series, New York, 1922.
*A Personal Word,* Pamphlet, New York, 1922.
*Men Versus the Man,* (in collaboration with Robert Rives La Monte), New York, 1910.
*Europe After 8:15,* New York, 1914, (George Jean Nathan and Willard Huntington Wright, co-authors).

PLAY

*Heliogabalus,* New York, 1920, (George Jean Nathan, co-author).

## EDNA ST. VINCENT MILLAY

Edna St. Vincent Millay was born at Rockland, Maine, February 22, 1892. She was graduated from Vassar College in 1917. She was married in 1923. She has been a frequent contributor of poems to the magazines and of stories and essays under a nom de plume. She was awarded the Pulitzer Prize for the best volume of poems published during 1923. Her present home is at Croton-on-Hudson.

---

REFERENCES:

*The New Era in American Poetry,* LOUIS UNTERMEYER, Holt.

*Miss Millay's Poems,* (Review of *Second April* and *A Few Figs from Thistles*) PADRAIC COLUM, *Freeman,* November 2, 1921.

*Taking the Literary Pulse,* JOSEPH COLLINS, Doran.

BIBLIOGRAPHY:

*Renascence,* New York, 1917.

*A Few Figs from Thistles,* New York, 1920.

*Second April,* New York, 1921.

*The Harp-Weaver and Other Poems,* New York, 1923.

PLAYS

*The Lamp and the Bell,* New York, 1921.

*Aria Da Capo,* London, 1920; New York, 1921.

*Two Slatterns and a King,* Cincinnati, 1921.

## FREDERICK O'BRIEN

Frederick O'Brien was born at Baltimore, Maryland. He was educated at the Jesuit College there and the University of Maryland. At eighteen he went to sea. He has traveled all over the world. He has been connected with newspapers in various countries. He is married and lives in Sausalito, California.

---

REFERENCE:

*The Author of "White Shadows," Bookman,* December, 1920.

BIBLIOGRAPHY:

*White Shadows in the South Seas,* New York, 1919.
*Mystic Isles of the South Seas,* New York, 1921.
*Atolls of the Sun,* New York, 1922.

## BURTON RASCOE

Burton Rascoe was born at Fulton, Kentucky, October 22, 1892. He was educated at the Shawnee, Oklahoma, High School and the University of Chicago. Beginning newspaper work at the age of fourteen, on the Shawnee *Herald,* he has been associated with various newspapers in various capacities, was for a year associate editor of *McCall's Magazine* and two and a half years literary editor of the New York *Tribune* and New York *Herald-Tribune.* He is married and has two children.

---

BIBLIOGRAPHY:

*H. L. Mencken* (a duograph with Vincent O'Sullivan), New York, 1920.

EDITOR

*Madame Bovary* by GUSTAVE FLAUBERT, (Borzoi Classics), New York, 1919.

*Manon Lescaut* by the ABBE PREVOST, New York, 1919.

*Mademoiselle de Maupin* by THEOPHILE GAUTIER, New York, 1920.

*Nana* by EMILE ZOLA, New York, 1921.

## EDWIN ARLINGTON ROBINSON

Edwin Arlington Robinson was born at Head Tide, Maine, December 22, 1869. He was educated at Gardiner, Maine, and at Harvard University, although he was never graduated from that institution. He is unmarried. He is a member of the National Institute of Arts and Letters. He has lived in Brooklyn and New York now for many years. He was awarded the Pulitzer Prize for the most important book of poems published in 1922 (his *Collected Poems*) and for many years has pursued his profession which is, simply, that of poet.

---

REFERENCES:

*E. A. Robinson,* LLOYD MORRIS, Doran.

*A Bird's Eye View of E. A. Robinson,* AMY LOWELL, *Dial,* February, 1922.

*Edwin Arlington Robinson,* JOHN DRINKWATER, *Yale Review,* April, 1922.

*A Critical Fable,* ANONYMOUS, Houghton Mifflin.

BIBLIOGRAPHY:

*The Torrent and the Night Before,* Gardiner, Maine, 1896.

*The Children of the Night,* Boston, 1897.

*Captain Craig,* New York, 1902.

*The Town Down the River,* New York, 1910.

*The Man Against the Sky,* New York, 1916.

*Merlin,* New York, 1917.

*The Three Taverns,* New York, 1920.

*Lancelot,* New York, 1920.

*Avon's Harvest,* New York, 1921.

*Collected Poems,* New York, 1921.
*Roman Bartholow,* New York, 1922.
*The Man Who Died Twice,* New York, 1924.

PLAYS

*Van Zorn,* New York, 1914.
*The Porcupine,* New York, 1915.

## STUART P. SHERMAN

Stuart Pratt Sherman was born at Anita, Iowa, October 1, 1881. He was graduated from Williams College in 1903, and his postgraduate degrees were taken at Harvard University. He was instructed at several American universities and is well known as a critic and essayist. His home has been for many years at Urbana, Illinois, where he is professor of English in the University of Illinois. He has now taken charge of the Literary Department of the New York *Herald-Tribune.*

---

REFERENCES:

*Many Minds,* CARL VAN DOREN, Macmillan.
*Social Criticism of Literature,* H. W. PECK, *Sewanee Review,* April, 1921.

BIBLIOGRAPHY:

*Matthew Arnold,* Indianapolis, 1917.
*On Contemporary Literature,* New York, 1917.
*Americans,* New York, 1922.
*The Significance of Sinclair Lewis* (pamphlet), New York, 1922.
*The Genius of America,* New York, 1923.

EDITOR

*Treasure Island,* New York, 1911.
*Coriolanus,* New York, 1912.
*A Book of Short Stories,* New York, 1914.
FORD'S *'Tis Pity and The Broken Heart,* Boston, 1915.

*Cambridge History of American Literature* (with W. P. Trent, John Erskine and Carl Van Doren), New York, 1917, 1921.

*The Scarlet Letter,* New York, 1919.

*The George Sand-Gustave Flaubert Letters,* New York, 1921.

WHITMAN'S *Leaves of Grass,* New York, 1922.

*The Poetical Works of Joaquin Miller,* New York, 1923.

W. C. BROWNELL'S *American Prose Masters,* New York, 1923.

## BOOTH TARKINGTON

(Newton) Booth Tarkington was born at Indianapolis, July 29, 1869. He was educated at Exeter Academy, Purdue University and Princeton University. He has been twice married. His published novels, plays, and short stories are many. He is a member of the American Academy of Arts and Letters and has been honored by many degrees and literary prizes. He lives in Kennebunkport, Maine, in the summer time; Indianapolis in the winter season.

---

REFERENCES:

*Booth Tarkington,* ROBERT CORTES HOLLIDAY, Doubleday, Page.

*Contemporary American Novelists,* CARL VAN DOREN, Macmillan.

*Some American Story Tellers,* FREDERICK TABER COOPER, Holt.

*Booth Tarkington at Home,* JOHN R. MCMAHON, *Ladies' Home Journal,* November, 1922.

BIBLIOGRAPHY:

*The Gentleman from Indiana,* New York, 1899.
*Monsieur Beaucaire,* New York, 1900.
*The Two Vanrevels,* New York, 1902.
*Cherry,* New York, 1903.
*In the Arena,* New York, 1905.
*The Beautiful Lady,* New York, 1905.
*The Conquest of Canaan,* New York, 1905.
*His Own People,* New York, 1907.
*The Guest of Quesnay,* New York, 1908.

*Beasley's Christmas Party,* New York, 1909.
*Beauty and the Jacobin,* New York, 1912.
*The Flirt,* Garden City, 1913.
*Penrod,* Garden City, 1914.
*The Turmoil,* New York, 1915.
*Penrod and Sam,* Garden City, 1916.
*The Ohio Lady,* New York, 1916.
(Julian Street, co-author. 60 copies; printed for the authors).
*Seventeen,* New York, 1916.
*The Magnificent Ambersons,* Garden City, 1918.
*Ramsey Milholland,* Garden City, 1919.
*Alice Adams,* Garden City, 1921.
*Gentle Julia,* Garden City, 1922.
*The Fascinating Stranger and Other Stories,* Garden City, 1923.
*The Midlander,* Garden City, 1924.

PLAYS

*Monsieur Beaucaire* (with E. A. Sutherland), 1901.
*The Man from Home* (with Harry Leon Wilson), 1906, published, New York, 1908.
*Cameo Kirby,* 1907.
*Your Humble Servant,* 1908.
*Springtime,* 1908.
*Getting a Polish,* 1909.
*Mister Antonio,* 1916.
*The Country Cousin* (with Julian Street), 1917, published, New York, 1921.
*The Gibson Upright,* 1919 (with Harry Leon Wilson), published, Garden City, 1919.
*Up from Nowhere* (with Harry Leon Wilson), 1919.
*Clarence,* 1919, published, New York, 1921.
*Poldekin,* 1920.

*The Wren,* 1921, published, New York, 1922.
*The Ghost Story* (one act), Cincinnati, 1922.
*The Intimate Strangers,* 1921.
*Tweedles* (with Harry Leon Wilson), 1923.
*The Trysting Place* (one act), Cincinnati, 1923.
*Magnolia,* 1923.

## LOUIS UNTERMEYER

Louis Untermeyer was born at New York City, October 1, 1885. He was educated at De Witt Clinton High School. His business has been the manufacture of jewelry, from which he has recently retired in order to study and to travel in Europe. His wife, Jean Starr Untermeyer, is a poet. As lecturer, critic, anthologist and poet he is gaining a wide reputation. His home is in New York City.

---

REFERENCES:

*New Voices,* MARGUERITE WILKINSON, Macmillan.

*An Introduction to Poetry,* HUBBELL AND BEATY, Macmillan.

*A Critical Fable,* ANONYMOUS, Houghton Mifflin.

*The Poetry of Louis Untermeyer,* H. H. PECKHAM, *South Atlantic Quarterly,* January, 1918.

*The Advance of English Poetry in the Twentieth Century,* WILLIAM LYON PHELPS, *Bookman,* May, 1918.

**BIBLIOGRAPHY:**

*First Love,* New York, 1911.
*Challenge,* New York, 1914.
*These Times,* New York, 1917.
*The New Adam,* New York, 1920.
*Roast Leviathan,* New York, 1923.

PARODIES AND TRANSLATIONS

*The Younger Quire,* New York, 1911.
———*and Other Poets,* New York, 1916.

*Poems of Heinrich Heine,* New York, 1917.
*Including Horace,* New York, 1919.
*Heavens,* New York, 1922.

ANTHOLOGIES AND CRITICAL ESSAYS

*The New Era in American Poetry,* New York, 1918.
*Modern American Poetry,* New York, 1919.
*Modern British Poetry,* New York, 1920.
*This Singing World,* New York, 1923.
*American Poetry Since 1900,* New York, 1923.

THE END